PAYPAL HACKS™

Shannon Sofield,
Dave Nielsen, and Dave Burchell

O'REILLY®

Beijing • Cambridge • Farnham • Köln • Paris • Sebastopol • Taipei • Tokyo

PayPal Hacks™

by Shannon Sofield, Dave Nielsen, and Dave Burchell

Copyright © 2004 O'Reilly Media, Inc. All rights reserved.
Printed in the United States of America.

Published by O'Reilly Media, Inc., 1005 Gravenstein Highway North,
Sebastopol, CA 95472.

O'Reilly books may be purchased for educational, business, or sales promotional use. Online editions are also available for most titles (*safari.oreilly.com*). For more information, contact our corporate/institutional sales department: (800) 998-9938 or *corporate@oreilly.com*.

Editor:	David A. Karp	**Production Editor:**	Jamie Peppard
Series Editor:	Rael Dornfest	**Cover Designer:**	Hanna Dyer
Executive Editor:	Dale Dougherty	**Interior Designer:**	David Futato

Printing History:

September 2004:   First Edition.

RepKover™ This book uses RepKover™, a durable and flexible lay-flat binding.

ISBN: 0-596-00751-5
[C]

Contents

Credits

About the Authors

Shannon Sofield is the personification of a hack: he takes anything that is supposed to do one thing and manipulates it to serve his own purposes, in both his life as a developer and his life in general. If it was originally supposed to do one thing, he probably has it doing something entirely different. Shannon began creating PayPal solutions more than three years ago using his original database-driven PayPal purchase system that integrated with Macromedia Dreamweaver UltraDev. Since then, he has gone on to implement unique fixes for common eCommerce problems using PayPal. He has written several tutorials and articles and has spoken on the topic of using PayPal in new ways. One of the first members of the PayPal Developer Network, he was added to the PayPal Developer Network Advisory Boards on its inception. He also served several terms as a member of Team Macromedia for their web development program Dreamweaver, which he uses in his daily PayPal development. His technical background extends back to the initial Internet boom, when he began picking up simple web design that evolved into web planning and programming using a variety of technologies, languages, and databases. Currently, he manages the PayLoadz Digital Goods eCommerce system that allows merchants to sell digital goods securely with PayPal. One of the first and most successful third-party solutions for PayPal, this system made headlines when it launched Madonna's "American Life" single higher on the Billboard music charts than any previous digital single (and he did it before selling digital music was cool). In addition, he continually contributes to the PayPal Developer Network Message Boards (*http://www.paypaldev.org*), which his company, Superfreaker Studios, hosts and maintains. When he's not slogging through code at his computer in a caffeinated, sleep-deprived state, Shannon enjoys outdoor activities that fit the time of year. In the summer, he surfs and volunteers for the surfboard manufacturer Wave Riding Vehicles; in the winter, he can be found on the slopes, working on his kicker spins. Year-round, he can be found reliving his BMX days on his 24" GT cruiser. In his undergraduate studies, Shannon majored in Finance and Accounting, while his Masters in

Business Administration includes a concentration in Finance. Ctrl-C is his best friend.

Dave Nielsen is a Technical Evangelist within the PayPal Developer Network, a member of SDForum's Executive Council, and the founder of the Web Services SIG of Silicon Valley. Dave has a Bachelor of Science degree in Business from Cal Poly, San Luis Obispo and is armed with an education in engineering and marketing, as well as many technical certifications. As a technical trainer in the early '90s, Dave taught classes in languages such as Visual Basic, SQL and ASP. Dave was an early Internet programming enthusiast and found himself hounding Microsoft for data-driven web developer tools. After taking a chance on early beta versions of IIS and Active Server Pages, Dave became one of the first technical trainers certified to teach the now popular ASP technology. At PayPal, Dave focuses his efforts on creating tools that help developers create great eCommerce web sites. These projects include the Payment Request Wizard, the JavaScript Button Factory, the PayPal SDK for ASP.NET and the PayPal Commerce Starter Kit. Dave can be found online at http://www.paypalhacks.com, at conferences, and "competing" in an occasional triathlon. At home, his girlfriend tries to stop him from selling everything he owns on eBay.

Dave Burchell got his start with computers by programming the Radio Shack TRS-80 in BASIC and the Commodore 64 in 6510 assembly. Currently, Dave's favorite programming languages are Perl and XSLT. A fervent proponent of XML, Dave enjoys solving content management problems with markup and open source software. His other interests include American history and Hellenistic philosophy. Dave lives with his wife, Renee, and children, Max, Gus, and Samantha Grace, in Lincoln, Nebraska.

Contributors

The following people contributed their writing, code, and inspiration to *PayPal Hacks*:

- Paulam Baldwin is a PayPal Developer Technical Support Agent. She started at PayPal in July 2003. Paulam holds a B.S. in Computer Science. She got her start with computers by creating an intranet workflow module, written in JavaScript and server-side JavaScript, for students reapplying to the Central University of Venezuela. Paulam enjoys origami and learning about the world's cultures. She believes that making people happy is the best way to live life.

- Loyal Bassett is one of the many content programmers in the PayPal Fraud Engineering group. He has been diligently working at PayPal for over two years. He enjoys cycling and his friendly cat, Mr. Kitty.

- Michael Blanton is a Technical Integrations Manager for PayPal, where he has helped integrate PayPal into such sites as B&H Photo/Video (*http://www.bhphotovideo.com*) and NewEgg.com (*http://www.newegg.com*). Prior to joining PayPal, Michael was an Architect/Developer for CyberSource Professional Services. At PayPal, Michael not only helps integrate the PayPal Payment Solution into their largest merchants, but he also helps develop new product ideas that work for enterprise-class customers. At home, he focuses all of his efforts on his wife, son, and his son's LEGO.

- Patrick Breitenbach, a Bay Area native, spent over four years as a UCSB Gaucho and over six years at American Express in New York before returning to San Francisco five years ago to work at X.com (now known as PayPal). Patrick is a manager of the PayPal Developer Network (*http://www.paypal.com/pdn*). He enjoys mountain biking, magazines, gadgets, and all things Apple.

- May Chen is a Product Manager within the Consumer Protections Product team. May has a Bachelor of Science degree in Business from Washington University in St. Louis, MO. Prior to PayPal, May worked for a financial services company and also for an online payment processing company. At PayPal, May previously was a part of the Customer Service and Operations Product Team, primarily focusing on internal customer service tools for PayPal's contact centers. Now on the Consumer Protections team, May focuses on products to improve dispute resolution processes.

- Rob Conery is a Microsoft Certified Trainer and Solutions Developer who has been using Microsoft technologies for the last 14 years, architecting and building enterprise applications for Fortune 500 companies such as SBC, KLA-Tencor, and WekeRoad. Rob has been described by his clients as both innovative and color-blind; one client likened his skill set to that of a homeless person's shopping cart, which he is still trying to understand. Prior to spinning the twirly on his nerd hat, Rob pretended to be a geologist while hogging VAX time in the computer lab at his alma mater, UC Santa Barbara. It is believed that his final for his Pascal class is still compiling.

- Souvik Das has a Master's degree in Computer Science. He started his engineering career in a company doing research on security policies. He has worked in various engineering positions at Netscape, AOL, and PayPal. His interests lie in building highly scalable, available, and reliable Internet applications. Outside of work, he loves to spend time with his son and listen to Hindustani classical music.

- Glenn Ellingson is a bold, strapping young man who spends a disturbing amount of time playing with cars. To fund this rather unfortunate habit, he also plays with computers. He has contributed to financial applications in Vermont, multiplayer gaming in Massachusetts, document management software in Illinois, telephony in Florida, and now online payments in California. He reports mixed feelings that Googling his name reveals he has "killed billions of sentient beings and should be treated with utmost caution."

- Gina Han is a product manager at PayPal, specializing in consumer protections programs for buyers and sellers. This involves online dispute resolution to help the community resolve issues around merchandise transactions. Gina has a long history of helping people, developing an e-mentoring program for science students, giving teens a way to shop online (okay, maybe this wasn't exactly altruistic), and building software that enabled people to trace their family trees. Her hobbies do not include karaoke, taxidermy, or participating in hotdog-eating contests.

- Stephen Ivaskevicius is the PayPal Developer Technical Support Supervisor who started at PayPal in January of 2001 and currently supports PayPal Web Services. Stephen has contributed to the enhancements of many PayPal features over the years. He has a strong inclination for eating cheeseburgers in paradise, searching for lost shakers of salt on his motorcycle, and shouting "Fins up!" at the top of his lungs.

- David A. Karp just likes to see his name in print. In addition to being the editor for this book, David is the author of *eBay Hacks*, the upcoming *eBay PowerSeller: The Missing Manual*, and the best-selling Windows Annoyances series (the latest installment of which is *Windows XP Annoyances*). His books are currently available in ten different languages, and his online help site, Annoyances.org, is one of the most popular of its kind. He has also written for a number of magazines—including *PC Magazine*, *Windows Sources Magazine*, *Windows Pro Magazine*, and *New Media Magazine*—and he is a contributing editor for *ZTrack Magazine*. Noted recognition includes *PC Computing* magazine, *Windows Magazine*, the *San Francisco Examiner*, and *The New York Times*. He uses PayPal as a means to acquire more junk on eBay.

- Sarah Livnat is a PayPal Product Manager who has worked with Limited Account Access and many of PayPal's compliance and risk products. Prior to joining PayPal, Sarah was a Product Manager at Chemdex/Ventro, a B2B marketplace application service provider. Sarah is an avid world traveler, just having returned from a year-long expedition to Southern Africa, Nepal, Southeast Asia, and the Oceana.

- Joseph Lowery's books on the Web and web-building tools are international bestsellers, having sold more than 300,000 copies worldwide in nine different languages. He is the author of the *Dreamweaver Bible* and the *Fireworks Bible* series (both from Wiley Publishing), and he coauthored *Dreamweaver MX 2004 Web Application Recipes* (New Rider Publishing) with Eric Ott, president of WebAssist (*http://www.webassist.com*). WebAssist is the leading provider of extensions (software add-ons) for the Macromedia platform. WebAssist hosts a self-service developer community with over 100,000 members registered. WebAssist's partners include Macromedia, PayPal, Affinity, Yahoo!, and Google.

- Dave Lundvall is a Senior Sales Consultant for Oracle, specializing in Oracle's Application Server 10g. He has a Bachelor of Science degree in Computer Science from the University at Buffalo. Dave began programming soon after his family purchased a Commodore 64 in the mid '80s. Now Dave has experience building everything from mobile phone applications to enterprise portals. Before Dave moved into the J2EE world, he was even once a Microsoft Certified Solutions Developer (MCSD). A couple of Dave's interests outside of software are competing in triathlons and volunteering for Team in Training, which raises funds for the Leukemia and Lymphoma Society. Dave can be reached at *davidlundvall@yahoo.com*.

- Dave McClure is Director of the PayPal Developer Network (*http://www.paypal.com/pdn*), and also a current geek and former entrepreneur (*http://www.500hats.com*). His interests and hobbies include finance and economics, entrepreneurship and venture capital, jazz and baroque music, politics and business, numerous sports and games, ultimate Frisbee, cartoons and animation, and an ever-growing collection of funny-looking hats. Dave is a huge fan of Dr. Seuss, *The Economist*, and the Muppets, and lives in the San Francisco Bay Area with his wife, Saya, a talented jazz pianist and composer (*http://www.saya.com*).

- Jeffrey McManus is a Senior Manager of Developer Relations at eBay and has over 15 years of experience as a developer, technology manager and technical writer. He is proficient in many development technologies and has written six books, including the *C# Developer's Guide to ASP.NET, XML, and ADO.NET* and the *VB.NET Developer's Guide to ASP.NET, XML and ADO.NET* (both from Addison-Wesley). In his spare time, Jeffrey enjoys helping high school kids build robots for competitions.

- Evan McPhillips is a Product Integration Specialist for PayPal and has worked with PayPal for almost two years. He started in Member Services, then moved to Resolution Services as a Customer Service Representative, then moved to Protection Services as a Seller Protection Agent, and has been in his current position for the last couple of months. He has over 10 years in the customer service industry. Evan has a Bachelor of Arts degree in Religious Studies and is an avid reader of science fiction and fantasy novels and an Everquest junkie.

- Hugo Olliphant is a PayPal Product Manager who has worked with eBay Gift Certificates, Merchant-Initiated Payment, and many of Pay-Pal's reporting tools. Prior to joining PayPal, Hugo was the CEO of gMoney Corp, a company that provides financial management solutions for groups involving roommates, ski houses, car pools, and the like. Hugo has a penchant for polar exploration literature and dinosaur origami.

- Patrick O'Neal is a PayPal Technical Support Senior Agent who has worked primarily with supporting PayPal's Merchant Features (e.g., web site payment buttons, IPN, and PDT). Before working at PayPal, Patrick was a Customer Service Analyst with Ameritrade. Patrick holds an Associate's degree in Computer Network Systems and a Bachelor of Science degree in Computer Science with an emphasis on Web Programming. In his free time, Patrick enjoys writing and producing hip-hop music and learning new programming languages.

- Ray Tanaka is the Technical Architect for the PayPal Sandbox and Web Services APIs. Prior to joining PayPal, Ray was with SkyGo, Inc. (now known as Enpocket), working on wireless marketing solutions. His hobbies include sleeping, foosball, racquetball, and spending time with his girlfriend.

- Alan Tien is a PayPal Global Product Manager. His primary claim to fame is releasing PayPal's Web Services. Prior to PayPal, Alan was a Senior Product Manager at the ASP aggregator Jamcracker, a $140M dot com flameout. Before the Internet era, Alan was a consultant at WESTT and Accenture (then known as Andersen Consulting). He graduated from Stanford with a Bachelor of Science degree in Electrical Engineering but carefully avoided any career that would actually use his education.

- Katherine Woo is a Director of Product Management at PayPal, where she manages the Merchant Features Product Team. Her prior experience includes product management at Netscape (AOL), strategy consulting at Mercer Management Consulting, and an MBA from Stanford. She dreams one day of making a line of greeting cards or designing wine labels.

- Mike Yeung, a Development Architect, is responsible for providing technical leadership and project management for major integration projects at Grand Central. Mike has over 12 years of experience in software development and technical management. He has previously worked at companies such as Chinadotcom, Netscape, and Oracle in various technical and management positions. Mike holds a Master of Science degree from Stanford University and a Bachelor of Science degree from UC, Berkeley, both in Computer Science.

Acknowledgments

The authors and contributors wish to thank Rael Dornfest, Kyle Hart, and Dan Woods. Jamie Peppard, Brian Sawyer and Darren Kelly were instrumental in cleaning up our work for this book.

Shannon Sofield

I'd like to thank the PayPal team for creating a great service and for their support throughout this process. I also would like to thank the "Daves" that helped get this book written: Dave McClure, for being there from the beginning, David A. Karp for putting up with my writing habits, Dave Nielsen for his expertise and management, and Dave Burchell for stepping up and helping us get this out the door. Also, thanks to my parents and friends for their motivation.

Dave Nielsen

I'd like to thank PayPalians, past and present, for creating this awesome payment platform; Dave McClure, my PDN mentor, for taking me under his wing; PB, for his mastery of the multitude of PayPal's intricate features; David A. Karp, cat-wrangler extraordinaire, for his encouragement and perseverance; Mom and brother Mark for putting up with my quest for answers to life's persistent questions; Dad for leaving me his wacky inventiveness; and Erika, my inspiration, who makes me smile every day. Erika, I feel so lucky to have found you. With you, every day is beautiful and new. Nothing would make me happier than to spend the rest of my life with you...Erika Anderson, will you marry me?

Dave Burchell

I wish to extend my thanks to the many coworkers who assisted me while working on this book, including Paulam Chang, Debbie Becker, Claudia Erickson, Stephen Ivaskevicius, Warren Lynch, Patrick O'Neal, Michelle Taylor, Patricia Truit, and Kim Weiss. My thanks also to marketing maven

Evelyn Schlaphoff of SourceLink/Los Angeles, guru Mike Lewis of The World Book, and to our masterful, patient, and dedicated editor, David A. Karp.

Preface

PayPal wasn't the first company to build an online payment system, but it might as well be the last. With over 50 million registered accounts, PayPal is rapidly becoming a household name. But, as indicated, there have been others; PayPal's predecessors attempted to capitalize on the Internet boom by building new forms of money. But whether this new currency was called Flooz, Beanz, or eCash, it didn't matter, because people didn't buy it. PayPal based its system on plain old dollar bills (not to mention yen, euros, and pounds sterling), which, in the end, turned out to be more valuable than Internet gold.

PayPal's next brilliant move was to identify each account by an email address. That way, anyone with an email account could send money to anyone else just by knowing the recipient's email address. The email proclaiming "You've got cash" turned out to be extremely motivating.

From its beginning, PayPal empowered the little guy to compete in the big world. It made doing business over the Internet easy for individuals, who could attach their bank accounts to their PayPal accounts without requiring a CFO's signature. And the little guy returned the favor. After all, it was the little guys who paved the way for PayPal to become the number one payment system on eBay.

PayPal also removed the technical challenges. PayPal made it possible for an HTML developer to accept online credit card payments from any web page without requiring the years of programming skills necessary to install credit card processing software on a web server. A simple Pay Now button in an eBay auction page became as empowering as the most expensive eCommerce site on the Internet.

For developers, it didn't stop there. Buy Now, Donate, Add to Cart, and Subscription buttons make Internet commerce in all flavors possible. And with innovations such as Website Payments, Instant Payment Notification, and PayPal Web Services, all the power of this eCommerce giant is only a few lines of code away. It's not surprising that PayPal is being touted as the payment platform of the future. But for those who learn what it can already do, it may mean making profits today!

Why PayPal Hacks?

The term *hacking* has a bad reputation in the press. They use it to refer to someone who breaks into systems or wreaks havoc with computers as their weapon. Among people who write code, though, the term *hack* refers to a "quick-and-dirty" solution to a problem, or a clever way to get something done. And the term *hacker* is taken very much as a compliment, referring to someone as being creative and having the technical chops to get things done. The Hacks series is an attempt to reclaim the word, document the good ways people are hacking, and pass the hacker ethic of creative participation on to the uninitiated. Seeing how others approach systems and problems is often the quickest way to learn about a new technology.

As any experienced merchant will tell you, there are plenty of tasks involved in accepting payments on the Internet, and anything that can be done to make those tasks easier, faster, or more effective will improve your profits and give you more time to grow your business. But despite the title *PayPal Hacks*, this book is also not about "hacking into a system" or anything so nefarious—quite the contrary. In fact, you'll find in this book a very real emphasis on trading responsibly and ethically, as well as extensive tools and tips for protecting yourself as both a buyer and a seller.

PayPal, on the surface, seems like a simple system allowing you to send and receive payments. But there's a whole lot more under the hood; there are many tips and tricks you can use to save time and improve sales with PayPal. The hacks in this book address the technological and diplomatic challenges faced by all PayPal members, and are written from the perspectives of both PayPal insiders and experienced solution providers. Essentially, you'll find the tools to help you buy and sell smarter and safer, make more money, and have fun doing it.

Getting Started with the Code in This Book

The sample code in this book should serve as a good jumping-off point for however you want to use each hack in the real world. To that end, *PayPal Hacks* provides real code you can type in and run yourself.

PayPal's home is the Web, a heterogeneous place governed by well-defined standards. The concepts presented in this book work with any programming language or platform you might be using with your web site. However, the example code is primarily kept to three language and platform combinations, each inhabiting its own niche of the Internet ecology: server-side scripting, client-side (browser) scripting, and desktop applications.

Server-Side Scripting

Server-side scripts are installed on a web server. When a user requests a web page that contains a server-side script, the script is processed on the web server and its output is converted to HTML and delivered to the end user's web browser.

Most of the hacks in this book that involve server-side scripting are written in VBScript (Visual Basic Script), which runs on a web server with support for Microsoft Active Server Pages (ASP). The ASP/VBScript combination is one of the most popular platforms among webmasters and developers using Microsoft systems. Microsoft's newest web platform, ASP.NET, is growing rapidly; it is backward-compatible and will also run ASP/VBScript code.

You can host the VBScript examples using a modern Microsoft operating system, such as Microsoft Windows XP Professional, Microsoft Windows 2000 Professional, or Microsoft Windows 2003 Server. Each of these products comes with Microsoft's Internet Information Server (IIS), an ASP-capable web server. In practice, you might not have (or desire to set up) your own web server; many ISPs offer affordable (or free) space on preconfigured web servers that are capable of hosting ASP/VBScript.

To create ASP/VBScript pages, simply type them into your favorite text editor, whether you're using Microsoft's default Notepad or the powerful Vim editor, which is popular amongst Unix jocks. If you're already using an ASP-compatible web site editor, such as Dreamweaver or Microsoft Visual Studio, you can use that instead. Once you have created your ASP/VBScript pages, upload them to your web server (typically via FTP) and view them with your web browser. (The steps to do this vary; check with your ISP for specific instructions.)

To browse ASP/VBScript pages, you (or your customers) need only an ordinary web browser, such as Internet Explorer, Netscape Navigator, Mozilla, Opera, or even Lynx. You will, however, need to know the URLs of your ASP/VBScript pages (e.g., *http://www.yourdomain.com/pagename.asp*). If you host the pages on the same computer as your web browser, the URL will likely start with *http://localhost/*. Because the VBScript is processed on the web server that turns it into HTML, your (or your customer's) web browser does not need any VBScript capabilities.

 Although many of the hacks in this book are written in ASP/ VBScript, Perl, Python, PHP, Java, and Cold Fusion are all good choices for developing eCommerce web pages that use PayPal as a payment method. No exotic features unique to VBScript are used, so the concepts and examples should readily translate to your favorite platform.

Client-Side (Browser) Scripting

Browser, or client-side, scripts are embedded in the HTML of the web page and are executed by the browser. The first and still most popular browser scripting technology is JavaScript. Since its introduction, JavaScript has been cloned by Microsoft (their offering is called JScript) and standardized by an international standards organization (resulting in ECMAScript). The bland flavor of JavaScript/JScript/ECMAScript used in the examples should be palatable to all modern JavaScript-capable browsers.

To try the JavaScript examples, you need only a text editor, such as Microsoft Notepad or VIM, or some other HTML authoring tool, such as Microsoft FrontPage, Macromedia Dreamweaver, NetObjects Fusion, or Adobe GoLive. Save your JavaScript-laden HTML pages to your computer's hard drive and view them in any modern browser with JavaScript support enabled.

Desktop Applications

The examples provided with PayPal's API hacks involve the building of desktop applications. Although they use the Internet and HTTP to access the PayPal API, these are standalone applications designed to work on your Windows desktop (as opposed to working from within a web browser).

While you can access the PayPal API from within any programming language that supports SOAP (.NET, Java, Perl, PHP), the examples in this book are all written in C# and require the Microsoft .NET Framework. To try these examples yourself, you need to first compile them with a C# development environment, such as Microsoft Visual Studio .NET or Borland C#Builder. (You can't use an older version of Visual Studio, because it won't support SOAP or .NET). To run the examples, you (and your employees or customers) need Microsoft's .NET Framework 1.1 installed on each computer on which your application is to run. The .NET framework is installed by default on Microsoft Windows XP and is freely available for previous versions of Windows, such as Windows 2000, from *http://windowsupdate.microsoft.com*.

Database Coding and Platform Choices

Many of the hacks in this book rely on your ability to set up a database and connect to it with code. A database table looks something like an Excel spreadsheet, with rows (records) and columns (fields). Table P-1 shows a simple *products* database table.

Table P-1. An extremely simple table with three fields (columns) and as many records (products) as you wish to store in it

ID	Description	Price
0001	Acme Widget	$37.94
0002	Industrial, Co. Wicket	$12.88
0003	Krusty Brand Tongue Depressor	$0.40

Here, each record corresponds to a single product. The data is divided into three fields: a unique numeric ID (ID), a product description (Description), and the unit price (Price). You'll not only need to choose a database application with which to create your tables and manage your data, you'll need to include code (specific to the platform you choose) to connect to your database.

Most of the database-enabled hacks in this book cite a Structured Query Language (SQL) query to retrieve data from a database or store data back into it. In order to put these hacks to use, you'll have to customize the code for use with your server and database platform.

There are two general platforms commonly used to host web sites: Windows and Unix/Linux. These two systems can provide similar functionality, but they do so in completely different ways. The problem is that some of the more advanced code, especially code that accesses databases, might work on one platform but not the other. For instance, Windows servers have a built-in web server capable of interpreting VBScript or JavaScript that is executed in Active Server Pages (ASP). On the other hand, Unix/Linux platforms typically use the Apache web server, which can understand Hypertext Preprocessor (PHP) code (i.e., code with a *.php* extension). Of course, you can run ASP pages on Unix/Linux platforms using ChiliSoft ASP, and you can run PHP scripted pages on a Windows machine by installing the Windows version of the Apache web server.

Once you've chosen a server platform, you'll need to choose a database technology that works with that system. For instance, Windows servers will likely be integrated with a Microsoft Access, MSDE, or Microsoft SQL database, whereas Unix/Linux servers will likely be using MySQL, Postgres, or Oracle.

 It almost goes without saying that a dynamic web site (dynamic in that the content is created on the fly) will be much more powerful with the benefit of a relational database management system (RDBMS). The examples that require a database were tested against Microsoft's SQL Server 2000 or better, but with some small modifications the examples will work with any popular RDBMS, such as MySQL or Oracle.

Many of the advanced hacks in this book reference a *recordset* in their instructions, so you'll need to do something like the following to deploy those hacks. This code creates a recordset named rsProducts using VBScript for ASP:

```
1  connStore="DRIVER={Microsoft Access Driver (*.mdb)};DBQ="C:/InetPub/wwwroot/
   database/dbPayPal.mdb")
2  set rsProducts = Server.CreateObject("ADODB.Recordset")
3  rsProducts.ActiveConnection = connStore
4  rsProducts.Source = "SELECT item_name FROM tblProducts"
5  rsProducts.Open()
6  Response.Write(rsProducts.Fields.Item("item_name").Value)
```

Line 1 defines the location of the database and specifies the database driver. Line 2 initiates a new recordset named rsProducts. Line 5 actually executes the database query, and line 6 sends the contents of a field to the output (in this case, the item_name column returned from the database is displayed).

To put this code to use, replace the SQL statement on line 4 with the SQL query shown in the hack you wish to use.

Further Study

To learn more about some of the aforementioned technologies used in this book, check out the following O'Reilly books:

ASP
  Programming ASP.NET by Jesse Liberty and Dan Hurwitz

Access (Database)
  Access Database Design & Programming by Steven Roman, Ph.D.

JavaScript
  JavaScript: The Definitive Guide by David Flanagan

MySQL (Database)

Managing & Using MySQL by George Reese, Randy Jay Yarger, and Tim King

PHP

PHP Cookbook by David Sklar and Adam Trachtenberg

SQL

SQL Pocket Guide by Jonathan Gennick

VB.NET

VB.NET Language in a Nutshell by Steven Roman, Ph.D., Ron Petrusha, and Paul Lomax

How to Use This Book

You can read this book from cover to cover if you like, but you'll probably be better off picking an interesting item from the table of contents and just diving in. Each hack stands on its own, so feel free to browse and jump to the different sections that interest you most. If there's a prerequisite you need to know about, a cross-reference will guide you to the right hack.

How This Book Is Organized

Each hack has been designed to show you how to complete a specific task, streamline a common practice, or overcome a PayPal limitation. Some hacks point to obscure features on the web site, while others present code to solve problems or unlock hidden features.

The 100 hacks in this book are distributed into eight chapters:

Chapter 1, *Account Management*

Use the hacks in this chapter to set up a PayPal account and keep it in good standing. If you're new to PayPal, make sure to verify your account [Hack #2] and confirm your address [Hack #3].

Chapter 2, *Making Payments*

PayPal's all about sending payments. This chapter covers the basics of buying with PayPal and protecting yourself when you do.

Chapter 3, *Selling with PayPal*

The real fun of PayPal starts when you begin accepting payments. Upgrade to a Business or Premier account and then hook up your PayPal account with your eBay auctions or eCommerce web site and watch the money roll in. Make sure you take steps to protect yourself from buyer fraud "Protect Yourself from Buyer Fraud" [Hack #24] and chargebacks "Protect Yourself from Chargebacks" [Hack #25].

Chapter 4, *Payment Buttons*

Integrate PayPal with your web site and begin accepting PayPal payments for goods and services in minutes. Although adding the most basic PayPal Buy Now button "Create a Buy Now Button" [Hack #28] to your site involves little more than copying and pasting a simple HTML form onto a web page, there are dozens of ways to extend and customize your online storefront and fine-tune your customer's purchase experience.

Chapter 5, *Storefronts and Shopping Carts*

Take payment buttons a step further and allow customers to purchase multiple items in a single transaction. PayPal provides everything you need to set up a simple shopping cart interface with your web site; just add a few buttons "Hack Shopping Cart Buttons" [Hack #45] to your pages to get started.

Chapter 6, *Managing Subscriptions*

Accept recurring payments from other PayPal members and provide paid access to online content and other membership-based products.

Chapter 7, *IPN & PDT*

Automate your business by setting up PayPal to notify your server whenever you receive a payment, allowing you to automatically record all transactions into a local database, offer instant fulfillment of digital goods, and provide instant access to online content.

Chapter 8, *The PayPal Web Services API*

Leave the PayPal web site behind and build applications and web sites using the PayPal Web Services API as a development platform.

Conventions Used in This Book

The following is a list of the typographical conventions used in this book:

Italics

Used to indicate URLs, filenames, filename extensions, and directory/folder names. For example, a path in the filesystem appears as */Developer/Applications*.

Constant width

Used to show code examples, the contents of files, and console output, as well as the names of variables, commands, and other code excerpts.

Constant width bold

Used to highlight portions of code, typically new additions to old code.

Constant width italic

Used in code examples and tables to show sample text to be replaced with your own values.

Color

The second color is used to indicate a cross-reference within the text.

You should pay special attention to notes set apart from the text with the following icons:

This is a tip, suggestion, or general note. It contains useful supplementary information about the topic at hand.

This is a warning or note of caution, often indicating that your money or your privacy might be at risk.

The thermometer icons, found next to each hack, indicate the relative complexity of the hack:

 beginner   moderate   expert

Using Code Examples

This book is here to help you get your job done. In general, you may use the code in this book in your programs and documentation. You do not need to contact us for permission unless you're reproducing a significant portion of the code. For example, writing a program that uses several chunks of code from this book does not require permission. Selling or distributing a CD-ROM of examples from O'Reilly books *does* require permission. Answering a question by citing this book and quoting example code does not require permission. Incorporating a significant amount of example code from this book into your product's documentation *does* require permission.

We appreciate, but do not require, attribution. An attribution usually includes the title, author, publisher, and ISBN. For example: "*PayPal Hacks* by Shannon Sofield, Dave Nielsen, and Dave Burchell. Copyright 2004 O'Reilly Media, Inc., 0-596-00751-5."

If you feel your use of code examples falls outside fair use or the permission given above, feel free to contact us at *permissions@oreilly.com*.

How to Contact Us

We have tested and verified the information in this book to the best of our ability, but you may find that features have changed (or even that we have made mistakes!). As a reader of this book, you can help us to improve future editions by sending us your feedback. Please let us know about any errors, inaccuracies, bugs, misleading or confusing statements, and typos that you find anywhere in this book.

Please also let us know what we can do to make this book more useful to you. We take your comments seriously and will try to incorporate reasonable suggestions into future editions. You can write to us at:

O'Reilly Media, Inc.
1005 Gravenstein Highway North
Sebastopol, CA 95472
(800) 998-9938 (in the U.S. or Canada)
(707) 829-0515 (international/local)
(707) 829-0104 (fax)

To ask technical questions or to comment on the book, send email to:

bookquestions@oreilly.com

The web site for *PayPal Hacks* lists examples, errata, and plans for future editions. You can find this page at:

http://www.oreilly.com/catalog/payhks/

Download sample code from:

http://www.paypalhacks.com

For more information about this book and others, see the O'Reilly web site:

http://www.oreilly.com

Got a Hack?

To explore Hacks books online or to contribute a hack for future titles, visit:

http://hacks.oreilly.com

## CHAPTER ONE

Account Management

Hacks 1–9

You can use PayPal to send and receive money, but you need a PayPal *account* to manage your payments and your business. There's something comforting about having your own account. Sure, it's yet another password to remember, but it's all yours. You can visit a site like PayPal, log in, and see your settings, your name, and your history—proof that you've been there before and that someone (er, something) remembers you. But a PayPal account [Hack #1], in particular, has the added bonus of being able to store cold, hard cash. You can't really touch it, but it's there, and it's yours.

You can use your PayPal balance to pay for stuff [Hack #11], or you can withdraw it [Hack #20] and add it to the shoebox under your mattress. You can also watch it grow, as your eBay bidders pay for your stuff, web site customers buy your products, or friends pay you back for sushi dinners.

But it's not about sending and receiving money; it's about finding new ways to handle transactions so that you can spend more time eating sushi (or curly fries, or whatever). The real power of PayPal is its invisibility; you can have strangers send you money and still keep your account all to yourself. Whether you're selling a single product [Hack #28], or a cart full of products [Hack #45], Pay-Pal can be as slick as you need it to be. If you take things even further, you can have PayPal notify your server "Receive Instant Payment Notifications" [Hack #65] when you receive money, or even write a standalone application [Hack #88] to manage your sales without ever having to log into your account.

But it all begins with learning the ins and outs of your PayPal account, and that's what this chapter is about. Chow down, and have fun, but don't linger; there's code to be written.

 If you want to get anywhere in this business, make sure you verify your account [Hack #2] and confirm your address [Hack #3], and then make sure you never forget your password [Hack #4].

Get to PayPal in Five Keystrokes or Fewer

"How many licks does it take to get the center of a Tootsie Roll Tootsie Pop? One, Two, Three?" The world may never know, but it takes exactly five keystrokes to get to *http://www.paypal.com*. But how can this be? There are 10 keystrokes in paypal.com (not including the Enter key), not 5!

The clues leading to the answer can be found only by examining the history of PayPal. PayPal was not always named PayPal. It was founded in January 1999 under then name FieldLink and renamed Confinity later that same year. In May 2000, Confinity merged with another company and the combined entities renamed themselves PayPal.

Can you name the company that merged with Confinity? The answer is the third-to-last letter in the alphabet: *X.com*, to be exact. X.com and Confinity were competitors who merged to form PayPal. The URL *http://www.x.com* now points to *http://www.paypal.com*. So, if you're in a real hurry, just type x.com and you'll get to PayPal (paypal.com) in half the keystrokes!

Internet Explorer users can get to PayPal even quicker by typing x into the address bar, then pressing Ctrl-Enter.

Create a PayPal Account

#1 Sign up for your own PayPal account, which is necessary if you'll be receiving payments or using just about any other hack in this book.

Although you can send money without creating a PayPal account [Hack #15], there are advantages to having an account, including PayPal Buyer Protection, receiving payments, and viewing account history. And since there is no cost to create or maintain an account, the benefits easily outweigh the costs.

Here's what you'll need to get started:

- Your email address
- Your postal mailing address
- Your phone number

You'll also be asked to provide two of the following four pieces of personal information, which will be used to verify your identity if you ever forget your account password:

- Your mother's maiden name
- The last four digits of your driver's license
- The last four digits of your Social Security number
- Your city of birth

To sign up for a Personal PayPal account (see the introduction to Chapter 3 for information on Business accounts), follow these steps:

1. Go to *http://www.paypal.com* and click Sign Up.

2. Select the Personal Account option, select your country, and then click Continue.

3. On the Account Signup page, enter your postal mailing address. PayPal will double-check the city, state, and Zip Code, so they must be valid. The address you provide should be the same as the billing address of the credit card you plan on adding to your account, although you will be given the opportunity to change it later.

4. Enter your telephone number, email address, and password. The email address must correspond to a valid email account to which you have immediate access, because you won't be able to use your PayPal account until you respond to the verification email that PayPal sends you.

> For security reasons, do not use the same password for your PayPal account and your email account. Otherwise, anyone who has access to your email account will also have access to your PayPal account and the money within.

You should also enter a real phone number, since it's one of the ways PayPal allows you to regain access to your account if you forget your password [Hack #4].

5. Enter your Security Question answers. If you're concerned about divulging real information here, then don't enter it! You can put any secret words or phrases into these fields, provided that you'll be able to remember them later on.

6. When asked if you'd like this to be a Premier Account, select No.

> If anyone sends you a payment funded with a credit card, PayPal will require that you upgrade to a Premier (or Business) account at that time to accept the payment. Although there are advantages to these account types, you'll be charged a small fee for each subsequent payment you receive, regardless of the funding source. See the introduction to Chapter 3 for further details.

7. Select Yes to indicate that you agree with the User Agreement and Privacy Policy, and check Yes again to indicate that you've read the Legal Disputes section. Enter the Security Measure characters as shown in the box [Hack #15].

8. Click Signup when you're done.

9. The next page instructs you how to confirm your email address, which involves nothing more than opening the email message PayPal has just sent you and clicking the link inside.

After you confirm your email address, you will be able to use your account. However, you will have limited abilities until you verify your PayPal account [Hack #2].

HACK #2   Verify Your PayPal Account

Provide PayPal with your necessary account information without waiting for your monthly bank statements.

Federal banking regulations require financial institutions to obtain proof of your identity before allowing you to open a bank account, and PayPal uses this fact to add security to their system. If you have a bank account, it proves you are a real person, at least in the eyes of PayPal. To unlock all the features of a new PayPal account, you'll have to attach a bank account and confirm it.

Once you do this, your account will be *verified* and the following will happen:

- You'll become eligible for Seller Protection "Protect Yourself from Chargebacks" [Hack #25].
- You'll be able to send as much money as you like. Unverified accounts are otherwise limited in the total amount of money that can be sent ($2,000 for U.S. accounts, for instance).
- You'll be able to pay instantly from your checking account, rather than having to wait for eChecks to clear "Choose How to Fund Payments" [Hack #11].
- You'll be able to withdraw money to your bank account "Get Your Money" [Hack #20].

Add a Bank Account

Here's how to become verified:

1. Log into your PayPal account, click the My Account tab and then click Profile.

2. Click the Bank Accounts link under the Financial Information heading.

3. Type the name of the bank that holds your checking account, and choose either Checking or Savings to indicate the type of account you're adding.

4. Grab one of the checks from your checkbook and type your bank's routing number and your account number, as illustrated in Figure 1-1.

Figure 1-1. Adding a bank account

5. Retype the account number in the next field to ensure there are no typos.

6. Click Add Bank Account when you're finished here.

The next page that appears will inform you that your bank account was successfully added, but you're not done yet; you still need to confirm your bank account.

Confirm an Account and Get Free Cash

PayPal makes two small deposits into your bank account, each in an amount between $.01 and $.99. Because you alone have access to your bank statement, only you and PayPal have access to the exact amounts deposited. When you receive your bank statement, return to PayPal and confirm your account by typing the respective amounts of the two deposits made to your account.

These two random deposits are yours to keep, so you can earn between two cents and $1.98 just by confirming your bank account.

Now, if you're the patient type, waiting up to a month for your paper bank statement to arrive in the mail should be no problem. However, in most cases, you won't have to. If your bank provides online access to your account (most do), all you need to do is log in and retrieve the two deposit amounts.

PayPal initiates these two small deposits into your bank account right away, but the banking system typically requires three to four business days to process them. So, even if you have online banking, you won't be able to confirm a bank account the same day you add it to PayPal. Instead, give it a few days and log into your bank's web site on the third or fourth day.

Once you have the amounts of the two deposits, log into your PayPal account. Click the My Account tab, click Profile, and then click Bank Accounts (under the Financial Information heading). Your newly added bank account should be listed here; select the account (if there's more than one), and then click Confirm. Enter the amounts of the deposits into the Confirm Bank Account page (as shown in Figure 1-2), and click Submit when you're done.

Your account is now verified, and you're ready to start sending as much money as you like.

Confirm Your Mailing Address

HACK #3   Add a credit card and a confirmed shipping address to your PayPal account to have your payments accepted by more sellers.

Whenever you buy something online using a credit card, the store from which you made the purchase checks that the address you provided matches the address on file with your credit card company. Retailers do this as a security precaution to guard against payments made with stolen credit cards; otherwise, a thief could use your credit card number to purchase something and have it shipped anywhere.

Address matching is done through a standard system called Address Verification System/Service (AVS), which is set up by all the credit card companies. PayPal does the same thing when you add a credit card to your PayPal account:

Figure 1-2. *Entering the random deposit amounts*

1. Log into PayPal, click the My Account tab, and then click Profile.
2. Select Credit Cards under Financial Information.
3. Any credit cards currently attached to your account will be shown here. Click Add to attach a new card.
4. Fill in your credit card number and mailing address; make sure the address matches the one on file with your credit card company as precisely as possible.
5. Click Add Card when you're done.

If PayPal is able to match the address through AVS, it will designate your address as Confirmed and you'll be able to use your credit card to fund payments right away. Plus, your payments will be eligible for PayPal's Seller Protection Policy "Protect Yourself from Chargebacks" [Hack #25], and sellers (especially on eBay) will be much more likely to accept your payments.

If you're an online seller, you'll need to decide if and when you'll consider shipping items to an unconfirmed address. See the introduction to Chapter 3 and "Protect Yourself from Chargebacks" [Hack #25] for account settings related to accepting payments from unconfirmed addresses.

Expanded Use Enrollment

If PayPal is unable to confirm your address through AVS, it will remain Unconfirmed and you won't be able to make credit card payments until you complete the Expanded Use Enrollment. Essentially, PayPal initiates the process by charging your credit card US$1.95 (don't worry; you'll get it back). When you receive your next credit card statement, a unique, randomly generated four-digit Expanded Use Number will accompany the charge.

If you have online access to your credit card account, check your statement online after three to four business days to view the Expanded Use Number. Otherwise, you'll have to wait for your credit card statement to arrive in the mail.

Once you obtain the Expanded Use Number, enter it into PayPal. Your address will be confirmed and you'll be able to make payments with your credit card. Plus, you'll get your $1.95 back in the form of a credit to your PayPal account.

If you can't complete the Expanded Use Enrollment, you'll have to complete Alternate Address Confirmation, which involves faxing several documents to PayPal. To qualify, you must be verified [Hack #2], a PayPal member for more than 90 days, and a U.S. member in good standing. You also must have a Buyer Participation buyer number [Hack #7] of more than 10.

Confirming a Second Address

Although some sellers ship anywhere you ask them to, most want to abide by PayPal's Seller Protection Policy "Protect Yourself from Chargebacks" [Hack #25] and thus will ship only to a confirmed address. Naturally, you might want to have more than one confirmed mailing address on your PayPal account.

There are two ways to go about this. The best way is to contact your credit card company and request that a second address be added to your credit card account. Most credit card banks will add an address to your credit card account for this purpose. You usually need to call your bank directly and provide them with the address. Some banks require you to fax or mail the request.

Once you have worked with your bank to have the new address added to your credit card account, you'll need to have it confirmed by PayPal:

1. Log into PayPal, click the My Account tab, and then click Profile.
2. Select Street Address under Account Information.

3. Click Add, fill in the new address, and click Save when you're done.

4. Select the address you just entered and click Confirm.

5. Fill in your credit card information and click Continue.

If everything goes smoothly, PayPal will now designate that address as Confirmed and you'll get all the benefits of using a confirmed address.

Alternatively, if the need arises, you can use the Alternative Address Confirmation (AAC) process described on the PayPal web site.

—*Patrick Breitenbach*

Pay When You've Forgotten Your Password

Use an extra credit card to pay when you can't get into your account and don't have time to recover a forgotten password

If you find you have forgotten your password, PayPal can help. But if you need to make a payment now and don't have time to recover your password (a process that can take from a minute to over a week, depending on how much you know about your own account and how current that information is), there is a shortcut: use a credit card that is not already attached to a PayPal account to make your purchase.

You can't use a credit card already attached to an existing PayPal account; the system won't allow it. If you have only one credit card, you're out of luck and will need to recover your password before you can make another payment.

Note that if your debit card doubles as a credit card, you can use it with PayPal, either for a one-time purchase or, more permanently, by attaching it to your PayPal account.

Here's how to do it:

1. Clear the cookies in your web browser.

2. Click the appropriate button to make the payment, such as a Buy Now button on a seller's web site or an eBay checkout flow.

3. Choose the option for paying with a credit card if you do not have a PayPal account ("If you don't have a PayPal account and want to pay with a credit card...").

4. You will be prompted to complete your payment.

Now that you have made your purchase, don't forget to recover your password! You have several choices at this point, depending on how much you know about your account and how current your account information is:

Security Questions and Answers

A forgotten password is a prime example of how PayPal uses the security questions you set up when you opened your PayPal account to protect you. Personal information (stuff that only you would know), such as your city of birth, your mother's maiden name, or the last four digits of your Social Security number, is used by PayPal to make sure you are who you say you are.

Make sure your security questions (and corresponding answers) are current and sufficiently private. To review your security questions or change your answers, open PayPal's Profile Summary page (My Account → Profile) and click Password. Choose the security questions from the list and click Edit.

Password reset by email

If one of your current email addresses is registered with your PayPal account, start the process by clicking the "Forget your password?" link in the Member Log In box on the PayPal home page. Type in your email address (one to which you currently have access), click Submit, and follow the further instructions in the email message you'll receive shortly. Click the link in the email to go to a page where you can answer questions about the bank and credit card accounts listed on your account or your personalized security questions (see the "Security Questions and Answers" sidebar). Once your identity has been verified, you'll be given the opportunity to choose a new password.

If you don't receive the email message, you might have an overly aggressive spam filter. Make sure to check your incoming spam folder or temporarily disable your spam filter (or your ISP's filter) and try again if you suspect that PayPal's confirmation email was deleted.

Telephone password recovery process

If you no longer use any of the email addresses registered with your PayPal account, but you do know the answer to your security questions and still use a telephone number registered with your account, you can use the telephone password recovery process:

a. First, click the "Forget your password?" link and enter your old email address as though you were still using it.

b. Next, click "I no longer have access to this email address." The system then verifies your identity by asking you to fill in some personal information. Provide this information and then click Submit.

    c. On the Password Recovery by Phone page, select the telephone number where you would like to be called and provide a current email address. Click Continue. A PayPal Confirmation PIN will be shown.

    d. Next, PayPal places an automated telephone call to the phone number associated with your account. Assuming you're able to answer, you'll be asked to enter the PIN provided by PayPal into the telephone keypad, followed by the pound key (#).

    e. Once you have done so, hang up and click Continue. You will be prompted to enter (and reenter) a new password and select and answer two security questions. Remember this password. Use it with the email address you just added to log in to your PayPal account.

If all else fails

If neither of these solutions works, you can recover your password by postal mail and other means. At this point, it's best to contact PayPal directly and have customer service help you recover your password.

Obviously, it's best to keep all your information (email addresses, postal addresses, and phone numbers) current, so that if you ever need to recover an inaccessible account, you can do so in minutes rather than days.

Restore Your Account if It Has Been Limited

In the event that PayPal limits your account as a result of suspected fraud or other problem, you can restore it to its original, unrestricted state.

If PayPal determines that you have been engaging in fraudulent or high-risk activity (such as selling fake merchandise or using stolen credit cards) or that you have not been abiding by the terms of the user agreement (e.g., you've been using PayPal to sell pornographic material or weapons), PayPal will impose limits on your account. Your account might also be limited if you initiate a bank transfer that then fails due to insufficient funds or if you accept a payment that is later disputed by its sender.

PayPal often limits the account's access to certain features, such as sending, withdrawing, or even receiving money. This helps protect any other PayPal users with whom you've been dealing and helps reduce subsequent losses that PayPal would otherwise have to incur.

        You know that PayPal has limited your account when your Account Overview page has a pink box that says Account Access Limited. As you might expect, click the "Click here for details" link for an explanation.

PayPal prides itself on being good at spotting high-risk behavior, but they also recognize that not all high-risk transactions are necessarily fraudulent or bad and not all disputes are the seller's fault. Thus, PayPal has an appeals process for those who have had their accounts limited.

Filing an Appeal

Needless to say, the best thing you can do if your account has been limited is to precisely follow the instructions on the web site and in the notification email you receive. Often, this entails completing a sequence of steps to provide PayPal with evidence of ownership of the PayPal account, ownership of the financials attached to the account, and verification of your own identity and address.

 Only after you have completed *all* the required steps will a PayPal Account Review Representative review your account. For instance, if PayPal asks you to fax several documents, your account will not be reviewed until you submit all requested documents and have completed all the remaining steps.

In addition, make sure to double-check the email you received notifying you of your account's limited access, because the PayPal Account Review Representative might have added extra steps for you to complete that are not listed on the web site. For instance, if you are a seller on eBay, PayPal will likely request tracking information for items you've delivered and proof of inventory for additional items you're currently selling.

 If you lose the email, you might not necessarily be able to find all the steps to complete on the PayPal web site; in this case, your best bet is to call PayPal **[Hack #9]**. However, if you no longer have access to your email account **[Hack #4]**, you might have bigger fish to fry.

A Last Resort

If you're really in a bind and cannot complete the steps requested of you for legitimate reasons, you can always escalate your issue by writing a letter to a PayPal executive, contacting the Better Business Bureau, or working with a legal representative.

Escalation in itself is not a guarantee that your issue will be resolved, but if your issue is legitimate, it is likely that a new pair of eyes, perhaps with more experience and background, will look at your issue and help reach a fair resolution.

Avoiding Suspicion

To prevent your account from being limited in the first place, keep your account in order by following these guidelines:

- Treat your PayPal account as you would your bank account: use secret passwords and keep them to yourself!

- Make sure your true name is on your PayPal account and that it matches the name on your bank and credit card accounts. If you are a business, make sure the bank account and credit card on your account are also in your business name.

- Use accurate addresses and phone numbers that match those on your credit card and bank account, and keep them current. False contact information can raise suspicion on your account and make it more difficult to regain access.

- Delete old or obsolete bank accounts and credit cards from your account. If you do not keep your account up-to-date, you might find yourself in a bind when your account is limited and PayPal asks you to prove ownership of a bank account with an old address.

- If you are a seller, always use electronically trackable shipping methods [Hack #24] so that if the shipment or receipt of a physical good is in doubt, you can easily prove your case. Also make sure to keep proof of inventory or merchandise, such as receipts, invoices, or proof of authenticity for older, collectible items. Maintain good relationships with your suppliers so that you can easily access this information when you need it.

- If you have any old or abandoned PayPal accounts, make sure to resolve your issues with those accounts and then close them. If your account has been limited and PayPal sees linked accounts with issues, such as a negative balance or outstanding buyer complaints, PayPal will probably ask you to resolve those issues as well before they'll be willing to lift the limitation on your active account.

See Also

There are lots of things you can do to protect yourself and your account, both before and after you encounter a problem. See the following hacks for more details:

- "Dispute Merchandise Payments" [Hack #16]
- "Protect Yourself from Buyer Fraud" [Hack #24]
- "Protect Yourself from Chargebacks" [Hack #25]

—Sarah Livnet

HACK
#6

Create a Separate Login for Each Employee

Use PayPal's Multi-User Access feature to provide a separate login for each employee in your organization.

Even though you might trust your employees to take care of your kids for the weekend, you might have second thoughts about giving them full access your organization's PayPal account. To that end, the Multi-User Access system enables you to add up to 200 different *users* to a single account, each with configurable account privileges. Each user is assigned a separate login ID and password.

Adding a New User

PayPal first has you establish an Administrative email address. PayPal will send all email notifications related to your account Profile to this email address. This is a security precaution so that PayPal can alert you at a different email address if someone tries to change the primary email address on your account.

PayPal steers you in this direction the first time you try to create a new user. Even before that, you should make sure you have at least two email addresses registered and confirmed in your account [Hack #8].

Once you have your two email addresses, you are ready:

1. Log in to PayPal, and go to Profile → Multi-User Access.
2. Select an address from the list; note that you won't be able to select your Primary address.
3. To create your first login, click Add and type in the user's name when prompted. It's best to use the person's actual name, but you could also consider using a job function or other nickname (e.g., *Customer Service 1*).
4. Choose a User ID (must be 10–16 characters).

> The length requirement and restriction against special characters make choosing a user ID is less than optimal. Further compounding the problem, these user IDs need to be unique for all of PayPal, not just for your account (e.g., *customerservice* and *jennifersmith* were taken a long time ago). A good approach is to think up a short prefix to append to the front of each user ID, perhaps something related to your business name—for example, *abcJohnSmith* and *abcMaryJones*. User IDs are not case sensitive, so you'll be able to log in with *abcJohnSmith* and *abcjohnsmith*.

5. Choose a password (must be eight characters or longer).

6. Check off the boxes that correspond to the privileges you want to grant this user. A good rule of thumb is to initially grant the fewest privileges possible when setting up a new user. You can always add more privileges later. But you can't undo mishaps!

7. Click Save when you're done.

You should now see something like Figure 1-3.

Figure 1-3. Adding new users to your account

You can add up to 200 users to your account, each with different login privileges.

Setting Privileges

You have a lot of flexibility in setting up different privileges for different users, as shown in Figure 1-4. To allow read-only access, leave all boxes unchecked.

Obviously, the users and privileges you assign depends on how many employees you have and how you run your business. A typical medium-sized business might use the following setup:

Customer Service Rep
Leave all boxes unchecked for read-only access.

Refund Rep
Check the Refunds option.

Financial Reconciliation
Turn on the View Balance and Settlement File options.

Head of Finance
Check View Balance and Withdraw Funds.

If your employees or partners used to log in with your password, it's a good idea to change it once you get everyone set up.

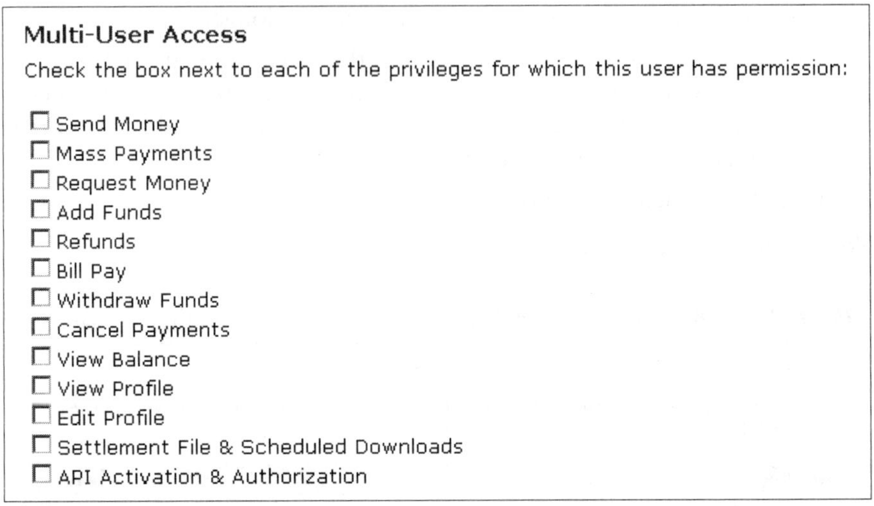

Multi-User Access

Check the box next to each of the privileges for which this user has permission:

☐ Send Money
☐ Mass Payments
☐ Request Money
☐ Add Funds
☐ Refunds
☐ Bill Pay
☐ Withdraw Funds
☐ Cancel Payments
☐ View Balance
☐ View Profile
☐ Edit Profile
☐ Settlement File & Scheduled Downloads
☐ API Activation & Authorization

Figure 1-4. Selecting any combination of privileges for each user

Adding an Administrative Account

An additional benefit of Multi-User Access is that you can create a user-name-based login for yourself. Traditionally, a user logs into PayPal with an email address and a password. I don't know about you, but my email address is pretty lengthy, and having to type the ampersand (@) and dot (.) characters gets annoying.

Just add a new user to your account, and check all the boxes to give yourself full access.

You'll probably want to leave API Activation unchecked; that setting is needed only for using the PayPal API **[Hack #88]**.

Responding if Something Goes Wrong

If you spot unexpected account activity, it's best to do some research before starting to point fingers. Review all the users and their privileges. If none appear to have the privilege to perform the activity you discovered, someone else might have used your login.

Unfortunately, the PayPal site doesn't indicate the name of the person who performed any given activity on your account. If you really get into a bind, you can contact PayPal's Customer Service and they will be able to pull up a list of user activity. PayPal usually also has the IP address of the computer that was

Protect Your Account Against Phishing

Phishing, the act of sending out bogus emails and creating fake web sites to trick users into giving up their passwords, has become a major problem on the internet. Phishers have become so adept at their profession that they have even managed to secure passwords from the most savvy of web users.

Creating PayPal logins for your employees with limited privileges can minimize the consequences if one of your employees yields to a phisher. If you suspect that you or one of your employees has unknowingly given their password to a phisher, you should first attempt to change your administrative password. Then, contact PayPal Customer Service to let them know what might have happened. They usually can shut down any nefarious activity before it happens, provided that you contact them promptly.

used, so you might be able to match it to one of your company's PCs or determine that the activity was performed from outside your company.

—*Patrick Breitenbach*

Access Member Information

Use the information PayPal publishes about members to scope out sellers and buyers, and see what they can learn about you.

While all human relationships are built on trust, you might not want to rely on blind faith alone when your money is at stake. To help you determine which vendors and customers to trust and which to avoid, PayPal offers information about its members' standing with PayPal.

Looking Up a User's Status

You can check any PayPal account's User Status by initiating (but not necessarily completing) a transaction with that user:

1. Log in to your PayPal account.
2. Click the Request Money tab.
3. Enter the email address of your prospective buyer, enter an amount to request (a single penny will do), and select the type Goods (other).
4. Click Continue.
5. The Request Money—Confirm page that appears (shown in Figure 1-5) will tell you the account type, Seller Reputation Number, and verification status of your buyer. Click the reputation link after Recipient Status: for information on the age of the account.

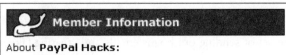

About PayPal Hacks:

To protect your security, PayPal offers information on the status of this member.

Seller Reputation:	(1426) Verified Buyers
Account Status:	Verified
Account Type:	U.S. Business
Account Creation Date:	Oct. 20, 2003
PayPal Member For:	6 months 8 days

- Member does not accept payments from Non-U.S. users
- Member only accepts payments with a Confirmed Address

Cust. Service Email: support@paypalhacks.com

Seller Reputation
The Seller Reputation Number measures how many Verified PayPal members have paid that seller. New transactions are added 30 days after they occur, to ensure that the Reputation Number reflects successful exchanges.

Account Status
U.S. Users are considered "Verified" if they have confirmed the bank account they have added to their PayPal account. Verification is a positive signal to the Community that a user has complied with Community security measures.

Account Type
Accounts can be Personal, Premier, or Business. Active sellers are required to have a Premier or Business account.

Please note that this information is not an endorsement or guarantee but a summary of a member's status with PayPal provided to help the Community evaluate the other members with whom they transact.

Figure 1-5. Checking a buyer's User Status

6. Because you are just making an inquiry here and don't actually intend to request money, click Cancel.

If you don't complete the transaction, the would-be recipient will not be notified.

Understanding the User Status

Here are some of the things you'll see in the Member Information box:

Seller Reputation
Although PayPal refers to these scores as *reputation numbers*, they are based solely on the number of transactions completed. Unlike feedback

scores at eBay and other community-oriented sites, PayPal reputation numbers are not in any way based on ratings from other PayPal members.

 PayPal's calculation of reputation numbers is delayed, such that any transaction in which you're involved won't be counted until 30 days after the transaction completes successfully. Also, only transactions $5.00 or greater in value with verified members are counted.

Account Status
This field shows whether or not the account is verified [Hack #2].

Account Type
This shows the country in which the account is registered and whether it is a Personal, Premier, or Business account (the differences between these account types are described in the introduction to Chapter 3).

Account Creation Date
This field is self-explanatory: the date that the PayPal account was created. (This information is restated in the PayPal Member For field.)

Checking Your Reputation as a Seller

Before conducting business or making payments with your PayPal account, you'd be wise to know what others can learn about *you* through PayPal.

If you have a Premier or Business account, a number will appear in parentheses after the word Verified or Unverified in the Account Overview page. Click the number to display your Member Information Box, the same box others see when they use the procedure in the beginning of this hack.

To find the Member Information Box for your Personal account, you'll need to use another PayPal account (either your own or a friend's) and follow the same procedure.

Checking Your Reputation as a Buyer

To find out your Buyer Reputation Number, go to *https://www.paypal.com/REPNUM*. If you have not logged in, you will be prompted to do so. Click "View your Buyer and Seller Reputation Numbers" near the bottom of the page to display your Buyer and Seller Reputation Numbers.

As confusing as it might be, your Buyer Reputation Number is not the same as your Seller Reputation Number. See the "Why Is My Seller Reputation Zero?" sidebar for more information.

Why Is My Seller Reputation Zero?

If you have used PayPal for some time as a buyer but are accepting payments for goods for the first time, you might be surprised to find your Seller Reputation Number is 0. The explanation lies with two numbers PayPal maintains for every account: a Seller Reputation Number and a Buyer Reputation Number.

Your Buyer Reputation Number measures the number of unique verified PayPal members you have paid, while your Seller Reputation Number tells you how many unique verified PayPal members have paid you.

Purchasing goods and services with PayPal can, over time, drive your Buyer Reputation Number into the stratosphere. But until you rack up qualifying *sales*, your Seller Reputation Number will languish.

HACK #8 Manage PayPal Email

Set up multiple email accounts and filtering to manage PayPal email notifications more efficiently.

PayPal sends a lot of email to its members, ranging from payment notifications to PayPal news and account updates. It's not uncommon for important emails to get lost in the shuffle. But there are several things you can do to make PayPal emails more manageable.

There are two primary strategies to make email more manageable:

- Set up multiple email accounts for different purposes.
- Use the routing and filtering capabilities of your email reader to segregate the different types of email.

Setting Up Multiple Email Addresses

As you've probably figured out, email addresses are very important at PayPal. You log in with an email address, send money to other email addresses, and receive "You've got cash" emails (the most-read email messages on the Internet, by the way!) in your own email inbox.

But PayPal doesn't limit you to one email address, and with good reason: by associating multiple email addresses with a single account, it can be easier to deal with incoming payments and the associated orders that need to be filled.

The first thing you can do is register a second email address to be used to notify you of changes to your account Profile. If you are using PayPal's Multi-User Access feature [Hack #6], you've already set up an administrative email address. But if not, consider doing so anyway, even if you don't intend to use the Multi-User Access feature.

PayPal uses the administrative email address to send notices when you make changes to your Profile. This is primarily a security measure intended to make it more difficult for a thief or phisher to gain access to your account and change your primary email address.

Before setting up an administrative email address, you should have access to at least two email accounts. Many ISPs allow single users to hold multiple email accounts, and if you have your own domain name, so much the better. Otherwise, you can use one of the free providers, such as Yahoo, Hotmail or Gmail.

1. Log into PayPal and click Profile.

2. Go to Email under Account Information.

3. Make sure you have at least two confirmed email addresses listed (there's no indicator that an email address is confirmed, but an Unconfirmed label will appear next to unconfirmed addresses). If you need to confirm an address, do so now by selecting an address and clicking Confirm. Or, click Add to enter a new address, and then confirm it.

4. PayPal sends an email to the new account; open it, click the link inside, and enter your password at the PayPal web site when prompted.

5. Next, set up your administrative email by returning to the Profile page and clicking Multi-User Access.

6. Select the email address that you want to use as the administrative email address and click Save.

Using Different Email Addresses

Probably the most beneficial aspect to using more than one email address is that you can more easily separate payments made for different purposes. For instance, you might have both *website@paypalhacks.com* and *ebay@paypalhacks.com* registered to a single PayPal account, one for web site payments and the other for eBay auction payments.

Not only does PayPal send the "You've got cash" notification to the email address to which the payment was sent, but PayPal also keeps track of that address for future reference. For example, in PayPal's downloadable logs, one of the columns lists which email address received the payment that was sent, making it easy to sort and group payments.

You can type either email address into your web site payment buttons [Hack #28], into eBay's Sell Your Item form, or even in text links [Hack #17].

Regardless of how you end up using them, you'll most likely want to filter your email so that different payment notifications are sent to different places.

Filtering Your Incoming Email

After setting up a second address, you'll still receive a lot of email from PayPal; it'll just be divided across both addresses. Most email applications, as well as many web-based email services, offer ways to filter, route, and automatically file emails in different folders.

A basic filter in Outlook Express, shown in Figure 1-6, sorts messages into different folders depending on the email address to which the payment was sent.

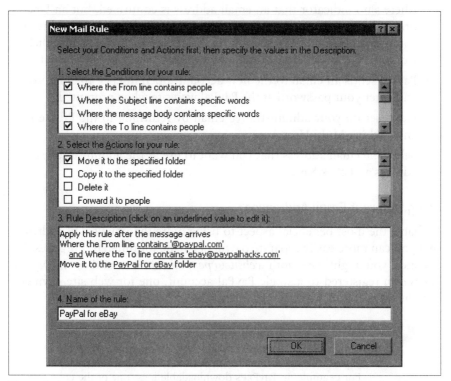

Figure 1-6. Setting up Outlook to automatically route emails to folders based on the From address or Subject line

Here's how to set up a Mail Rule in Outlook Express for Windows to separate your PayPal email:

1. Start Outlook Express
2. Right-click on Local Folders and select New Folder.
3. Type PayPal for eBay and press Enter to create a new mail folder.
4. Go to Tools → Message Rules → Mail.
5. Turn on both the "Where the From line contains people" and "Where the To line contains people" option in box 1.
6. Turn on the "Move it to the specified folder" option in box 2.
7. In box 3, next to "Where the From line," click "contains people" and type @paypal.com. Click Add and then OK when you're done here.
8. In box 3, next to "Where the To line," click "contains people" and type the first of your email addresses on file with PayPal (e.g., *ebay@paypalhacks.com*). Click Add and then OK when you're done here, too.
9. Click "specified" in box 3, and select the new PayPal folder you created in step 3.
10. Name the rule something like *PayPal* in box 4, click OK, and then click OK again when you're done.
11. Repeat these steps for each additional email address you have on file for PayPal, specifying a different folder for each address.

That's just a start; you can be creative, doing such things as automatically sending "Thank you for your purchase" emails to all your eBay customers, for instance.

You can also prioritize your mail by severity: set up a mail rule that looks for "Notification of Reversed Transaction" in the Subject line and route it to a *Reversals* folder.

Setting Notification Preferences

PayPal sends out a lot of email to its members, but luckily, most of it can be turned off by using the Notifications settings in your account Profile, as shown in Figure 1-7.

> As desirable as it might be, you won't be able to turn off every single notification. PayPal will still send the occasional email describing changes to the Terms of Use and major product changes.

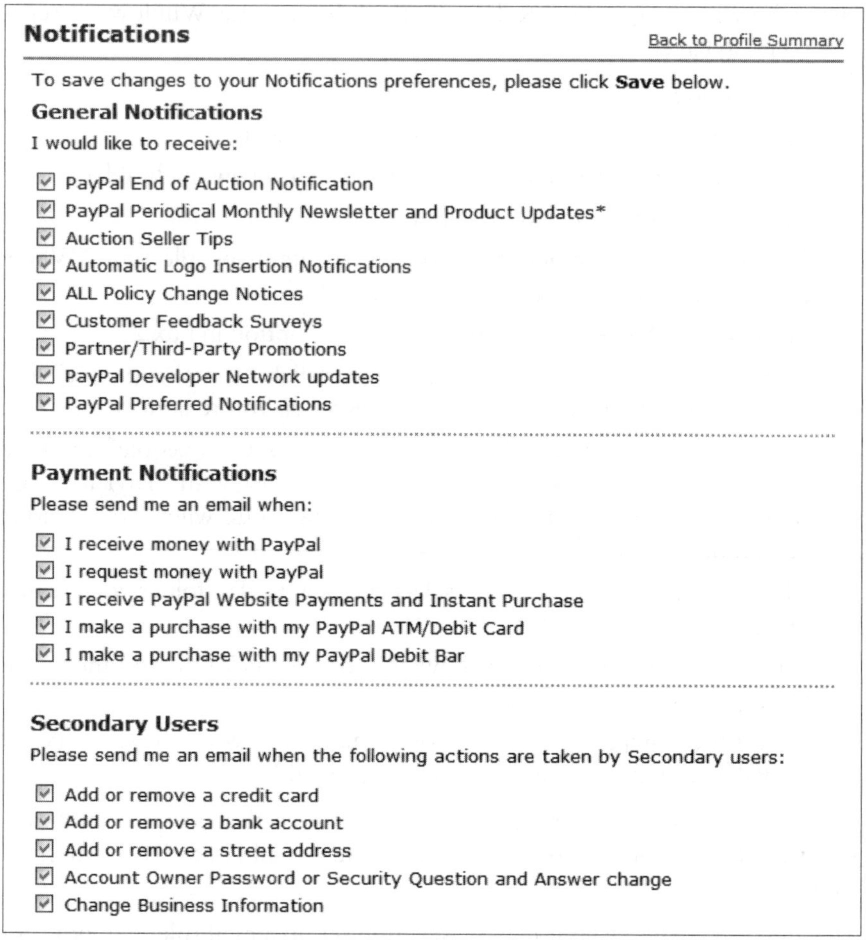

Notifications   Back to Profile Summary

To save changes to your Notifications preferences, please click **Save** below.

General Notifications

I would like to receive:

- ☑ PayPal End of Auction Notification
- ☑ PayPal Periodical Monthly Newsletter and Product Updates*
- ☑ Auction Seller Tips
- ☑ Automatic Logo Insertion Notifications
- ☑ ALL Policy Change Notices
- ☑ Customer Feedback Surveys
- ☑ Partner/Third-Party Promotions
- ☑ PayPal Developer Network updates
- ☑ PayPal Preferred Notifications

Payment Notifications

Please send me an email when:

- ☑ I receive money with PayPal
- ☑ I request money with PayPal
- ☑ I receive PayPal Website Payments and Instant Purchase
- ☑ I make a purchase with my PayPal ATM/Debit Card
- ☑ I make a purchase with my PayPal Debit Bar

Secondary Users

Please send me an email when the following actions are taken by Secondary users:

- ☑ Add or remove a credit card
- ☑ Add or remove a bank account
- ☑ Add or remove a street address
- ☑ Account Owner Password or Security Question and Answer change
- ☑ Change Business Information

Figure 1-7. Choosing which emails you want to receive from PayPal

Some PayPal users actually prefer to receive every email that PayPal sends, and given the sensitive nature of the business, this is understandable. Since you can automatically filter the various email messages PayPal sends you, you might be more inclined to sign up for all of PayPal's emails. Of course, if a message subsequently sneaks through the Mail Rule, you can easily modify the rule or create a new filter to catch it the next time. That way, you'll always have an archive of messages relating to your account, without having them clutter up your Inbox.

—*Patrick Breitenbach*

Get Help from PayPal

When things go wrong, don't run screaming for the hills. Use PayPal's various forms and phone numbers to get help fast.

Even if you aren't much of a fan of online help systems, it's probably the best place to start if you run into a problem with your account. PayPal Help is especially useful when it comes to PayPal's vast assortment of policies and procedures.

You'll find a link to Help in the upper-right corner of every page of the PayPal site. There are two main ways to use PayPal Help:

- Browse by category (e.g., Making Payments, Seller Tools, etc.)
- Search using natural language questions (e.g., "how do I earn interest?")

As with most search engines, you don't have to type a whole question to get good results. "add email" works just as well as "Can I add another email address?"

> If the answer you find is particularly good or bad, you can do your good deed for the PayPal community by pressing the "Was the answer helpful?" buttons. We're told that PayPal actually does modify the Help system based on this feedback. In fact, PayPal performed a large-scale redesign of the Help system in early 2004.

Unfortunately PayPal's Help URLs do not remain constant, so don't try to bookmark specific pages for future reference. If you need to refer a friend or customer to a PayPal Help page, it's best to indicate a search term that brings up the article in question.

Email Support

Like many companies, PayPal doesn't let you send a regular email directly to Customer Service. You must navigate through some web forms and give the web site the chance to answer your question. But eventually, you can write an open-ended question to PayPal. PayPal has a large support staff in Omaha, Nebraska, as well as in Omaha's unofficial sister city, Dublin, Ireland, to answer your questions and process your requests.

> If you have a PayPal account (and are able to log in), you should always log in before sending your message. Doing so makes it much easier for PayPal to locate and reference your account.

As with any email inquiry, it's crucial that you provide as specific and clear information about your situation as you can. Instead of paraphrasing error messages or web page text, copy and paste the exact passage. PayPal gives you up to 1,000 characters with which to write your question, which should cover most situations.

> You should never type your password or complete credit card number in a web form or email, even when sending it to PayPal.

Telephone Support

Let's be honest; some situations require talking to an actual person on the phone:

- If you're in the U.S., call PayPal toll-free at 888-221-1161.
- If you are outside the U.S. or for any reason need to use a non–toll-free number, call 402-935-2050. European customers can call 0870-730-7191.

PayPal Customer Service representatives can talk only to the primary contact listed on the account. To verify this, they will likely ask you for your telephone number, email address, or last four digits from your credit card or bank account number, so make sure to have these on hand when you call.

If you don't have access to a live Internet connection while calling, try to prepare for the call ahead of time by collecting all the specific information about your inquiry. This information might include such details as the PayPal transaction ID, payment date and amount, payment recipient, eBay auction number and username, online store web site address, and so on.

Support Forums

There are several online support forums that can also be good places to ask questions and get answers. PayPal has two official forums:

- The PayPal forum at the eBay Discussion Boards (*http://forums.ebay.com/db2/forum.jsp?forum=97*)
- The PayPal Developer Forums (*http://developer.paypal.com*)

Good independent forums include:

Fatwallet (http://www.fatwallet.com)
    For general information about a variety of online commerce topics.

Vendio Community (http://www.vendio.com/mesg/)
> For discussions about online auctions. See the eBay boards, as well as the PayPal board under Vendio Partner Services.

PayPalDev.org (http://www.paypaldev.org)
> An independently operated board for PayPal programmers.

eBay University

Finally, eBay offers hands-on courses in which you can learn a lot about trading on eBay from expert instructors. While eBay University is heavily focused on eBay, PayPal is becoming an increasingly popular topic. Furthermore, instructors usually stick around after the course to answer any PayPal questions you might have. To find out when eBay University will be in your area, check the eBay site (*http://www.ebay.com/university/*).

—Patrick Breitenbach

Making Payments
Hacks 10–16

So, you've just bought a genuine Zapp Brannigan Atomic Ray Gun on eBay, and now it's time to pony up the dough. You might be able to mail a personal check, but most sellers won't take them (and when they do, there's an extra week to wait for them to clear). Money orders and cashier's checks usually cost money and take several days to arrive, and then there's still no protection if the seller takes the ray gun and runs. Some sellers accept credit cards directly, but few provide online ordering or other safe means of sending your payment information.

This is where many buyers are introduced to PayPal. With a few clicks and usually no typing, you can send large or small sums of money across the country or around the world almost instantaneously and get fraud protection while doing it.

The first thing to remember when making a payment with PayPal is to be certain you've got it right. Review the details of the payment you're about to make on the Check Payment Details page, because once you hit the Pay button, there is no going back. You won't be able to rescind the payment, change the recipient in the case of a typo, or change the way the payment is funded [Hack #11].

> Keep a close eye on the source of funds [Hack #11]; if you don't have enough money in your checking account and would prefer to use your credit card instead, you'll need to make that selection before you pay. Even if your recipient were to refund the payment immediately [Hack #21], the funds would still be pulled from your bank account or charged on your credit card.

Now, none of this means that PayPal doesn't have policies in place to protect you. If the recipient doesn't claim a pending payment within 30 days, for example, you'll get it back automatically. And you'll be able to dispute payments made for merchandise [Hack #16] in the event of fraud. But the person in the best position to protect your money is you, so use that position wisely.

Send Money to Anyone

Use PayPal's most basic feature to send money to anyone with an email address, even if the recipient doesn't have a PayPal account.

It's a little-known fact that you can send money to anyone who has an email address: the person to whom you send money doesn't need a PayPal account! The only information you need is the recipient's email address and, of course, the amount of money you would like to send.

Back in the days when PayPal was giving away $10 for each new account referred, some entrepreneurial students would send $.20 payments to every kid in their school in hopes that the recipient would create an account. If no one claimed the payment, the money would eventually go back to the sender. Not a bad moneymaking scheme, even if only 1 in 20 recipients signed up! Today, with over 50,000 new users each day, PayPal doesn't offer such a bounty for referral. However, you can still enjoy the fun of surprising someone with a "You've got cash" email.

Sending a Payment via Email

To send money to someone (whether they have a PayPal account or not):

1. Log into your PayPal account.
2. Click the Send Money tab, and then click the Pay Anyone subtab.
3. Enter the recipient's email address.
4. Enter the amount to send and select the currency you wish to use.
5. For Type, select Goods or Service if you are paying someone back for a good or service they provided you.

> If you select Quasi-Cash and pay with a credit card or debit card, your card issuer might treat the transaction as a cash advance and charge you a cash advance fee.

6. Enter a Subject and a Note (both are optional). The Subject is important, because it appears as the subject of the email sent to the recipient of your payment. The note, however, is less likely to be seen, because it appears buried in the email. If you need to include important details, it is best to send them in a separate email.
7. Click Continue when you're finished with this page. The next page shows a summary of the payment.

> At this point, if the recipient does not have a PayPal account, you'll see, "This recipient is not yet registered. PayPal will send an email to the recipient explaining how to open an account and receive your transaction." See the next section of this hack for details on what to do if your recipient doesn't open an account.

8. Click More Funding Options to choose how to fund your payment [Hack #11].

9. If you are just sending money to a friend, select "No shipping address required" in the Shipping Information section. Otherwise, if you are paying for an item that will be shipped to you, you'll most likely want to provide your address. Note that some sellers will refuse your payment if you don't include a confirmed address [Hack #3].

10. Click Send Money when you're done.

To confirm that everything has gone as planned, PayPal will send you a "Receipt of your payment" email to notify you that you have indeed sent the money. If the recipient has a PayPal account, she will receive a similar email letting her know that she has received money. If the recipient doesn't have an account, PayPal will send a "You've got cash" email, along with instructions to sign up for a PayPal account. Only after signing up for an account will the recipient be able to access your payment.

If you pay with a credit card and the recipient has a Premier or Business account, the money will be deposited directly into the account. If you're sending money to a friend, you might want to send it to her personal account to avoid the PayPal fees, although this means you won't be able to fund the payment with a credit card [Hack #11].

What If They Don't Sign Up?

If you send money to someone without a PayPal account, it's possible that the recipient won't sign up and claim the money. This can happen, for instance, if the recipient confuses PayPal's "You've got cash" email with unsolicited spam. Also, many people feel uneasy about signing up for a service like PayPal, thinking that they might be charged a bunch of fees or that they'll be victimized if they share their financial information over the Internet. For this reason, you might need to reassure skittish payees before sending them money with PayPal.

If, for whatever reason, the recipient doesn't sign up and claim the payment within 30 days, PayPal will return the funds to your account (or refund your credit card, if that's how you funded the payment). PayPal will also reverse the payment if you try to send a credit card–funded payment to a Personal account and the recipient doesn't upgrade to a Business or Premier account within 30 days to accept the payment. Either way, you can try to resend the money, but your best bet is to contact the recipient separately via email to ensure you have the right email address and that they understand what they need to do to get the money.

> Just as you would look someone in the face before handing over a fistful of cash, be sure to double-check the email address of the recipient before you send money, because there isn't any easy way to get your money back if you send it to the wrong person. See "Dispute Merchandise Payments" [Hack #16] if this happens to you.

If you decide to cancel an unclaimed payment for any reason, you can reverse the transaction before the 30-day automatic reversal period *only* if the recipient has not signed up and claimed the money. To cancel a pending payment, log into your PayPal account and click the History tab to view your transaction history. Find the payment you'd like to reverse and click the Cancel button.

HACK #11 Choose How to Fund Payments

Select your preferred payment funding source each time you make a payment, a necessary step if you want to pay with a credit card or alternate bank account.

While a primary reason so many people use PayPal (PayPal reports over 45 million users as of March 31, 2004) is to send and receive credit card payments, there are several other ways to make a payment without using a credit card at all.

Each time you make a payment [Hack #10], PayPal displays the Source of Funds (as shown in Figure 2-1) that will be used to make the payment on the Check Payment Details page and gives you an opportunity to switch sources if you so desire. Always review how you're making your payment and switch payment sources if necessary.

Source of Funds

       Credit Card: $75.00 USD from American Express XXXX-XXXXXX-1006

More Funding Options

Figure 2-1. Choosing a source of funds

Click More Funding Options to display the Funding Options page, as shown in Figure 2-2. Each time you make a payment, you can select a funding source among several choices.

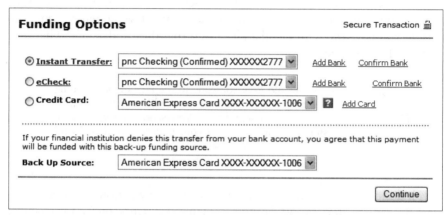

Figure 2-2. Selecting funding options

PayPal offers several different ways to fund your payment:

PayPal Balance
If you have funds sitting in your PayPal account, they are always used first when making a payment. Only if the amount of your payment exceeds your balance will you be able to choose the source for the remaining funds. The exception is the eCheck option, which can be used whether or not you have funds in your PayPal account. See the next section of this hack for a workaround.

Instant Transfer
The funds necessary to make the payment will be drawn from your bank account. Although PayPal does not actually get the funds from your bank for several days (thus, the transfer is not technically *instant*), the payment recipient will have immediate access to the funds you have sent.

Because of this, PayPal requires that you set up a backup funding source to be used in the event that the bank transfer fails (i.e., the transfer bounces). Your credit card is normally used as the backup funding source; if you don't have a credit card on file with your PayPal account, you might have to send an eCheck instead.

Credit Card
An immediate charge to your credit card or debit card will be made. In the U.S., PayPal supports Visa, MasterCard, American Express, and Discover. In the UK, Switch and Solo are also supported.

One reason people like to pay with a credit card is the added protection afforded by credit card issuers. Fortunately, if you use PayPal to pay for an eBay auction (and some other terms are met), you might be eligible for the Buyer Protection Policy [Hack #16], regardless of the funding source you choose for the payment.

eCheck

An eCheck is a noninstant bank transfer, in which your payment will remain pending until PayPal receives the funds from your bank. When the bank transfer clears, PayPal switches the payment status to Completed and deposits the money in the recipient's account. This usually takes two to four business days. eChecks are useful for large payments (greater than $1,000), since they can be used when other payment options aren't available (if, for example, you have maxed out your credit card).

The maximum fee assessed to an eCheck recipient is $5.00. This means that eChecks are a good way to lower your seller fees [Hack #23], at least for any payment of US$162.07 or more. Although you, as the buyer, will not directly benefit from this price advantage, you might be able to negotiate a discount on the purchase, since the seller will be saving quite a bit on PayPal transaction fees. For example, on a $1,000 purchase, the seller could stand to save $17.90 to $24.30 in transaction fees.

Overriding the Funding Source Hierarchy

As mentioned in the previous section, if you have a balance in your PayPal account, it will be used to fund all your payments. Only if the amount of a payment exceeds your balance will you be able to fund your payment with a credit card or checking account transfer. (An eCheck can be sent regardless of your PayPal balance, however.)

To work around this limitation, bring your account balance down to zero before making your payment. Here's how to do it:

1. Make a payment to an email address that you control but that isn't registered with PayPal. Set the amount of the payment equal to the balance in your PayPal account.

As described in "Send Money to Anyone" [Hack #10], the status of the payment will be *pending*, because it was sent to an email address that is not registered with PayPal.

2. Make the payment you were originally intending, and fund it with a credit card or Instant Transfer.

3. Once you've completed the payment, go to your payment history and cancel the pending payment you made to yourself. The funds will then be moved back into your PayPal account.

This is a quick and effective way to use a credit card or Instant Transfer, without having to withdraw any funds in your account [Hack #20].

eBay-only Payment Methods

eBay buyers have the benefit of three additional PayPal payment methods not available elsewhere:

eBay Anything Points
> eBay Anything Points is a loyalty program, similar to airline frequent flyer miles, introduced by eBay in 2003. You can earn points from:
>
> * Companies who have partnered with eBay to offer points for joining their service (for example, Hilton, American Airlines, and Earthlink)
> * Individual eBay sellers who offer points to the winning bidders of their auctions
> * Every purchase made with the eBay Credit Card
>
> Once you've saved up enough Anything Points, you can use them with PayPal to make purchases for eBay auctions. When you go through the eBay checkout process, before you get to the PayPal payment screen, you have the option of using eBay Anything Points to pay the entire amount or just a portion of it. For more information, visit *http://anythingpoints.ebay.com*.

eBay Gift Certificates
> If someone emails you an eBay Gift Certificate, it shows up in your PayPal account, just like an ordinary payment. You can apply it to any auction you win, provided that you go through the eBay checkout process. For more information, visit *https://certificates.ebay.com*.

PayPal Buyer Credit
> PayPal Buyer Credit is basically a personal loan extended to you by PayPal (actually, by PayPal's lending partner, GE Credit), that can be paid down over time. As with most forms of credit, not everyone gets approved, and if you don't pay your bill on time, you will pay penalties. PayPal Buyer Credit can be used only on eBay listings in which the seller explicitly offers the Buyer Credit option.

Buying from Outside the USA

The funding sources available to non-U.S. users is more limited. For most countries, credit/debit cards and PayPal balances are the only methods available. Visa, MasterCard, American Express, and Discover can generally be used in any country, and UK users also have the option of Switch and Solo.

While the Instant Transfer and eCheck payment methods are not available outside the U.S., it is possible for German and Dutch users to load up their PayPal accounts from a bank account. You must prepare ahead of time, however, because this takes several days. PayPal provides all the bank account information needed to use the standard interbank transferring systems of Germany and the Netherlands.

PayPal expects to be able to offer an Instant Transfer–like payment method in Germany sometime in 2004.

Use Your PayPal Funds Anywhere

Use the PayPal Virtual Debit Bar to pay for goods or services at web sites that don't normally accept PayPal.

It's possible for you to pay someone via PayPal even if the recipient doesn't have a PayPal account [Hack #15], but only if you know the email address of the person or business to whom you wish to send money and only if the recipient is willing to sign up and accept your payment. But what do you do if you want to buy something from an online retailer that doesn't accept PayPal?

There is, as it turns out, a way to pay with PayPal as though your account were a debit or credit card. There's a hard-to-find page at PayPal that allows you to set up and use the virtual Debit Bar to turn your PayPal email address into a virtual MasterCard debit card number. To get a virtual debit card number, you'll need to do all of the following:

- Have a PayPal balance of at least one U.S. dollar
- Add and confirm control of a checking account [Hack #2]
- Add a credit card to your PayPal account and complete your Expanded Use Enrollment [Hack #3]

To use the virtual debit card, start by opening the virtual Debit Bar:

1. Log in to your PayPal account.
2. Visit the PayPal virtual Debit Bar web page (shown in Figure 2-3) at *https://www.paypal.com/us/cgi-bin/webscr?cmd=p/shop/vdebit*.

PayPal has removed most links to the virtual debit card from its web site, but you might still find it at this URL.

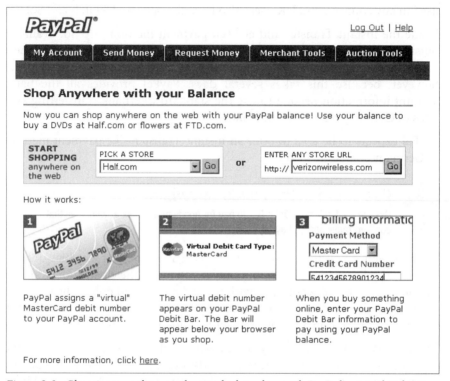

Figure 2-3. Choosing an online retailer at which to shop with PayPal's virtual Debit Bar

3. From the drop-down list, pick an online store from which you want to make a purchase; or, in the second box, enter the URL of the store (as shown in Figure 2-3). Either way, you can switch web sites at any time without affecting your virtual debit card.

4. Click the appropriate Go button. The online store you specified then opens in a new browser window and the virtual Debit Bar appears at the bottom of your screen in another browser window (as shown in Figure 2-4) and remains visible while you shop.

5. When you're ready to make a purchase, use the debit card information in the virtual Debit Bar just as you would any MasterCard debit card.

6. You will find all the debit card information on the Debit Bar. Fill out the billing information (name, billing address, debit card type, debit cart number, and expiration date) on the web site, just as you would with

Figure 2-4. The virtual Debit Bar

any other debit card. You can copy and paste the debit card information in the virtual Debit Bar to save time.

7. For the security of your PayPal Account, close the PayPal virtual Debit Bar browser window when you are finished shopping. Close the bar the same way you would any other web browser.

Keep the following in mind while using the virtual Debit Bar:

• You'll need at least one U.S. dollar in your PayPal account to activate the virtual Debit Bar, and you'll need sufficient funds in your account to cover any purchase you make. If you try to spend more than your current balance, your card will be declined.

• The spending limit for the virtual debit card is $150 per day.

• The virtual debit card does not have a three-digit Card Verification Value (CVV), so it won't be accepted by online retailers that require one.

• For those retailers that will ship only to your credit card billing address, your virtual debit card billing address is the same as the address listed with the primary credit card registered to your PayPal Account.

• The expiration date for your virtual debit card (displayed on the upper-right corner of the virtual Debit Bar window) is set for two years from the date the card number was issued.

 If you need a plastic debit card that is linked to your PayPal account, you can apply for a PayPal ATM/debit card **[Hack #20]**. You can also apply for a PayPal Providian credit card (*http://www.paypalcreditcard.com*), although it won't be linked to your PayPal account balance. Both plastic cards are available only to U.S. members.

Pay from a Cell Phone
Send a payment or request a payment with a WAP-enabled cell phone.

Imagine rummaging through items at a garage sale and finding a priceless antique. Now imagine checking in your wallet only to discover that you don't have the $19.00 to pay for it. What do you do? Hide the antique behind a box, run to the nearest ATM, and hope the item is still there when you return? No, you use your head, the power of PayPal, and the wonder of technology: pull out your web-enabled cell phone and use it to send a Pay-Pal payment on the spot!

To navigate to PayPal's Wireless Application Protocol (WAP) site, open your phone's browser, choose "Go to URL" (or something similar), enter paypal.com, and click OK.

 PayPal's WAP site is shown automatically to anyone access-ing *http://www.paypal.com* from a WAP-enabled cell phone or PDA. It's a secure (*https*) connection, but must already have a PayPal account before you can use it.

Sending Money

After you have successfully logged in, you can select the Send Money link from the main menu, as shown in Figure 2-5. Next, enter the recipient's email address, the amount in dollars, and the amount in cents.

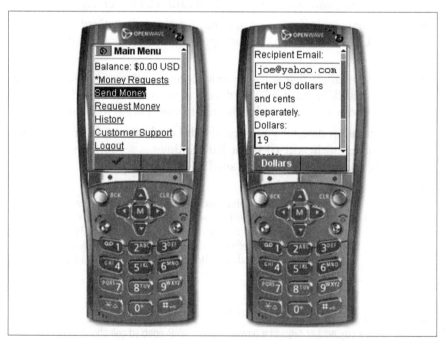

Figure 2-5. Sending a PayPal payment from a WAP-enabled cell phone

When you're done, click Submit. This brings you to a screen where you can confirm the payment by selecting Yes, as shown in Figure 2-6.

Figure 2-6. Select Yes to confirm your payment

Checking the Payment

After you have made the payment, the recipient might want to verify that the transaction has completed.

If you're feeling charitable and the recipient is standing next to you, you can simply log out on your phone, hand it over, and let her verify your payment.

To check the status of a payment, log into PayPal on your phone and select the History link to display a transaction log that lists transaction amounts (debit or credit) and transaction dates in chronological order (newest to oldest). Select a transaction to view more details, such as who sent the money and whether the transaction has completed successfully.

Requesting Payment with a Text Message

You can send an SMS message directly from your own cell phone, from the web site of your recipient's carrier, or from email. Each cell phone and carrier has a slightly different procedure; refer to your phone or calling plan documentation for details.

When you enter the text message, make sure to include paypal.com. If the recipient is using a WAP-enabled phone, he simply clicks the Go option button that appears and is taken to the PayPal WAP site to complete the transaction.

HACK #14 Pay Seller Fees when Buying

Send a payment along with the respective seller fees using the Mass Pay feature, so that your recipient gets precisely what you promised.

Whether a product is sold or a service is performed, most people generally accept that the product or service provider is responsible for paying any applicable processing fees. But there are plenty of scenarios in which the recipient of your payment is not expecting or willing to pay any fees:

- Someone who has loaned you money should not have to pay a fee to get paid back.
- Members of your web site's affiliate program [Hack #77] are not likely to expect to lose 2.9% of their referral fees.
- Those new to selling on eBay often don't realize that accepting PayPal for their auctions generates enough additional business to be worth the applicable PayPal fees. If you're buying something from an eBay seller who is unwilling to accept PayPal because of the fees, you can often grease the wheels by offering to cover the fees yourself.

Of course, PayPal doesn't charge seller fees for payments received into Personal accounts, but these accounts have their own limitations (described in the introduction to Chapter 3), rendering them useless for this purpose. If you need to make a payment to a recipient's Premier or Business account for a specific amount without generating fees for him, you have two options: calculate the seller fees yourself or use Mass Pay.

Calculating the Fees Yourself

The first solution is to include the applicable fees with your payment, so that when PayPal deducts the fees, the recipient ends up with the intended amount. The equation (yes, there's some math involved) to calculate the total amount received is as follows:

Amount Received = Amount Sent – PayPal Fees

Seller fees for Business and Premier accounts are typically 30 cents plus 2.9% of the amount sent. If you send someone $40, PayPal takes $1.46 (2.9% x $40 + $.30), leaving $38.54 for the recipient.

Non-U.S. account holders and those doing business with non-U.S. account holders might be subject to additional fees or a different fee rate. See [Hack #7] for a way to determine whether your recipient has a Personal account, in which case, no seller fees at all will be incurred.

If you're having trouble remembering your high-school algebra, you might think that all you'd have to do is pay an extra $1.46 for the recipient to get the correct payment, but it doesn't turn out that way:

Amount Received = Amount Sent – PayPal Fees
Amount Received = $41.46 – (2.9% x $41.46 + $.30)
Amount Received = $41.46 – $1.50
Amount Received = $39.96

It's close, but you've still underpaid by 4 cents. The reason is that the goal, $40 in this case, was plugged into the wrong part of the equation. Here's the correct calculation:

Amount Received = Amount Sent – PayPal Fees
$40 = Amount Sent – (2.9% x Amount Sent + $.30)
$40 + $.30 = Amount Sent – (2.9% x Amount Sent)
$40 + $.30 = Amount Sent x (1 – 2.9%)
($40 + $.30) / (1 – 2.9%) = Amount Sent
$41.50 = Amount Sent

Plugging $41.50 back into the original equation, you can see that it does indeed work:

Amount Received = $41.50 – (2.9% x $41.50 + $.30)
Amount Received = $41.50 – $1.5035
Amount Received = $39.9965 or $40.00

When dealing with fractions, PayPal rounds to the nearest penny.

Here's a general equation you can use to calculate seller fees:

Amount to Send = (Amount to be Received + $.30) / (1 – 2.9%)

Covering the Recipient's Fees Using Mass Pay

Another, more direct way to cover the seller fees is to use an underused Pay-Pal tool called Mass Pay [Hack #77]. With Mass Pay, PayPal deducts the fees from the sender's account rather than the recipient's account. In addition to being a simpler method than the arithmetic above, using Mass Pay in this way can make your bookkeeping easier, because the fees appear in your transaction history more clearly.

But the best part about Mass Pay is that the fee is a flat 2% and is capped at $1.00 per transaction (e.g., per recipient). In the scenario described earlier in this hack, the recipient would get the full $40 and you'd be charged only $0.80 instead of $1.50.

See "Lower Your Seller Fees" [Hack #23] for other ways to reduce PayPal's seller fees.

Send Money Without Creating a PayPal #15 Account

Pay someone quickly without going to the trouble of setting up an account.

If you don't have a PayPal account and you want to see what the fuss is about, send someone money using PayPal. After all, everyone owes someone for something. Perhaps you owe a coworker for lunch, a friend who bought you a ticket to the big game, or another friend who sold you his old DVD player. Why not pay them via PayPal?

But to send someone money, you'll have to sign up for an account. Or will you? The answer is no, as long as the recipient has a PayPal account!

Using this procedure, you can also request and accept payments without requiring the customer to sign up for a PayPal account. Just fill in your own email address into the URL discussed here and send it to your customers.

To send money without creating a PayPal account, open up any web browser, and type this address (URL):

http://paypal.com/xclick/business=

Add the email address of the recipient of the money to the end of the URL, like this:

paypal.com/xclick/business=reg@paypalhacks.com

After pressing the Enter key (or Return on the Mac), the email address (*reg@paypalhacks.com*, in this case) will be sent to the PayPal web site, which will look up the user's account. If the email address refers to an existing PayPal account, you will see the Payment Details page (shown in Figure 2-7) with the following information:

Pay To
> The email address of the recipient of your payment.

Payment For
> An optional field, into which you can enter a note describing what the payment is for.

Currency
> The currency it expects you to use; the default is U.S. dollars.

Amount
> In this example, you will be required to enter the amount you wish to pay, since you didn't put the amount in the URL

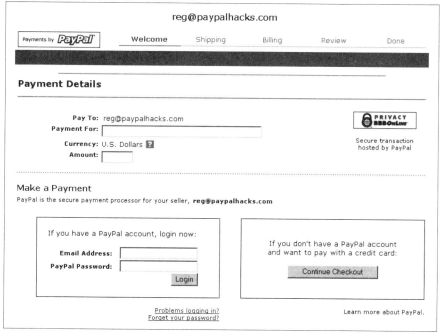

Figure 2-7. Payment Details screen for customers sending money to registered PayPal sellers

If, on the other hand, the email address of the recipient does not refer to an existing PayPal account, you will see a slightly different Payment Details page, as shown in Figure 2-8. In this case, you'll be required to sign up for a PayPal account as a part of the payment process.

At this point, you'll have two choices:

- If you have a PayPal account, you can type your email address and password here and click Login to pay with your account.

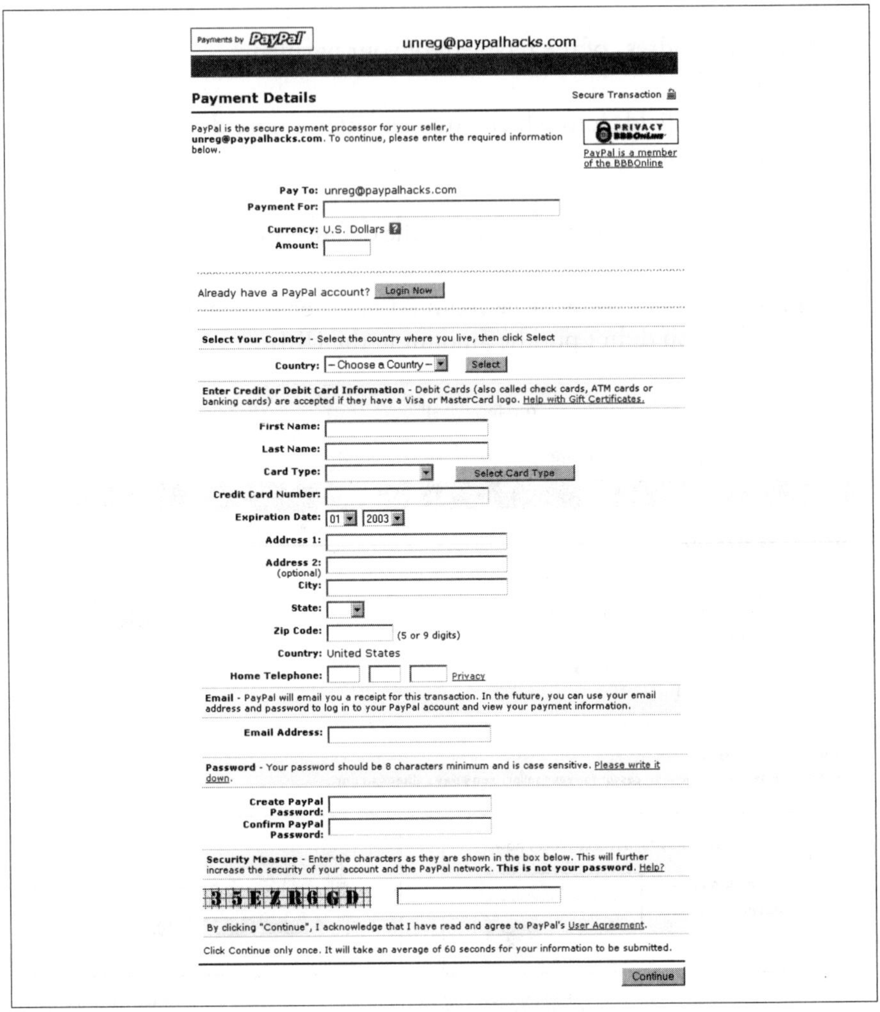

Figure 2-8. Payment Details screen for customers sending money to unregistered users

- Otherwise, click the Continue Checkout button. Use this option if you don't want to pay with your PayPal account, or if you don't have a PayPal account and want to pay with a credit card.

If you or someone else has previously accessed a PayPal account on your computer, the Payment Details page might look a little different, as shown in Figure 2-9. You will see the email address of the PayPal customer who previously used your computer, and you'll be prompted for a password. But you can still get to the *new user* page shown earlier in this hack by clicking the Click Here button, at which point you'll be able to pay without logging in.

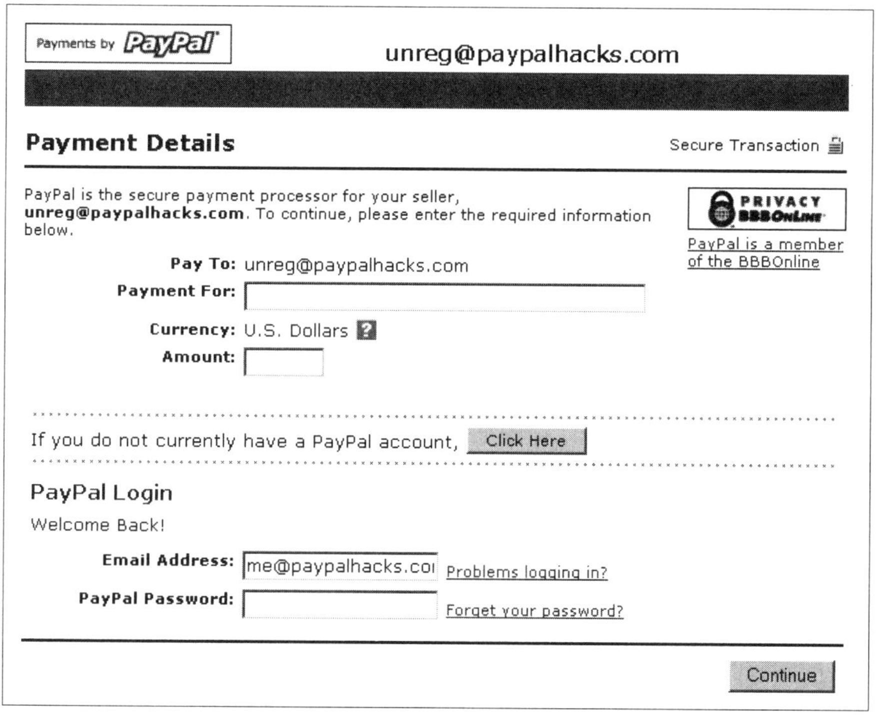
Payments by PayPal
unreg@paypalhacks.com
Payment Details
Secure Transaction
PayPal is the secure payment processor for your seller, unreg@paypalhacks.com. To continue, please enter the required information below.
PRIVACY BBBOnLine
PayPal is a member of the BBBOnline
Pay To: unreg@paypalhacks.com
Payment For:
Currency: U.S. Dollars
Amount:
If you do not currently have a PayPal account,
Click Here
PayPal Login
Welcome Back!
Email Address:
me@paypalhacks.coi
Problems logging in?
PayPal Password:
Forget your password?
Continue

Figure 2-9. Payment Details screen with cookies enabled

Cookies and Personal Information

Cookies are tidbits of information that web sites store on your computer for future reference; they typically contain just enough information for the web site to identify your login or user ID.

A good example of how cookies can work to your advantage is the way both eBay and PayPal use cookies to keep you signed in and remember you the next time you visit.

To experience PayPal as a new PayPal user would, find and delete your PayPal cookie. If you're using Internet Explorer, look for a text file containing the characters `@paypal.com` in your *Cookies* folder (or *Temporary Internet Files* if you're using Windows 2000). If you're using Netscape or Mozilla, go to Tools → Cookie Manager. In either case, deleting this cookie is harmless, so give it a try and see what happens when you return to the PayPal web site.

Next comes the Shipping Information page; for purchases that do not require shipping (e.g., for repaying a friend or for a digital download), select the No Shipping Required option and click Continue Checkout.

If PayPal skips the Shipping Information page and instead shows you the Billing Information page, then the person you are trying to pay does not have a PayPal account. You will be asked to create an account before sending the money.

Otherwise, if you're purchasing a physical product that must be shipped, enter your shipping address here. Select Yes at the bottom if this address is the same as your credit card billing address, and click Continue Checkout when you're done.

On the Billing Information page, enter your credit card information and email address. (If you indicated that your billing and shipping addresses are the same on the previous page, your billing address will appear here; otherwise, you'll need to fill it in.) You'll also need to fill in your phone number and security code.

The security code, typically a word embedded in a pattern, is an extra step that PayPal requires to ensure that you are a real person and not a computer trying to gain automated access to PayPal. In theory, only human beings have the patience to read the code and enter it.

You'll also have another chance (in addition to the aforementioned Payment For field) to leave a message to the seller in the Message to Seller field.

When you're done, click Continue Checkout. On the Review Information page, review the details of your payment and click Pay to complete the transaction. Assuming your credit card is accepted, you have just made a payment!

When you are finished making your payment, one of two things will happen:

- If the email address to which you sent the money is registered with PayPal, the money will be deposited directly into the email owner's PayPal account.

- If the email address is not registered with PayPal, a "You've got cash" email will be sent to the owner of the email address. The recipient will then need to follow the instructions in the email to sign up for a PayPal account and accept the money. Note that your email address will be used as the return address, suggesting its origin and allowing the recipient to reply to the message and easily email you.

Either way, after accepting the money, the recipient will be able to use your payment to pay someone else, transfer the money into her bank account, or even have a check sent to her from PayPal [Hack #20].

Truth be told, this process isn't all that easy. In fact, it's more involved than paying with an existing PayPal account. It is, however, easier (in the short term, anyway) for those who don't yet have PayPal accounts, and this fact might be enough to attract customers who otherwise might be scared off by PayPal.

On the last page of the payment process, you will be invited to create a PayPal account using the credit card information you have just provided. If you plan on using PayPal to pay again or perhaps to even accept payments yourself, go ahead and accept the invitation. There is no easier way to create a PayPal account than at this moment. And the next time you need to make a payment, the process will be even easier, because you won't have to enter all your payment information again.

HACK #16 Dispute Merchandise Payments

Know your rights! Use PayPal's Buyer Protection policy to get your money back in the event that a seller has defrauded you.

Let's say you just found an unbelievable deal for a plasma screen TV on eBay and you pay for it with PayPal. But it's been two weeks and still no TV has been delivered, and the seller doesn't respond to any of your emails.

Or you buy a high-end coffee grinder from eBay, pay with PayPal, and it's shipped to you quickly. But when you plug it in, nothing happens. In fact, upon closer inspection, there is nothing inside the grinder at all: it's just a shell with no parts. You get ahold of the seller, but he is uncooperative.

Fortunately, PayPal can help resolve merchandise disputes. The key is to understand the delicate processes and etiquette involved so that your dispute can be handled quickly and painlessly.

If you're a seller, see "Handle Merchandise Disputes Effectively" [Hack #27] for ways to defend yourself against disputes filed against you.

PayPal Buyer Protection

PayPal Buyer Protection uses online dispute resolution to address transaction-related disputes between buyers and sellers. For transactions that are eligible for PayPal Buyer Protection (look for the blue and white shield on the eBay listing), buyers can report a problem with a purchase as long as it's tangible merchandise that has been shipped by a courier that uses online package tracking.

What isn't covered? Vehicles (e.g., cars and boats), intangible goods such as online subscriptions, and anything in violation of PayPal's Acceptable Use Policy are not covered.

There are two kinds of claims you can file as a buyer:

- You did not receive a package.
- You received a package, but it is not as described (which includes getting an empty box).

A bunch of rules and conditions apply; see the "PayPal Buyer Protection Fine Print" sidebar for details. Buyers don't do anything to qualify, but there are rules that must be followed to retain coverage.

PayPal Buyer Protection Fine Print

Look for the blue and white shield in the Seller Information box. Those are the only listings eligible for PayPal Buyer Protection.

Covers up to $500 USD. If your transaction is over $500, you might still get all your money back if the seller has it in his PayPal balance. If he doesn't, you'll get $500 and then PayPal limits the seller's account until he pays you back.

File within 30 days. PayPal counts down to the very second. If you miss the window, they won't help you.

Limit of one claim per payment. Even if there are multiple listings within a single payment, you can file only once for the entire *order*.

Limit of two refunds per calendar year. You can file as many claims as you want, but only two listings will be refunded up to $500. The others will fall under the standard Buyer Complaint Process where recovery is not guaranteed (although PayPal will make a best effort to get your money back from the seller when appropriate).

Pay the seller's PayPal account under which he listed the item. As long as you use any of the eBay/PayPal checkout processes, the funds automatically go to the right account. If you send money, make sure you send it to the PayPal account associated with the listing and not to some other account the seller asks you to use.

To file a PayPal Buyer Protection claim, log in to your PaypPal account, click the Resolution Center tab, and read the instructions. When you're ready, click File a Claim and fill in the information as prompted.

The first thing you'll be asked for is the PayPal Transaction ID, a unique 17-digit code that corresponds to the transaction you're disputing. To find the code, click Get PayPal Transaction ID and then wade through your PayPal history until you've found the transaction. Simply click the code in the Transaction ID column, and PayPal will automatically insert it into the claim form.

> You might have a stack of proof you think PayPal should review, but hold onto it for now; PayPal might never even ask for it. PayPal typically cares only about objective evidence that they can verify with a third party.

Each claim opens a case at PayPal and notifies the seller to respond. Once you have filed a claim, click the Resolution Center tab to check the status of your claim.

Buyer Protection Etiquette

Before you transact with a seller, make sure you read the merchandise description carefully for details and disclaimers. If the deal seems too good to be true, beware! A brand new iPod for half the price you'd normally pay should raise a big red flag. (You can also buy a plasma screen TV off the back of a truck in a dim alley.) Great deals can be found online, but don't ignore your common sense.

Always contact the seller before filing a claim; sellers appreciate this and might be willing to work things out to avert the claim going on their PayPal record. (If your neighbor's dog is barking all night, try talking to your neighbor before calling animal control about a rabid dog.) A lot of issues can be resolved with simple communication, leaving both the buyer and seller on good terms.

Allow the seller time to ship the merchandise to you. Sellers are required to ship within seven days to qualify for the Seller Protection Policy, that this does not include the time it might take for the courier to deliver the package. International shipments might take longer, due to customs and fundamental shipping delays. Obviously, filing a claim an hour after you pay makes you appear irrational and only angers your seller. An angry seller will be less likely to be reasonable and responsive to your claim.

Buyers must file a claim under PayPal Buyer Protection within 30 days from the date of the PayPal transaction. Sellers might have legitimate reasons for not immediately responding to emails or for delaying your shipment, but beware of sellers who repeatedly put off your inquiries about when the merchandise will be shipped.

Finally, be patient. Instead of contacting PayPal in multiple ways at multiple times, allow the claim process to work. Multiple contacts just add clutter to your case and might actually delay it.

Can I Get My Money Back?

Filing a claim does not necessarily mean that you'll get your money back. As with any online dispute resolution forum, both parties involved in the dispute tell their sides of the story and are asked to submit information to substantiate their statements. Most claims are resolved without any intervention from PayPal at all; for instance, you might cancel your claim after receiving a tracking number from the seller.

Does PayPal just take the buyer's word? PayPal uses a variety of checks and balances to vet the buyer's claims. This might include requiring you to fax a letter of inauthenticity from a third-party dealer on claims for counterfeit goods or fax a police report for higher-priced merchandise.

Buyers who abuse PayPal Buyer Protection are investigated by fraud specialists and are dealt with appropriately (which might include escalation to law enforcement), so don't file reports frivolously.

What does significantly "not as described" mean? "Not as described" claims are handled on a case-by-case basis because there are millions of items that change hands every day, and it's impossible to generalize about the meaning: a scratch on a priceless violin cannot be compared to a scratch on a Frisbee™.

If it's an eBay item, the original eBay listing is the main decision factor: what exactly did the seller advertise? Only claims for significantly "not as described" merchandise will be granted. (If a shirt is light blue instead of dark blue, you'll probably be denied a refund.)

In almost all cases, a buyer has to return (at her own expense) the significantly not-as-described merchandise to the seller before getting a refund. Buyers do not get to keep both the item and the money.

Where does the refund come from? Although PayPal might find that you're due a refund, PayPal never draws money from a seller's bank account or credit card without the seller's permission (this would be considered an unauthorized transaction and is therefore illegal). PayPal might not be perfect (in some people's opinions), but they're not stupid. For this reason, don't dawdle when it comes to filing Buyer Protection claims.

PayPal Buyer Protection ensures that buyers are refunded up to $500 no matter how much sellers have in their PayPal balances.

If a seller's PayPal balance has insufficient funds to complete a refund, the PayPal account balance will become negative as soon as the buyer has been refunded and the acouunt might be limited. See "Restore Your Account if It Has Been Limited" [Hack #5] for more information on what you can do if your account has been limited.

What happens to bad sellers? I want justice! Even if a buyer's claim is denied, there is a record of every claim on the seller's account. Sellers with a high claim rate quickly trigger investigation by PayPal. Fraudulent sellers have been taken to court, convicted, heavily fined, put in jail, and blacklisted. Every now and then, you'll read about these cases in the newspaper.

Unfortunately, due to privacy concerns, PayPal never reveals what actions have been taken against a seller (if any). You can, however, subsequently check the status of the seller's PayPal account "Access Member Information" [Hack #7].

If you made your purchase on eBay, you can also check out eBay's Security Center to read about ways to protect yourself. In 2003 or earlier, eBay might have paid you under their $200 ($25 processing fee) purchase protection program, but now that eBay and PayPal are one company, there is sufficient coordination such that you'll be directed to the right place to file a claim. If your purchase was paid for with PayPal, eBay will ask you to work with PayPal to get your money back. For other issues, you will find various forms in the Security Center to report sellers asking for additional money after the listing ends, suspended sellers selling under another ID, sellers abusing feedback, and so on. In addition to getting your money back from PayPal, you can alert eBay to problem sellers.

Selling with PayPal
Hacks 17–27

From accepting occasional donations to receiving payments from thousands of customers, PayPal provides the tools and support you need to build your business. Rather than having to complete a complicated and costly application for a merchant account so that you can accept payments, all you have to do is fill out a form at *http://www.paypal.com*, and PayPal will handle all the dirty work. To get started, all you have to do is to set up your PayPal account for accepting payments.

PayPal offers three types of accounts. All of them can be used for making and accepting payments, but each has its own unique features:

Personal
> Personal accounts "Create a PayPal Account" [Hack #1] are the most common, because they are what most new PayPal members choose by default. Most buyers who use PayPal to make payments have a Personal account.
>
> There is no fee for sending or receiving payments with a Personal account, but there are limitations. Personal accounts cannot receive payments funded by credit cards; since many PayPal buyers like to fund their payments with a credit card, a Personal account severely limits a seller's customer base. Also, Personal accounts are limited to receiving $1,000 in payments per month.

Premier
> Premier accounts can accept payments funded with credit cards. There is no fee for sending payments with a Premier account, but there is a fee for accepting payments, no matter how they are funded. Premier accounts also include a host of features to help make your business successful and efficient, such as the Seller Protection Policy, the PayPal Shopping Cart, Subscriptions, Recurring Payments, and a listing in PayPal Shops.

Business

Business accounts are nearly identical to Premier accounts, but they offer a few added features of interest to businesses. For instance, your PayPal account is identified to your customers as your business name instead of your personal name (as it is with both Personal and Premier accounts). The fee structure for Business accounts is the same as for Premier accounts.

> Choosing a Business account over a Premier account can be a good way to protect your privacy and reinforce your business presence. If you're an eBay seller, for instance, you can set your PayPal business name to be the same as your eBay user ID.

If you're serious about making it easy for your customers to pay you, you will want to hold a Premier or Business account.

> PayPal's policies allow each person to hold no more than two accounts. If you do hold two accounts, one must be Personal and one must be Business or Premier. See "Lower Your Seller Fees" [Hack #23] for reasons you might want to hold a separate Personal account.

Upgrade to Business Class

If you have only a Personal account, you can easily upgrade it:

1. Log into your PayPal Personal account.
2. Click Upgrade Account.
3. On the Upgrade Your Account screen, click Upgrade Now.
4. On the Choose a Name to Do Business As page, choose either Premier or Business. Choosing Business allows you to enter business information, such as customer service contact information for your business, on the next screen.

When you're done, your account will immediately be capable of accepting payments funded by credit cards .

> Should you change your mind, you can downgrade a Premier or Business account to a Personal account only once. If you think you might want to use a Personal account after upgrading, it's best to open a separate account.

Set Your Payment Receiving Preferences

Before using your account, you might want to take a moment to review your Payment Receiving Preferences, as shown in Figure 3-1. You can set your PayPal account to accept or reject payments based on your business needs.

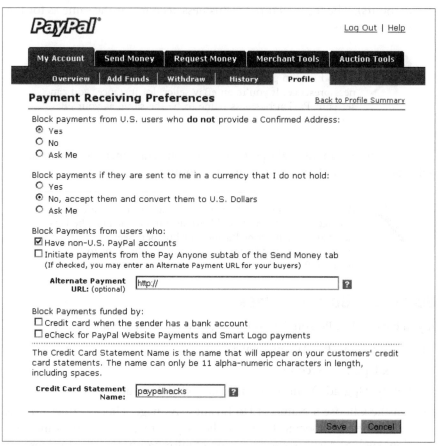

Figure 3-1. Using the Payment Receiving Preferences page to choose which types of payments to accept

Here's how to access these settings:

1. Log into your PayPal Premier or Business account.
2. Click the My Account tab, and then click the Profile subtab.
3. Click the Payment Receiving Preferences tab under the Selling Preferences heading.

Here you can make your choices about whether to accept payments:

From unconfirmed addresses

You might choose to accept, block, or decide on a case-by-case basis whether to accept payments from members without confirmed addresses "Confirm Your Mailing Address" [Hack #3]. If you intend to accept payment only for goods covered by the Seller Protection Policy, this is a good option.

In a foreign currency

You can block payments in currencies you do not currently hold, automatically convert them to your primary currency, or decide on a case-by-case basis. You might not want to automatically accept payments in foreign currencies if you might want your customers, rather than yourself, to pay the fee for converting money from one currency to another.

For example, suppose you are a U.S. account holder and a customer wants to pay you in pounds sterling. The newspaper reports the current exchange rate as 1.8 USD to 1 GBP, which prompts you to sell $18 worth of coffee for≥£10. You now have a balance of £10 in your PayPal account. When you withdraw that money from your PayPal account to your U.S. bank account, you need to convert the money to dollars. PayPal will do this for you, but you won't get the exchange rate listed in the newspaper. You will get a rate, determined by PayPal, that might be considered a retail rate; for example, you might see your £10 converted into only $17.

 If you choose the Ask Me option for either the "From unconfirmed addresses" or "In a foreign currency" settings, you will get an email from PayPal each time you receive such a payment, allowing you to accept or deny the payment. This allows you to choose on a case-by-case basis or simply gives you the time to learn more about the buyer before you accept the payment.

From non-U.S. account holders

You might want to avoid the cross-border fee by refusing payments from non-U.S. accounts (this fee applies to U.S. PayPal accounts only).

The cross-border payment fee, assessed on payments made to Business and Premier accounts receiving a payment from someone in a different country, is an additional 1% for payments in U.S. dollars and .5% for payments in Canadian dollars, euros, pounds sterling, and yen. (This cross-border fee is waived for Canadian sellers receiving payments from U.S. buyers.)

Another reason to restrict foreign payments is that most non-U.S. PayPal members cannot confirm their addresses, which means that payments from these customers will not be covered by PayPal's Seller Protection Policy [Hack #24].

Made from the Pay Anyone subtab of the Send Money tab
This option forestalls payments made directly from your customers' PayPal accounts, allowing you to require that all payments you receive come through, say, your online shop or directly through eBay checkout. This can be useful if, for instance, you need special information from the customer to accompany each order.

Fill in the Alternate Payment URL if you want customers who try to pay through the PayPal interface redirected to your web site.

Funded by a credit card when the sender has a bank account
You can force customers who have a bank account attached to their PayPal account to use it when paying you. This discourages customers from paying with credit cards unless it's their only choice. Doing so might reduce the risk of chargebacks [Hack #25], a possible problem when accepting payments funded by credit cards.

Funded by an eCheck for Website and Smart Logo payments
Instant Transfer payments are instant payments funded with a bank account; they appear in your PayPal account immediately. However, processing payments through the banking system usually takes three to four business days, and PayPal can't be assured of receiving the money until the bank transfer is complete. Because PayPal is opening itself up to some risk with this policy, PayPal allows a buyer to send an Instant Transfer payment only if the sender's account has a backup funding source, such as a valid credit card or second bank account.

An eCheck is also an electronic bank transfer, but it requires no backup funding source and is therefore not credited instantly to your account. Instead, during the waiting period of three to four business days, the payment is listed in your PayPal account as Pending. The payment will not be credited to your PayPal balance (achieving a status of Completed) until the buyer's funds have been transferred to PayPal.

 If you receive an eCheck and the buyer's bank account lacks sufficient funds for the transaction or has been closed, the transaction might never be completed and you might never receive those funds. For this reason, you should never ship your product until an eCheck payment has cleared and its status is listed as Completed.

If you would prefer to receive only payments that will be completed immediately, you might want to block eChecks. This setting applies to payments sent through your web site, such as with Buy Now buttons, as well as Smart Logo payments, such as those sent through eBay checkout. Customers will still be able to send eChecks through the PayPal interface, unless you also check the "Made from the Pay Anyone subtab of the Send Money tab" setting.

Identify Yourself to Your Customers

Building a relationship with your customers translates into satisfied buyers who return to your site (or eBay auctions) again and again. A basic step in building a relationship is establishing your identity; your customers need to know who you are and what you are about. Here are some ways PayPal can help you establish your identity:

Set the string that appears on credit card statements. When a buyer who funded her payment with a credit card opens her monthly statement, she will see a payment to PayPal. Unfortunately, some consumers have a notoriously short memory and might not recall using PayPal and a credit card to make a payment to your eCommerce site a month ago. To jog their memories, PayPal allows you to choose an 11-character string to be displayed on your customers' credit card statements. To edit this string, go to the Payment Receiving Preferences page (shown earlier in Figure 3-1) and enter up to 11 letters and numbers that will identify your business to your buyers.

Add appropriate email addresses. Your PayPal account can have up to eight email addresses listed, all of which can be used to receive payments. If you are running two or more separate businesses, each with its own identity or branding, you might want to add an email address for each one.

If you import both organic coffee and hand-rolled cigars from Bolivia and would rather not be known to your coffee customers as a cigar outlet (or vice versa), you can set up two email addresses, such as *sales@bolivian-cigars-4u.biz* and *sales@bolivian-coffee-4u.biz*. Each address can be used to receive payments to your single PayPal account, but without confusing your two brands to your probably mutually exclusive sets of customers. See "Manage PayPal Email" [Hack #8] for more information on adding multiple email addresses to your account.

Customize PayPal's checkout process. See "Customize Checkout Pages" [Hack #51] for ways to customize PayPal's payment pages to match the look and feel of your web site.

If you're an eBay seller, see Chapter 4 for eBay-specific hacks.

Request Money the PayPal Way

#17 Use PayPal's Request Money feature to ask someone for a payment, whether you need to invoice a customer or collect money from a friend.

Anyone who goes to lunch with friends regularly knows the uncomfortable feeling of not having enough cash to cover your portion of the meal. One solution is to offer to pay for everyone with a credit card and then ask the others for cash to cover their portions. This works out well, because the card holder doesn't have to borrow money and it saves a trip to the bank.

But what if there are two or even three of you with the same cash flow problem? Then it becomes tricky. That's when you can say, "I'll pay with my credit card and the rest of you can PayPal me." This way, no one has to worry about having the right amount of cash. The only problem is having to remember to send the money requests, but PayPal makes this easy.

When requesting money from friends, use your Personal PayPal account to avoid paying the associated fees. If the payment is optional, send the request via email **[Hack #18]** so that the request doesn't show up in your PayPal history.

Use these steps to request money from anyone with an email address:

1. Log into your PayPal account, and click the Request Money tab.
2. Enter a subject and a note (both are optional).

The subject is more important than the note, because it is used as the subject for the email your recipient gets. The note, however, is less likely to be seen, because it appears buried within the email. If you need to include important details, it is best to send them in a separate email.

3. For the Payment Type, select Goods (other), Service, or Quasi-Cash. You can also select eBay Items or Auction Goods (non-eBay) if you want to bill someone for an auction.
4. Click Continue to view the confirmation page. Double-check the email address to make sure you have the correct email address.
5. Click Request Money.

PayPal generates a payment transaction record in its database and sends a custom email (shown in Figure 3-2) with a link that will enable the recipient to pay the amount requested.

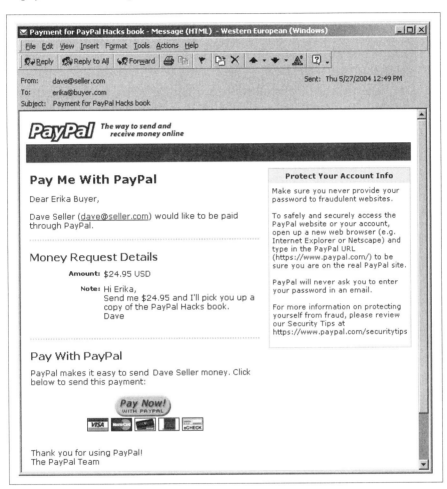

Figure 3-2. Request Money email

Requesting Money from Multiple People

Sending single money requests to several people can be repetitive and time-consuming; not only do you have to enter the email address, amount, currency, and payment type for each person, you might also need to personalize each request.

To make this process easier, PayPal provides a feature called Request Money—Group, which lets you request money from multiple people all at once. This is most useful when you are requesting money from people for a specific occasion, such as a group lunch or group movie tickets, wherein the email subject and note are the same. The Request Money—Group feature also lets you specify additional details, such as an event name, event date, and a different amount, if necessary, for each person on your list.

To use Request Money—Group, follow these steps:

1. Begin the standard Request Money procedure, as explained earlier in this hack.

2. After entering the first email address, enter a comma, followed by a second email address. Continue this process until you have entered the email address for each of the individuals from whom you want to request money.

> If you've requested money from any of these people previously, their email addresses might already be listed in the drop-down listbox. If so, you can save time by selecting the applicable recipients from the list (one by one) and inserting them into the email address field instead of having to type them all in.

3. After you have entered all the email addresses, enter the amount that each person should pay and select the currency. If each recipient is to pay a different amount, don't worry about that here; just type any amount. You'll have a chance to specify individual amounts on the next page.

4. Enter the optional email subject and note, and click Continue when you're done.

5. The next page, Request Money—Group, differs from the standard Request Money confirmation page. Here, you can type an Event Name and Event Date, along with the standard Email Subject and Note fields.

> Keep in mind that everyone gets the same message, so make the details (event name, event date, subject, and note) appropriate for everyone.

6. In the bottom half of the page, you'll see the total number of recipients of the email, followed by a total amount you will receive from the group (provided that everybody pays!). The total amount is initially calculated by multiplying the amount from the last page by the number of recipient emails, but you can change it freely and click Calculate to update the individual amounts. Alternatively, you can enter the individual

amounts of the money requests and then click Calculate Total Cost to update the Total Amount field. Either way, make sure that everything adds up before you continue.

7. Click Continue to view the Request Money—Confirm page. Be sure to confirm that each email address and corresponding request amount is correct. If you're sure that the information on the page is correct, press Request Money.

Each recipient in your group will receive an email requesting payment, complete with all the information you've entered here. You can confirm that each individual email has been sent by clicking the Overview tab.

Sending Custom Requests to Multiple Recipients

While the Request Money—Group feature can make multiple requests easier, it allows for only a single note and email subject for all recipients. To send a custom note to each person from whom you are requesting money, you'll need to send separate requests. Here's a way to make this process easier:

1. Use the Request Money feature as described in the beginning of this hack. After sending the first Money Request, you'll find yourself on the Money Request Sent page.

2. Click your web browser's Back button to return to the Request Money—Confirm page, as shown in Figure 3-3.

> If you're using Microsoft's Internet Explorer, you will see a "Warning: Page has Expired" message. Click Refresh, and you'll see a Retry/Cancel dialog box that reads, "This page cannot be refreshed without resending the information...". Click Retry to continue.

> If you're using Netscape/Mozilla, you'll see an OK/Cancel dialog box that reads, "The page you are trying to view contains POSTDATA that has expired from cache...". Click OK to continue.

3. Click the Edit button to modify the details of the previous money request. Simply replace the email address, make any other changes, and click the Continue button to send another request.

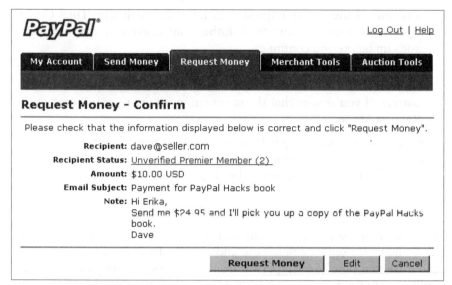

My Account | Send Money | Request Money | Merchant Tools | Auction Tools

Request Money - Confirm

Please check that the information displayed below is correct and click "Request Money".

Recipient: dave@seller.com
Recipient Status: Unverified Premier Member (2)
Amount: $10.00 USD
Email Subject: Payment for PayPal Hacks book
Note: Hi Erika,
Send me $24.95 and I'll pick you up a copy of the PayPal Hacks book.
Dave

Request Money | Edit | Cancel

Figure 3-3. Returning to the Request Money—Confirm page to send another money request

For security reasons, PayPal has a five-minute timeout, which means that if you wait more than five minutes before viewing another page at PayPal, you'll be required to log in again. If this happens while you are sending multiple money requests, you'll lose the data from the last money request.

Ask for Money in Your Own Way

Generate your own PayPal payment links for use in email or your web site, and get a little more flexibility in how to ask people for payments. There are more ways available than using the Request Money feature.

Using Request Money [Hack #17] is a useful technique if you're sending invoices to customers for items already sold or services already rendered, especially when PayPal is the likely form of payment. (For example, an eBay seller who accepts PayPal might use Request Money to send a payment request to a customer who has just won an auction.)

However, Request Money isn't a good idea when you're uncertain whether a payment will take place at all. For example, recipients might find it presumptive and uncomfortable if a fundraising volunteer used Request Money to send donation requests. Likewise, it would be inappropriate to use Request Money to send a customer a product brochure or other advertising. Instead, use a more passive payment link.

The simplest way to ask for money is to send a PayPal payment link with the payment details inside, but without registering the request at the PayPal site. When the recipient sees the link, he can click it and be whisked to *http:// www.paypal.com* to make the payment, or he can simply delete the email and be rid of it.

Creating a Request URL

Here's an example of a request URL to pay $10.00 for a baseball jersey, where *me@mysite.com* is your PayPal email address and the account into which the payment will be deposited:

```
http://paypal.com/xclick/business=me@mysite.com&amount=10.00&item_
name=baseball_jersey
```

Sending a link like this, along with some instructions, is easy to do and can be used almost anywhere, such as in an email message body:

```
Here is your last chance to get your own Cubs 2003 pennant race jerseys. On
sale while supplies last:

Cubs 2003 Jersey Size Small: http://paypal.com/xclick/business=me@mysite.
com&amount=10.00&item_name=smalljersey

Cubs 2003 Jersey Size Medium
http://paypal.com/xclick/business=me@mysite.com&amount=10.00&item_
name=mediumjersey

Cubs 2003 Jersey Size Large http://paypal.com/xclick/business=me@mysite.
com&amount=10.00&item_name=largejersey
```

Choosing the Best Approach

So, between requesting money the PayPal way [Hack #17] and requesting money via email, which is the best way to request money?

Here are the benefits of using PayPal's Request Money feature over sending custom payment requests:

- PayPal sends a PayPal-branded email to the recipient with one tamper-proof PayPal payment link.
- The money request shows up as Unpaid in the recipient's and sender's accounts until the recipient denies the request, the sender cancels the request, or the money request is paid.
- The recipient gets the payment request just by logging into PayPal, even if the email gets lost or deleted.

And here are the benefits of creating your own PayPal payment links over using the Request Money feature:

- You're able to send a customized email directly to the recipient.
- You can send a single email to multiple recipients as easily as to one.
- You have the option to include multiple payment links in a single email, including one or more custom payment buttons [Hack #38].
- The request does not show up in the recipient's account (or yours) until it has been paid.
- The recipient might feel less obliged to pay, which is useful for advertising or collecting donations.

Probably the most compelling difference between these two methods involves the record keeping. Unless you want PayPal to record your money requests, you'll probably want to create your own custom payment links. In the end, you might want to use both methods, either in unison or individually on a case-by-case basis.

Request Money Without an Account

Send a PayPal payment request without having to create a PayPal account, and send payment requests on behalf of other PayPal users.

Collecting small debts can be tricky, and most of us aren't good at it. It's easy to sound petty when asking for small amounts of money, so many people often don't. And borrowers often forget to pay. But if the subject comes up, it can be an awkward moment as the two individuals try to decide what's worse, being petty or being a deadbeat. Then there's the issue of exact change. If you remind them of the debt and they don't have enough money on hand, it means you have to go through the uncomfortable scenario all over again.

No one wants to be a debt collector, so wouldn't it be great if there were a service that would ask for money on your behalf? PayPal's Request Money feature will send an email to someone and politely request money on your behalf. Asking for money via email is a great way to get paid, because it allows you to make your request without requiring them to respond immediately. Offering PayPal as the payment method is even better, because others don't have to pay you in person and can make their payment for the exact amount they owe, using whatever means is most convenient (PayPal balance, credit card, electronic bank transfer, etc.).

However, to use Request Money you must have and log into your PayPal account. Or must you? Few people know that you can create your own payment request by adding a special link in your own email. And you don't even have to have a PayPal account.

To request money without using the PayPal web site, open any email program and start a new message.

Type this URL somewhere in the body of your email:

```
http://www.paypal.com/xclick/business=
```

Add the email address to which the money should be sent (e.g., your email
address):

```
http://www.paypal.com/xclick/business=yourname@paypalhacks.com
```

You'll probably want to specify an amount by adding the optional amount
parameter, like this, where 17.00 is the dollar amount you'd like the recipient to send you:

```
http://www.paypal.com/xclick/business=yourname@paypalhacks.com&amount=17.00
```

Finally, add text to your email, explaining why you are asking for money,
and include a note that makes PayPal sound like the greatest thing since
sliced bread (be careful not to sound like a spammer, however):

```
Hi Joe,
Thought I'd send you a friendly reminder to pay me the $17 you
owe me for that book I picked up for you last week. If you'd like,
you can pay me via PayPal by clicking this link and following the
instructions:
http://www.paypal.com/xclick/business=yourname@aol.com&amount=17.00
```

When you're done, send the email!

When the recipient opens your message, he will read your note and (hopefully) click the PayPal link. Most people will be thankful that you have
offered them an easy way to pay, or at the very least, you'll know that *they*
know that you haven't forgotten.

See Also

- For a taste of what your recipient will see, see [Hack #15].
- To send a payment request from the PayPal site, see [Hack #17].
- See [Hack #38] for another way to request money via email.

HACK #20 Get Your Money

Retrieve the money in your PayPal account with an electronic bank account
transfer or other means.

PayPal makes sending money a cinch. But getting your money out of PayPal
is also pretty easy. You might have money in your PayPal account if anyone
has sent you cash or a payment for an item you sold on eBay or your own
web site. Money is also deposited to your account when you receive a refund

for a payment you made with a PayPal balance, when you transfer funds from your bank account into PayPal, or when you receive a bonus for referring a new user to PayPal.

Your balance (or balances, if you have multiple currencies) is always displayed prominently, under the My Account tab, whenever you log into PayPal. Click Withdraw to reveal the range of money retrieval options at your disposal.

Withdraw Without Withdrawing

Of course, you can always use the money in your PayPal account to fund a payment to someone else, such as to pay for an item you won on eBay or to shop at an online store. In fact, your PayPal balance will be the default funding source the next time you send money.

This is popular among eBay users who do a lot of both buying and selling, yet don't want their checking account or credit card statements cluttered with lots of transactions. In fact, some of the best-selling items on eBay are seller supplies such as boxes and bubble wrap! You can send and receive all the payments you want (subject to PayPal limits), instantaneously and without clutter.

Be careful when using PayPal funds to pay for high-risk purchases on eBay, because you won't have the extra purchase protection afforded by other means. See "Dispute Merchandise Payments" [Hack #16] for details.

Transfer to a Bank Account

Certainly, a common means of retrieving money from PayPal is to withdraw it to a bank account. Once you've registered a bank account with PayPal, you'll be able to ask PayPal to transfer your funds to the bank account.

First, you'll need to attach a bank account to your PayPal account [Hack #2], if you haven't done so already.

Once you've registered a bank account, you can immediately request a withdrawal to it. Click the My Account tab, and then click Withdraw to display the Withdraw Funds by Electronic Transfer page, as shown in Figure 3-4.

Your current balance is shown at the center of the page; immediately underneath, type the amount you'd like to withdraw. Choose the bank account to which the funds should be sent, and click Continue

Figure 3-4. Withdraw Funds by Electronic Transfer

Your account will be subject to a withdrawal limit of $500 per month until you do at least two of the following three tasks [Hack #2]:

• Verify your PayPal account.

• Enter your Expanded Use Number.

• Confirm your social security number

Withdrawals take a few days to show up in your bank account, a delay that can be caused by any of the following:

• PayPal initiates bank transfers several times throughout the day. If you miss the last cutoff (about 5:00 p.m. Pacific time), your request won't be processed until the next business day.

• The transfer is made over the standard bank Automated Clearing House (ACH) network that all U.S. banks use to transfer funds between bank accounts. These transfers take two to four business days on average and sometimes take longer.

• After transfers are made, they can then take a few hours or even a day or two for your bank to post the funds to your account and make them available to you. This varies by bank and is usually explained in your account details.

PayPal currently can processes bank withdrawals to accounts in the following countries: Australia, Austria, Belgium, Canada, Denmark, Finland, France, Germany, Hong Kong, Italy, Korea, Mexico, Japan, the Netherlands, New Zealand, Norway, Singapore, Spain, Sweden, Switzerland, Taiwan, the United Kingdom, and the United States.

Each transfer typically must be performed in the native currency of the country in which your PayPal account has been established. This means that you won't be able to make a withdrawal in U.S. dollars to a Canadian bank account, even if the bank account is denominated in U.S. dollars. Avoid currency conversion as much as possible, since PayPal's rates are not favorable for large amounts.

 Unlike withdrawals to U.S. bank accounts (which are free), PayPal assesses a fee on withdrawals to non-U.S. accounts. For a complete listing of these fees, see *https://www.paypal.com/us/cgi-bin/webscr?cmd=_display-withdrawal-fees*.

Another option for sellers outside the U.S. is to use the PayPal debit card (provided that you have a U.S.-based PayPal account), as described later in this hack.

Auto-Sweep

You can have PayPal transfer funds into your bank account automatically every business day using PayPal's Auto-Sweep feature.

You must contact Customer Service to activate Auto-Sweep. Thereafter, an Auto-Sweep option will appear in your Profile. Once activated, PayPal tallies your balance once each business day (usually early in the morning) and initiates a transfer for the entire amount. The transfer happens over the same ACH network as ordinary transfers and thus is subject to the same delays and limitations.

 Auto-Sweep is free. Once you have it set up, it continues to operate until you log in and switch it off.

Auto-Sweep is a good option if you primarily receive payments and do little or no spending through PayPal. Plus, you'll consistently have one funds transfer per day, which might make subsequent bookkeeping easier.

PayPal also offers an automatic withdrawal option designed for large sellers who need precise reconciliation details. To find out more about this option, contact PayPal and ask about Automatic Settlement Withdrawal.

Just Send Me a Check

As a last resort, PayPal can mail U.S.-based sellers a paper check through postal mail. You won't want to do this too often, because PayPal charges $1.50 per check. The check will be made payable to the name listed on your account (or your business name if you have a Business account). Further, PayPal will mail the check only to a confirmed mailing address listed on your account, so make sure to confirm a shipping address [Hack #3].

PayPal can send checks only within the United States, drawn on a U.S. bank, and made out in U.S. dollars. If you are outside the U.S., you should make sure that one of the other withdrawal methods discussed in this hack works for you before you start receiving a lot of payments. Otherwise, the only thing you'll be able to do with the money is use it to fund PayPal payments to other people.

Get Paid to Use the PayPal Debit Card

The most profitable and flexible way to retrieve your PayPal balance is to use the PayPal MasterCard debit card. PayPal pays you up to 1.5% cash back (in the form of credits to your account) every time you use your card to make a purchase. The money comes from MasterCard every time you use your card, and PayPal passes these bonuses on to you when you follow certain guidelines.

The card works just like a MasterCard credit card, except that instead of getting billed each month for all your charges, the funds will come right out of your PayPal account immediately every time you make the purchase.

> Since there's no delay, the PayPal debit card is the fastest way to retrieve your PayPal balance. Another option is to use the virtual Debit Bar [Hack #12], which allows you to use your PayPal funds at web sites that don't accept PayPal.

To be eligible for the PayPal debit card, you must meet these conditions:

- You need to have a U.S.-based PayPal account, and the account needs to be active and in good standing for at least 60 days.
- You need a Premier or Business account, as described in the beginning of this chapter.
- You must attach a credit card that has its monthly statement sent to a physical street address (not a P.O. box).
- You must be verified [Hack #2].

To apply for the card, log into PayPal, click the My Account tab, and then click Withdraw. Click "Shop with a PayPal debit card" and then click Continue. The next page displays your name and confirmed address, as listed with the aforementioned credit card. Double-check your information here, check the box to indicate that you have read and agree to the user agreement, and click Submit when you're done. PayPal then processes your application and sends you a physical card in the mail.

Now, to get cash back from PayPal when you make debit card purchases, you have to become PayPal Preferred. To qualify, you must be an eBay seller and agree to choose only PayPal when specifying the payment methods in eBay's Sell Your Item form. You can still accept checks and money orders, and you can even mention other online payment services in your end-of-listing email to buyers, but you need to advertise PayPal exclusively in your actual eBay listing. To get started, click PayPal Preferred in the Enhance Account box to the left of your Account Overview page.

The PayPal debit card can also be used like an ATM card to withdraw money at automated cash machines that display the Cirrus or MasterCard logo; this covers most ATMs, including many outside the U.S. However, you won't earn any cash back when you use the ATM card to make cash withdrawals. And since PayPal charges $1.00 for each ATM withdrawal (regardless of the amount), it's best to make cash withdrawals only in emergencies.

 PayPal sets a daily limit on debit card usage. The limit typically falls between $1,000 to $3,000 per day for debit purchases and $300 to $400 per day for ATM withdrawals. You can view your limits by logging into PayPal and selecting View Limits on the Overview page.

Some users have found the debit card to be a good way to transfer money to other parts of the world. While PayPal issues debit cards to U.S.-based PayPal members only, it's possible for someone outside the U.S. to make ATM withdrawals or debit card purchases.

If you already have one debit card, you will most likely be eligible to receive a second debit card, which can be used by your partner, spouse, child, or whomever you allow to access your PayPal account funds. All the same cash back credits and charge limits will apply. If eligible, PayPal will provide a Request a Second Debit Card link on your account Overview page in the What's New section.

Refund a Payment

#21

Return payments to your customers without doubling up PayPal's fees.

No one likes to have to return a payment; the fact that keeping money is better for business isn't rocket science. Sometimes, however, refunds are unavoidable: a buyer might need to cancel an order, a seller can run low on inventory, or a purchased item might not work out as planned. Fortunately, PayPal makes refunding payments easy.

PayPal also allows you to make partial refunds. This can be handy when a dispute with your buyer is just about the item's price. If a buyer believes the condition of a used item is not as good as expected, you might offer to refund 20% of the purchase price as compensation. Your buyer will have the option to accept or decline your refund offer.

To refund a payment:

1. Log in to your PayPal account and click History.

2. Scroll through or search your account history and find the payment you need to refund, and click the corresponding Details link.

3. Near the bottom of the Transaction Details page, click the Refund Payment link.

4. On the Refund Offer page, fill in the amount of the refund you want to make, or leave the default amount to make a full refund. Fill in a note to your buyer if necessary, and then click Submit.

5. On the Confirm Refund Offer page, check the details of the transaction and click Process Refund when you're done.

The payment will then show up in your account history with the status Refunded.

When working with refunds, keep this in mind:

- You may offer a refund only for a limited time, usually 60 days. If you need to make a refund after that time, you will need to initiate a new PayPal payment to your buyer.

- If you offer the buyer a partial refund, she has 10 days to decline it if she wishes. (Full refunds are automatically processed.) As with most eCommerce, good communication with your customer can be especially helpful here; discuss the partial refund with your buyer to make sure she will be satisfied and will not decline it.

- Be sure you know where the funds are coming from; the Refund Offer page provides information about this. If the money will be transferred

Why Not Just Make Another Payment?

PayPal lets you make and receive payments, so you might wonder why you would want to bother issuing a refund when you can simply make another payment back to the person who paid you originally.

First, if you refund a payment, the person who originally paid you will see the status of that payment as Refunded rather than Completed. This might prevent the confusion that otherwise might arise if the buyer has to reconcile the original *sent* payment with a separate *received* payment.

Second, when you refund a payment, you'll get all the PayPal seller fees back. If you refund a $10 payment, for which 59 cents in fees were incurred, your customer will get a refund of $10 and you'll get a credit to your account for 59 cents. If you were to send a separate payment for that same $10, PayPal would charge each of you the 59 cents in fees.

from your bank account, be sure there are sufficient funds there to cover the refund.

Quick-Link to Transaction Details

#22 View the details of past purchases and sales without having to wade through the PayPal history listings.

If you buy and sell a lot with PayPal, you undoubtedly often need to look up past transactions in order to get the payment status, shipping address, customer notes, and other details, as well as issue refunds. Unfortunately, getting to the details of past transactions can be laborious, requiring that you click through three or four screens before you can search for a payment by transaction ID.

The good news is that there's a better way. PayPal provides a special URL that takes you directly to a payment's details page. You might have seen links like this in confirmation emails, where *xxxxxxxxxxxx* is the transaction ID:

```
https://www.paypal.com/vst/id=xxxxxxxxxxxx
```

For example:

```
https://www.paypal.com/vst/id=4WC420852U475861R
```

Click the link in the email or type it into your browser's address bar, and you'll be sent straight to the payment details for the specified transaction ID (after logging in, if necessary).

Whenever you click on a link that takes you to a PayPal page, you should make sure that *https://www.paypal.com/* is then displayed in your web browser's address box (the *s* in *https* is especially important). Otherwise, you might unwittingly try to log into a *spoof* site—one that looks like PayPal, but exists only to divert your login information to an unauthroized third party.

Where to Get Transaction IDs

Since transaction IDs are the definitive way to reference a payment on PayPal, you'll see them in a lot of places at PayPal:

- The Payment Details page, shown immediately after making a payment or in both PayPal History logs (for both buyers and sellers)
- Downloaded logs obtained from the PayPal History page
- Payment confirmation emails, such as "Receipt for your Payment" emails (for buyers) and "Notification of an Instant Payment Received" emails for eBay sellers
- Instant Payment Notifications (IPNs) [Hack #65]
- Payment Data Transfers (PDTs) [Hack #85]

If you're developing with the PayPal Web Services API, see Chapter 8 for several ways to obtain and use PayPal transaction IDs.

This technique works for both the sender and the recipient who are looking up the payment details by either transaction ID. It's also common for the other person involved in a payment to reference the transaction ID when emailing or calling you to inquire about an order.

One thing to watch out for is that PayPal assigns a different transaction ID to the sender and recipient of a transaction. This can sometimes be confusing when, for example, you look up a transaction using an ID given to you by the payment sender and you see a different transaction ID on the Payment Details page.

You will, of course, not be able to see the details for a payment that you weren't involved in!

Making a Web Interface

Once you have the transaction ID or a list of IDs, you can write a script to output a list of links that you (or your customers) can use to easily get to the transaction details page for each payment:

```
<html>
<body>
<a href="https://www.paypal.com/vst/id=4WC420852U475861R">
4WC420852U475861R</a>
<a href="https://www.paypal.com/vst/id=93H8WR41HAV710IU9">
93H8WR41HAV710IU9</a>
</body>
</html>
```

Or, create a simple web-based tool that includes an ID field and a Submit button, allowing you to look up a single transaction without having to remember the aforementioned URL:

```
<html><body>
<form action="https://www.paypal.com/cgi-bin/webscr">
<input type="hidden" name="cmd" value="_vst">
Transaction ID: <input type="text" name="id" value="">
<input type="submit" value="Get Details">
</form>
</body></html>
```

See "Display the Merchant Transaction ID on Your Return Page" [Hack #52] for a way to obtain the transaction ID programmatically (necessary to create a web interface like this one). Of course, the slickest way to do it is with the PayPal Web Services API [Hack #94].

Lower Your Seller Fees
#23

Here are five ways to lower the commissions PayPal charges you when you receive money.

Many sellers using PayPal don't sell enough to really care about an extra 0.7% transaction fee. For them, the convenience of PayPal is enough. With no startup fees, no monthly fees, and no long-term commitment, PayPal is a no-brainer. However, when you start doing $5,000 per month in sales, those fees start to add up. Many merchants don't realize there are extra steps they can take to reduce or offset their transaction fees.

Apply for the Merchant Rate

The *standard rate* (known as the *discount rate* by credit card merchants) for accepting a payment with a PayPal Premier or Business account is 2.9% plus $0.30 per transaction. (This rate applies to transactions between U.S.

accounts; fees vary for oversees or international transactions.) You can reduce your rate to 2.5%, 2.2%, or even 1.9% (plus US$0.30 per transaction) by qualifying for the PayPal *merchant rate*. Table 3-1 illustrates this new tiered fee structure.

Table 3-1. Tiered structure for the PayPal merchant rate (in USD)

Tier	Rate
$0.00–$3,000.00	2.9% + $0.30
$3,000.01–$10,000.00	2.5% + $0.30
$10,000.01–$100,000.00	2.2% + $0.30
>$100,000.00	1.9% + $0.30

> The rates in Table 3-1 apply to payments from U.S. buyers. Payments from non-U.S. buyers are assessed an additional 1%.

To qualify for the lower rates, you must have a Premier or Business account in good standing that has been open for at least 90 days and you must have received at least $3,000 in payments in a single calendar month. (Note that these criteria apply to U.S. account holders only; international accounts might need to meet other requirements.)

To apply, follow these steps:

1. Log in to your PayPal Premier or Business account (if you're still using a Personal Account, refer to the introduction to this chapter for upgrade details).

2. Click Fees at the bottom of the page.

3. On the Receive Funds row, click the rate link in the Premier/Business Account column (for U.S. sellers, this link reads "1.9% + $0.30 USD to 2.9% + $0.30 USD"). Click Merchant Rate at the top of the next page, and then click Apply Now on the page that appears.

4. Fill out the Merchant Rate Application, as shown in Figure 3-5.

5. Click Submit when you're done.

The confirmation screen will tell you if your request was accepted, denied, or queued for review. If all goes well, the new, lower rate should go into effect immediately!

PayPal®   Log Out | Help

| My Account | Send Money | Request Money | Merchant Tools | Auction Tools |

Merchant Rate Application

Although some fields are optional, the more fields you complete, the more likely your application is to be approved.

Business Name: PayPal Hacks

User Name: One of the Daves

Business Type: – select one –
(optional)

Industry: Other

Website URL: (optional)

eBay User ID: paypalhacks

I sell from: ☐ Online Auction site   ☐ Business website
(check all that apply) ☐ Physical Store   ☐ Other
                       ☐ Home

Social Security #: ☐ – ☐ – ☐

☐ Click here if you are NOT the owner of this business.

☐ Click here if you have proof of a **competitive offer** from a comparable merchant account provider for less than our Standard Rate.Click here if you have proof of a **competitive offer** from a comparable merchant account provider for less than our Standard Rate.

☐ Click here to indicate that you have read and agree to the **User Agreement**.

                                              Submit   Cancel

Figure 3-5. Using the Merchant Rate Application form to lower your discount rate

 Receiving fees are determined at the beginning of every month, based on your receiving volume in the previous calendar month. Once you complete the aforementioned one-time merchant rate application, PayPal automatically assigns the appropriate rate for each month.

Ask for eChecks

There is a maximum fee of US$5.00 for each eCheck payment you receive. To put this in perspective, the standard fee to accept a US$1,000 payment funded by a credit card is $29.30, nearly six times the measly $5 fee for a $1,000 eCheck. If you use eChecks for all your large payments, you will enjoy significant savings. See the beginning of this chapter for more information on eChecks.

Receive Money into Your Personal Account

If you hold both a Personal and a Premier or Business account, you can ask any customers who prefer to make payments funded by their bank account or PayPal balance to send payments to your Personal PayPal account. Receiving a payment into your Personal account incurs no fee, but you won't be able to accept payments funded by credit cards.

Personal accounts are also limited to receiving US$1,000 (or the equivalent in other currencies) per month. This limit is reset each month on the anniversary of the account's opening. To view your Personal account's limit:

1. Log into your PayPal account.
2. Click the My Account tab, and then click the Overview subtab.
3. Click View Limits.

Enroll in the PayPal Money Market

The PayPal Money Market Fund allows you to earn returns on your PayPal balance by turning your PayPal account into an investment from which you can earn dividends. To enroll in the PayPal Money Market, click the Money Market link in the Enhance Account section of your account overview page and follow the directions.

At the time of this writing, the current yield is 0.99%. There is no limit on withdrawals and no minimum investment.

Be advised that rates of return fluctuate and enrolling in any money market account carries risk. The money market account is not insured and might lose value. Read the prospectus carefully (it is available on the PayPal site) and consider consulting a qualified financial advisor.

Use the PayPal ATM/Debit Card

PayPal pays you a 1.5% cash-back bonus for every purchase made with the PayPal ATM/debit card when you use it as a MasterCard. The bonus does not apply to ATM withdrawals or point-of-sale purchases when you use your ATM card PIN. To take advantage of this offer, you need to have a Business or Premier account, add a credit card, and add (and confirm) a bank account [Hack #2].

If you use your PayPal debit card to pay your eBay seller fees, you'll effectively lower your eBay fees by 1.5%!

Let Your Customers Pay

Naturally, if your customers pay your seller fees for you [Hack #14], you won't pay any fees at all. Among other things, a buyer can use PayPal's Mass Pay feature to not only cover the seller's fees, but to do so at only 2% (as opposed to the 2.9% plus $.30 normally charged).

Protect Yourself from Buyer Fraud
#24

Use PayPal's Seller Protection Policy to ensure that you don't lose money to fraudulent payments.

Whether you use PayPal as a buyer or a seller, you need to be on the lookout for fraud. If you don't take the proper steps to protect yourself, PayPal might need to retract a payment from your account, even after you've filled the customer's order.

For instance, a credit card holder can dispute any credit card payment, even after you've received the payment and delivered the goods or service the customer agreed to buy. This is the customer's right and it can be an effective means of buyer protection, but dishonest buyers can also abuse this service to intimidate or cheat honest sellers.

Furthermore, a person using a PayPal account to pay you might have hijacked the account from its rightful owner, or someone might have funded a PayPal payment with a stolen credit card. Either way, the rightful owner will, understandably, dispute any such charges once she has discovered them.

PayPal's Seller Protection Policy can mitigate the risk, often to the point of allowing you to keep disputed funds, but the best way to avoid fraud is to spot it going in. Here are some ways to minimize your risk as a seller.

Qualifying for Seller Protection

If you are a U.S. or Canadian seller dealing with U.S. buyers or a UK seller transacting with UK or U.S. buyers, you might qualify for PayPal's Seller Protection Policy, which covers up to $5,000 per year of reversals. To qualify, you must do all of the following:

- Ship a tangible product. (See [Hack #26] for a cute workaround.)
- Ship only to a confirmed shipping address [Hack #3].
- Ship promptly and use some form of package tracking.
- Respond quickly to any complaints, either from the customer or from PayPal.

- Meet additional requirements discussed at *https://www.paypal.com/ sellerprotection* and *http://www.paypal.com/cgi-bin/webscr?cmd=p/gen/ua/ policy_spp-outside.*

If you follow these guidelines diligently, you might be able to avoid losses to buyer fraud completely.

Checking the Buyer's User Status

Use the information resources that PayPal provides to learn about your prospective buyer. The Seller Reputation Number [Hack #7] gives you a feel for how much selling your buyer has been doing with this PayPal account. Because many PayPal users do only selling or only buying with any given PayPal account, a buyer's reputation as a seller might not be the most useful information.

As a seller, you will be more interested in your customer's Buyer Reputation Number. However, this score is not readily available; PayPal makes this information available to you only when you are asked to accept or deny a payment sent without a confirmed address.

> See the beginning of this chapter for more information on the settings that affect whether you're asked to accept or deny payments.

Possibly the best indicator of a buyer's reputability is his accounts Status. Holders of verified [Hack #2] accounts have shown PayPal that they are in fact in control of the email addresses on file with PayPal and have legitimate bank accounts. PayPal trusts these members more than unverified account holders, so it makes sense for you to trust them as well.

Your prospective buyer's account creation date tells you how long the buyer has been a PayPal member. Buyers using relatively new PayPal accounts or accounts with low reputation numbers have a short track record as PayPal members, but this doesn't mean they can't be trusted. However, you might want to avoid doing business with buyers until they become better established. A long-standing account is less likely to have been set up with the commission of fraud in mind. On the other hand, accounts of any age can, and sometimes are, hijacked by phishers and crackers.

Conducting a Little Reconnaissance

Here are some tips to help you decide whether to do business with any particular person:

Consider the buyer's reputation. In addition to the user status information provided by PayPal, do you have other sources you can use to gather information? If you're conducting business via eBay or another auction site, check your buyer's feedback rating or community reputation. Also, look for a history of fraud or payment disputes in the recent comments from other sellers.

> If you're at all suspicious, take it one step further and look for any recent purchasing activity that appears out of the ordinary (such as numerous high-value items). At the eBay site, go to Search → By Bidder, type the customer's user ID, indicate that you want to include completed items, and click Search.

Contact the buyer. For any item, especially one that is expensive and easily resold, it makes sense to contact the buyer directly. Email to confirm purchase details or on the premise of confirming that the product will really suit the buyer's needs. Be particularly wary if the buyer takes little interest in your questions. Some social engineering and a nose for fraud can save major headaches.

Use common sense. If you sell only Beanie Babies, ball bearings, and body oil on your eCommerce web site and a single buyer suddenly orders ten boxes, bushels, and bottles of each, ask a few questions before shipping.

In the end, you will probably choose to do business with most of the customers you encounter. But a little common sense and awareness can protect you from most types of fraud.

HACK #25 Protect Yourself from Chargebacks

Reduce or eliminate the risk of having disputed payments reversed from your PayPal account.

A *chargeback* is the result of a credit card charge being rejected by the credit card holder, typically in cases where the credit card was stolen and used fraudulently. But such charges can also be disputed by customers who feel that they've been defrauded by sellers.

If you accept credit cards, in person or through PayPal, you might encounter a chargeback from a buyer, just as a seller accepting personal checks might receive an occasional bad check. Chargebacks are an unfortunate but realistic cost of doing business, so most sellers factor this cost into their business plans.

When a customer initiates a chargeback with his or her credit card company, PayPal may deduct the amount of the transaction from your account if you're not covered under PayPal's Seller Protection Policy [Hack #24]. All sellers who accept credit card payments run this risk and might be liable for chargebacks.

Even if you have a low-volume online business, you cannot avoid the risk of chargebacks. According to a study by the Gartner Group, approximately 1.1% of online transactions are estimated to result in fraudulent buyer chargebacks. That's like paying an extra 1.1% fee for each and every transaction! Of course, chargeback risk varies a good deal depending on the type of goods you sell, but nearly everyone who accepts credit card payments faces some chargeback risk.

Of course, none of this applies to non–credit card transactions, such as payments funded by a bank account transfer or PayPal balance.

Protecting Yourself

Whereas most merchant account providers and payment companies simply pass all of the chargeback risks and associated fees and liabilities on to sellers, PayPal is different. As long as you follow PayPal's guidelines (the Seller Protection Policy outlines these guidelines), PayPal helps protect you against fraudulent chargebacks.

Be sure to familiarize yourself with this policy; click the User Agreement link on the bottom of any page on the PayPal web site, and then click Seller Protection Policy. When you follow the policy's guidelines strictly, PayPal protects you from chargeback liability on all qualified transactions. In addition, PayPal takes chargeback claims seriously and, when appropriate, investigates and vigorously contests chargebacks on your behalf.

PayPal is able to guarantee protection against reversal of funds only if a chargeback occurs for nonreceipt of the product or in the event of an unauthorized charge (resulting from a stolen credit card or account takeover). Even then, you're entitled to this protection only if you have followed the terms of the Seller Protection Policy.

Here are some best practices you should follow to prevent chargebacks from occurring:

- Make sure the item you're selling is described (on your site or in your eBay listing) in as much detail and as accurately as possible. You should not assume that simply providing a picture in your listing will sufficiently answer any quality questions that your customers might have. Avoid merely stating that the merchandise is being sold "as-is." This won't protect you as much as you might expect. A detailed item description will help your defense in the event that a buyer claims that your item was not as described.

- Get to know your customers. Although selling in an online environment doesn't make it easy to build a face-to-face rapport, it doesn't have to keep you from learning about your customers. While the volume of your business might prevent you from contacting all your buyers, you should make every effort to respond to any customer inquiries regarding the transaction or the purchased items, both before and after the transaction. Plus, this practice will help get you more repeat customers.

- Keep any and all records and correspondence with your customers. This allows you to provide further evidence that you adequately described the item to the customer or responded to the customer's inquiries.

- Take some time to review the online resources listed at the PayPal web site. Click Security Center at the bottom of any page for further help. For more tips on how to avoid fraudulent transactions, see "Protect Yourself from Buyer Fraud" [Hack #24].

Shipping Products

When a customer disputes a transaction (e.g., files a chargeback) with her credit card company for an unauthorized charge or undelivered item, the first item of information the credit card company will expect from PayPal (and you) when disputing the chargeback is proof that the customer received the merchandise.

Providing verifiable proof that the customer received the item in question does not mean simply being able to prove that you shipped the merchandise. You must also prove that the package was delivered and, if applicable, signed for. To that end, you should always use a shipping service that provides some type of online package tracking.

To further protect yourself, make a habit of requiring a signature for delivery, a feature required for items worth US$250 (or the equivalent in the currency of the transaction) or more. Checking the box on the shipping form that indicates that a signature must be obtained overrides any waiver of signature that the customer might have on file with that shipping company.

Use the PayPal Shipping Tool by clicking the Ship button in your transaction history, as shown in Figure 3-6.

Figure 3-6. Using the PayPal Shipping Tool

This way, your customer's shipping information is automatically inserted into the shipping label (saving you time), and the resulting shipment tracking information is automatically stored along with the transaction details (streamlining any subsequent chargeback defense), as shown in Figure 3-7.

2004	Payment						USD	USD	USD
Mar. 30, 2004	PayPal Services	To	United States Postal Service	Completed	Details	Track Package	-$3.85 USD	$0.00 USD	-$3.85 USD
Mar. 30, 2004	PayPal Services	To	United States Postal Service	Completed	Details	Track Package	-$3.85 USD	$0.00 USD	-$3.85 USD
Mar.							-$23.50	$0.00	-$23.50

Figure 3-7. Tracking any package shipped with the PayPal Shipping Tool

If you don't use the PayPal Shipping Tool, you can still provide PayPal (and your customers) with your tracking information. Just open the transaction in your account history and click the Add button next to Shipment Tracking Information. Among other things, this feature will also eliminate a large portion of customer complaints and possible disputes filed prematurely by impatient or otherwise confused customers for nondelivery of items.

For eBay auctions, use PayPal's Post Sale Manager (located under the Auction Tools tab of your account) to help manage shipments, as shown in Figure 3-8.

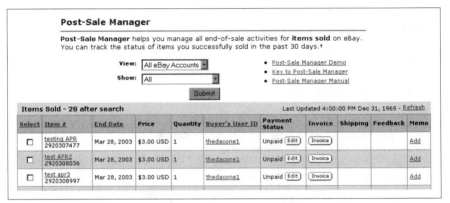

Figure 3-8. Using PayPal's Post-Sale Manager to manage shipments for eBay sales

Responding When You Receive a Chargeback

Unfortunately, no matter what steps you take during the transaction process, you still might receive a chargeback. Whether it is due to nonreceipt of an item, an item not as described, or a transaction that was reported as unauthorized, it can happen to you.

The first step when you receive a chargeback notification is to make sure that you respond with accurate information and do so within the requested timeframe. This allows PayPal to effectively dispute the chargeback case on your behalf. Keeping good records of transactions and shipment of goods and communications, as described earlier in this hack, will make this an easy task.

> Keep in mind that the rules governing a chargeback resolution are not the same as policies for PayPal's buyer-protection process. Credit card companies provide their customers with different timeframes in which to dispute transactions (and thus initiate chargebacks), and each card association (Visa, MasterCard, American Express, Discover, etc.) has different chargeback processing rules.

When a chargeback is first received, PayPal places a temporary hold on the associated funds in your account until PayPal is able to investigate the transaction and determine whether you're covered under the Seller Protection Policy. This does not mean your PayPal account will be debited; rather, it means the funds are, in essence, *frozen* and that a reversal is *pending*, which means that you cannot withdraw or otherwise use those funds. Upon review of your case (which can take up to 30 days), either of the following can happen:

- If PayPal determines that you are protected under the Seller Protection Policy, the temporary hold of funds will be cancelled (the funds will be *unfrozen*) and released back to your PayPal account. You will not be held liable for the chargeback case.

- If it turns out that you (and the transaction) are not protected under the Seller Protection Policy, PayPal might still dispute the chargeback on your behalf. (Obviously, providing as much information to help PayPal support the dispute on your behalf is crucial.) If this is the case, PayPal will, unfortunately, have to recover these funds from you while the chargeback is being disputed with the buyer's credit card company. If PayPal ultimately wins the chargeback dispute, the credit card company will reimburse PayPal for the chargeback and PayPal will reverse the recovered funds back to your account. This process may take up to 75 days, depending on the card type in the chargeback dispute.

As soon as PayPal notifies you of a chargeback, open the Transaction Disputes page by logging into your PayPal account and clicking the Resolution Center tab (or by going to *https://www.paypal.com/SRVCTR*). Next, select Open Disputes to go to the transaction in question, and click the Resolve button in the action column. Read the status details of the complaint and click the Resolve Chargeback Now button. At this point, you'll have three options:

- Provide valid tracking information in order to dispute the chargeback.

- Provide valid proof of a refund (either within or outside of PayPal) in order to dispute the chargeback.

- Accept liability for the chargeback.

Click Continue and follow the instructions provided.

Providing Additional Information About Your Case

PayPal welcomes any additional information that might aid the dispute process; the information that might be helpful depends on the type of chargeback you're fighting:

Nonreceipt of merchandise
    The information that PayPal needs to successfully dispute this type of chargeback is proof of delivery to the buyer's confirmed address. In

most cases, this proof will be in the form of a tracking number that can be entered into your courier's web site. (You did use a courier with online tracking, right?) Many larger couriers also provide a copy of the recipient's signature online, evidence that can you use to prove that your customer actually received the product in question.

Unauthorized credit card transaction
If you can provide proof of delivery of the item to the customer's confirmed address [Hack #3], plus any records of correspondence, PayPal will have a higher chance of successfully disputing the chargeback. In short, do your best to prove that the transaction was indeed legitimate and not "unauthorized" as the customer might be contending.

Merchandise not as described (quality of merchandise disputes)
PayPal needs any description or details of the merchandise in question. If you sent a replacement item for the original item being disputed, you should provide tracking for that replacement item. If you already provided a refund for the disputed transaction, you should provide proof of the refund. If the original merchandise has been returned to you from the customer, provide the details regarding that return.

Duplicate processing
If the customer has indicated that he was charged twice for the same transaction, you'll need to provide a separate tracking number for each transaction or item, such that you can correlate each charge with a distinct, tangible product that you've shipped. Or, if the second PayPal transaction ID number is indeed a duplicate transaction, you'll need to provide proof that you have refunded the duplicate transaction.

If, at any time, you discover additional information pertinent to an open case, you should send it through PayPal's secure web server. Simply log in to the PayPal web site, click Contact Us at the bottom of any PayPal page, and then click Contact Customer Service. When completing the Ask Your Question web form, make sure to include the chargeback case ID number (e.g., PP-xxx-xxx-xxx) in the subject line of the Transaction Disputes page. This allows PayPal's Chargeback Department to quickly associate the response with the appropriate case. If you are unable to provide all of the information you have through the PayPal web site, you can send an email to *chargeback-response@paypal.com*. Again, be sure to include the PayPal chargeback case ID in the subject line.

When sending emails to PayPal, keep in mind that you will not be able to include attachments. However, if you need to provide additional documentation that cannot be described easily in an email, you can fax additional chargeback dispute information to PayPal's Chargeback Department at

Timing and Chargebacks

Because chargebacks usually happen in response to a claim or discovery that occurs well after the initial transaction, it can be weeks or even months before you learn that a chargeback has been initiated by the issuer (on the buyer's behalf) and that the transaction is going to be reversed.

Although there might be a delay before a chargeback is initiated, you (and PayPal) typically do not have the same luxury. PayPal is limited by the time-frame provided to PayPal by the buyer's credit card company, so they attempt to work toward the quickest possible resolution of the issue.

In general, upon initial notification of a chargeback case, you should provide all supporting documentation to assist in the chargeback dispute within three business days. Under certain circumstances during the processing of charge-back disputes, PayPal might ask for additional information from you to sup-port the dispute. Any additional information should be supplied within the same timeframe of three business days.

(402) 537-5755. Of course, you should always include your PayPal Case ID as a reference.

Avoid Chargebacks on Digital Goods

Make purchases of digital goods eligible for PayPal's Seller Protection by mailing physical goods.

PayPal's Seller Protection Policy [Hack #25] limits your exposure to fraud, pro-vided that you follow its guidelines to the letter. The problem is that the pol-icy applies "only to the sale of physical goods, and not to any services, intangible goods or sales or licenses of digital content." So what's a digital-goods merchant to do?

Shipping a Physical Version

The solution is to sell physical goods. Ship media, such as a CD-ROM, con-taining your software or e-book. You can still grant your customers immedi-ate download privileges for the material they will be receiving on CD or floppy, but ship a physical product as well. Be sure to offer tracking of the package.

Thinking Outside the Disk

If you want to avoid the cost of a disk, mailer, and added postage every time you ship a CD, use paper instead. Encode your digital item with base64,* and then print it with a small font on both sides of plain letter-sized paper. Half a megabyte of data can easily be stored on 15 pages, which should weigh no more than three ounces.

Your customer can then scan the sheets with a scanner, convert them back into digital data with OCR software, and then decode the base64 code to recreate the original product. Obviously, it's unlikely that any customer will bother doing this, but since it's technically possible, your shipment will qualify for the Seller Protection Policy.

Be careful what you end up shipping. For instance, the User Agreement specifically states that "this protection applies only to the sale of physical goods, and not to any services, intangible goods or sales or licenses of digital content." This means that sending only a paper license or *certificate of ownership* would be insufficient for eligibility.

HACK #27 Handle Merchandise Disputes Effectively

Here's what to do when a buyer disputes a payment sent to you.

If you're a seller and a buyer has filed a claim against you [Hack #16] or initiated a chargeback [Hack #25], you should respond online through PayPal's Resolution Center within 10 days. If you don't, you'll forfeit your defense and PayPal will refund the buyer.

First Response

When you respond, you'll be able to choose how to resolve the dispute from a menu of options, including disagreeing with the buyer's claim.

Most claims involve nonreceipt of merchandise. Nervous buyers sometimes file claims before sellers have had a chance to ship merchandise. The most effective way to respond to such a claim is to promptly provide an online tracking number for your shipment. This allows the customer (and PayPal) to confirm that the merchandise was not only shipped, but also delivered to an address attached to the buyer's PayPal account.

---

* Go to *http://www.fourmilab.ch/webtools/base64/* for one of many publicly available base64 encoder/decoder utilities.

Never ship to a gift address, a friend's address, or any address in a country different than the one listed on the customer's PayPal account.

Without verifiable proof (e.g., a tracking number) that your package was shipped, you'll lose the dispute and forfeit the payment.

Preventive Maintenance

Overcommunicate with your buyers, especially *newbies*. Email them when you expect to ship, and email them again when you actually do ship (include a tracking number whenever possible). This allows your customer to check delivery status, which helps to reduce buyer anxiety about transacting with a stranger and thus reduces the likelihood that a dispute will ever be filed.

Also, be compulsive when writing your product or eBay listing descriptions. (Good descriptions often garner more buyer interest anyway.) If the item is used, say so, and exhaustively describe all wear and tear. Include actual photos you took yourself (e.g., a picture of the actual iPod you're selling rather than one you grabbed from Apple's web site).

Finally, to protect yourself against fraudulent chargebacks, ship to your customer's address as listed on the Transaction Details page, and ship only if you see that the transaction is eligible for the Seller Protection Policy [Hack #25].

Unfortunately, there is no way to automatically refuse payments that are ineligible for the Seller Protection Policy. Keep in mind that such transactions are not necessarily bad or risky. For instance, the buyer might simply live in a country in which some of the eligibility requirements are not available.

As a seller, you can pick and choose with whom you do business. If someone makes a payment you subsequently decide is not worth the risk, you can always issue a refund [Hack #21] and make other arrangements.

## CHAPTER FOUR

Payment Buttons
Hacks 28–44

The most common question of PayPal's merchant support staff might be, "How do I start using PayPal as a seller?"

For a buyer, PayPal is straightforward: sign up for an account and start using it to pay for goods and services on the Internet. But for merchants, PayPal offers so many options to fit each seller's needs that it can seem overwhelming when you first endeavor to sell online. Unless you plan to sell only on eBay (in which case you should see *eBay Hacks* by David A. Karp), here is the basic information you need to get started.

PayPal is an online payment processor; it allows buyers and sellers to make monetary transactions easily and securely. PayPal is not, however, a credit card gateway; to accept payments with PayPal you do not have to pass a rigorous credit check, install any equipment or special software, make agreements with a bank, or send in signed documents. You also do not need to gather credit card numbers from your buyers or subsequently safeguard such sensitive financial information.

Buyers using PayPal can either open PayPal accounts (which is recommended, especially if you use PayPal often) or just enter their credit cards for each purchase. Sellers who accept PayPal must have PayPal accounts, and merchants who are doing serious business with PayPal will want to have a Business account, which allows acceptance of payments funded by credit cards. There is no fee for opening or holding a Business account—only a per-transaction fee of 2.9% plus $0.30 on each payment received.

Non-U.S. account holders, and those doing business with non-U.S. account holders, might be subject to additional fees or a different fee rate.

The best way to start using PayPal to sell merchandise online is to add one or more PayPal buttons to your web site. You can do this by logging into your PayPal account (create one now [Hack #1] if you don't have one yet), generating a button with the Merchant Tools PayPal provides, and copying it to a page on your site. You can literally start offering items for sale in 10 minutes.

PayPal buttons are nothing more than HTML forms. They live on your web pages, but they direct your customers to PayPal for processing payments. All the software and complexity of processing those payments is done for you.

PayPal offers four types of payment buttons to meet the various needs of online enterprises, all at no additional charge:

Buy Now

> The most basic payment button is the Buy Now button. It lets your customers easily buy a single item from your site. One click directs a buyer to the PayPal system, where they can make their payment. See "Create a Buy Now Button" [Hack #28] to start hacking Buy Now buttons.

Add To Cart

> The Add To Cart button lets a buyer accumulate a group of items in a shopping basket and then pay for them all at once. You should add an individual Add To Cart button for each item you sell. When they are ready, customers click the Checkout button (also on your site) to go PayPal and complete their payment. See "Hack Shopping Cart Buttons" [Hack #45] and all of Chapter 5 to get started.

Subscribe

> A PayPal subscription button lets your customer easily set up a *subscription* (a recurring payment) from the customer's PayPal account to yours. You can set the terms of the subscription to fit your business model, and you or your customer can cancel the subscription at any time without further obligation. See Chapter 6 for more details on subscription buttons.

Donate Now

> The PayPal donation button is nearly identical to a Buy Now button. The wording of the payment screens, however, indicates the processing of a donation rather than the purchase of a product or service. See "Accept Donations" [Hack #40] for an introduction and "Display Donation Goals on Your Web Site" [Hack #79] and "Display a Recent Donor List" [Hack #80] for ways to take donation buttons further.

PayPal is a flexible system. With your own software, you can use it to accommodate just about any business process, such as delivering digital goods instantly, collecting conference registration fees, or cooperating with an extant shopping cart system. If you are just getting started, PayPal's buttons are the way to do it. The rest of this book should fire your imagination with ideas of where to go from there.

Create a Buy Now Button

Accept payments on your web site with a simple button that sends the customer, along with all necessary payment information, to PayPal.

The most basic way to accept payments on your web site is to deploy a Buy Now button, which essentially consists of an HTML form.

In order to use the Buy Now system, you need to have a Business or Premier account at PayPal.

Use the Merchant Tools section of the PayPal web site to generate the necessary code to sell goods from your web site. Once you have the code for one item, you can modify that code for any of your other products by changing a few variable values.

The Code

To generate a simple block of button code, follow these steps:

1. Go to *http://www.paypal.com*, log into your account, and click the Merchant Tools tab.

2. Click the Buy Now link under the Website Payments section to open the PayPal Button Factory, as shown in Figure 4-1.

3. Create a basic button by entering the item name and item number. Leave the Buyer Country as is, and enter 1 for the amount. Skip the rest of the settings, but make sure to change the Encrypt Button option to No.

4. When you're done, click Create Button Now to generate the code.

The resulting code should look like this:

```
<form action="https://www.paypal.com/cgi-bin/webscr" method="post">
<input type="hidden" name="cmd" value="_xclick">
<input type="hidden" name="business" value="sales@payloadz.com">
<input type="hidden" name="item_name" value="Widget">
<input type="hidden" name="item_number" value="Wid-001">
<input type="hidden" name="amount" value="1.00">
<input type="hidden" name="no_note" value="1">
<input type="hidden" name="currency_code" value="USD">
<input type="image" src=
    "https://www.paypal.com/en_US/i/btn/x-click-but23.gif" border="0"
    name="submit">
</form>
```

Most of the variables will not change, regardless of the item you're selling. The variables on lines ❶, ❷, and ❸ are the only ones you'll need to customize for each particular product.

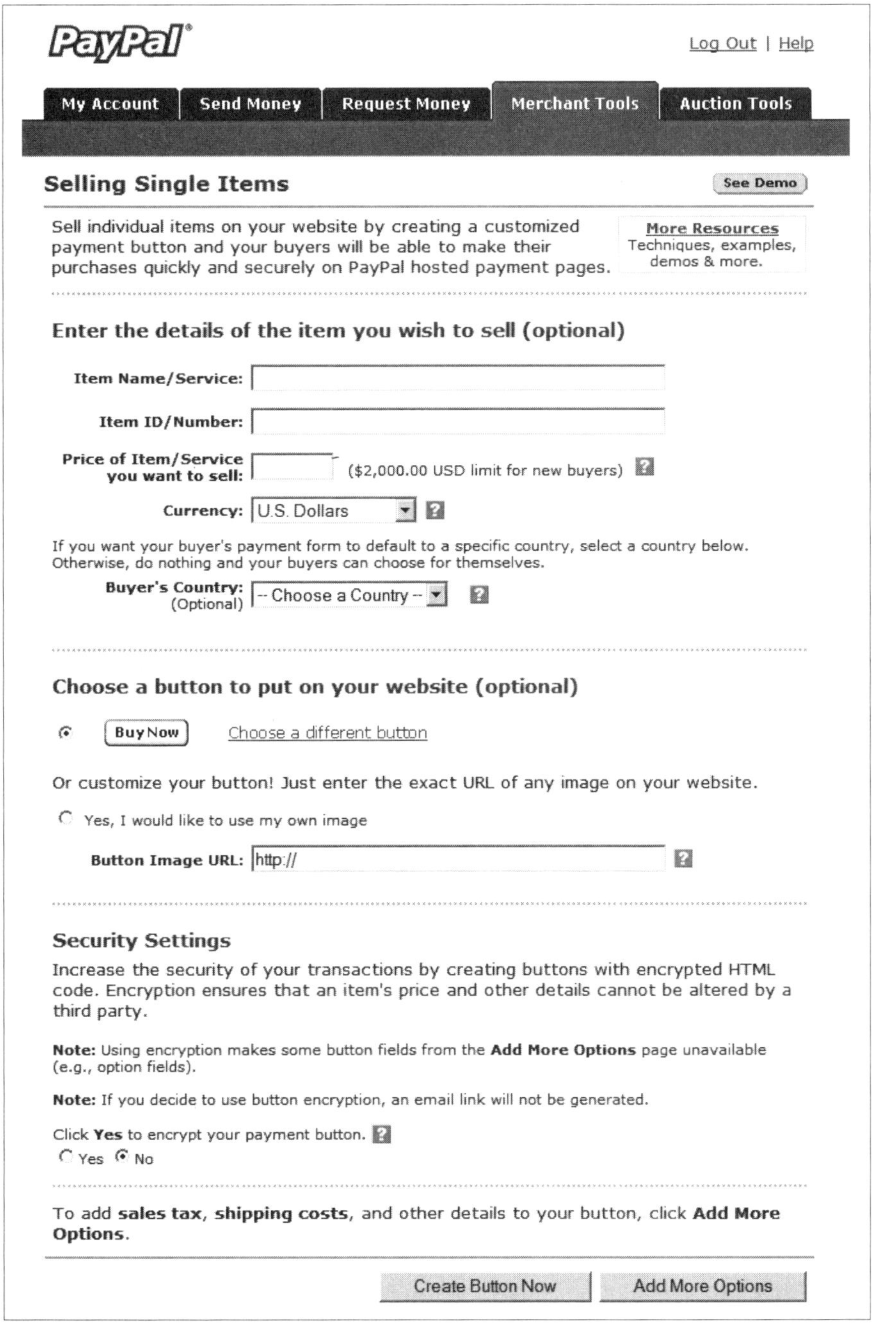

Figure 4-1. Using the PayPal Button Factory to create generic button code you can modify later

Modifications to the variables are straightforward and can be done directly in the HTML. For instance, to specify a price, replace 1.00 on line ❸ with the price of your item, in dollars and cents (but no dollar sign). Likewise, set the item_name variable to the name of the product, and set the item_number variable to a unique product number or SKU code that makes sense for your store.

Hacking the Hack

In addition to the aforementioned variables, there are also other PayPal-supported options you can add to your purchase buttons. For example, the return and cancel_return variables define the addresses of web pages to which the user should be taken after the payment process has been completed or if the process is cancelled, respectively:

```
<input type="hidden" name="return" value="http://yoursite.com/thankyou.html">
<input type="hidden" name="cancel_return" value=
    "http://yoursite.com/cancel.html">
```

Simply insert additional variables anywhere in your button code, so long as they appear between the opening <form> and closing </form> tags. Other variables include:

cn
> The text label to appear above the note field (maximum of 40 characters).

cs
> Sets the background color of your payment pages to black (1); the default is white (0).

currency_code
> The three-digit code indicating the currency in which the payment is to be made.

custom *and* invoice
> Both custom and invoice are pass-through variables, never shown to customers, to be returned to you when the payment process is complete.

handling
> The shipping surcharge, applied regardless of the number of items ordered.

image_url
> The address (URL) of your company logo. The image can be up to 150x50 pixels. If this variable is omitted, the customer will see your business name if you have a Business account or your email address if you have a Premier account.

`no_note`

> If this variable is set to 1, the customer will not be allowed to include a note. It's probably best to specify the `no_note` option (as in the example earlier in this hack) if you'll be automating your operation and are unlikely to see any notes your customers would enter here.

`no_shipping`

> See "Override Shipping and Handling Preferences" [Hack #34] for more information on this setting.

`on0, on1, os0,` *and* `os1`

> See "Include More Than Two Option Fields" [Hack #33] for more information on these four settings.

`page_style`

> Sets the Custom Payment Page style for payment pages. This variable should be the name of one of the styles listed on the Custom Payment Page Styles page. To add or edit custom payment pages, click the My Account tab, click Profile, and click the Custom Payment Pages link. See "Customize Checkout Pages" [Hack #51] for further details.

`return`

> The URL of the page on your web site to which the customer will be sent when the transaction is complete.

`rm`

> Specifies the behavior of the return URL (see the `return` option). If this variable is set to 1, the buyer will be sent back to the return URL using a GET method, and no transaction variables will be submitted. If `rm` is set to 2, the buyer will be sent back to the return URL using a POST method, to which all available transaction variables will also be posted. If `rm` is omitted or set to 0, GET methods will be used for all Shopping Cart transactions in which IPN is not enabled and POST methods with variables will be used for the rest.

`shipping, shipping2`

> The amount to charge the customer for shipping, per item. If you specify an amount for `shipping2`, the `shipping` amount will be charged only for the first item ordered and `shipping2` amount will be charged for each additional item (all of which applies only if the customer orders a quantity of more than one).

`tax`

> If this variable is omitted, the sales tax specified in your account preferences will take effect. Otherwise, use `tax` to specify a flat tax (in dollars and cents, rather than a percentage) to apply to the order.

Use a Custom Button Image

Customize the appearance of the Buy Now button with a few changes to the Button Factory code

The PayPal Button Factory generates HTML code that you insert into your payment pages to facilitate sales. The code you initially get depends on the values you type into the form, but you can subsequently edit it manually before you install it onto your site. This simple hack walks you through the modification of your button code to use your own custom Buy Now button images.

Preparing the Image and Code

First, you'll need to prepare another button image for use in the form. It can be either a GIF or JPG image file, but it must be located somewhere on your web site or elsewhere on the Internet so that you can reference its location in your code. See the next section for button design tips.

Start by generating the code for an ordinary Buy Now button [Hack #28]. Copy the HTML code and paste it into your favorite HTML editor, such as Dreamweaver, FrontPage, or any plain-text editor (e.g., Notepad). Find the piece of code that references the image:

```
<input type="image" src="https://www.paypal.com/images/x-click-but23.gif"
    border="0" name="submit" alt="Make payments with PayPal - it's
    fast, free  and secure!">
```

The `src` parameter contains the location (URL) of the image to be used:

```
src="https://www.paypal.com/images/x-click-but23.gif"
```

Simply change this source to the address (URL) of your button image:

```
src="http://www.anothersite.com/yournewimage.gif"
```

Or, if the image is located on the same site as your button code, it could be as simple as this:

```
src="/images/ournewimage.gif"
```

So, the final code should look like this:

```
<input type="image" ="http://www.anothersite.com/ournewimage.gif"
    border="0" name="submit" alt="Make payments with PayPal - it's
    fast, free and secure!">
```

Button Design 101

The PayPal Button Factory provides some options for button appearance, though most of the supplied images are branded with the PayPal look and might not integrate cleanly with your web site's design. The previous section shows how to use any image you like, provided that you have one at the ready. With a simple web search, you can find images of buttons at web sites that specialize in shopping cart buttons. But for even more seamless integration, you can create your own image in an image-editing program, such as Photoshop or Paint Shop Pro.

The ideal sizes for your buttons, based on the sizes PayPal uses for their buttons, are 68x23 pixels for Buy Now buttons and 87x23 pixels for Shopping Cart buttons. You do not have to use these exact sizes for your own buttons, but do use them as guidelines when choosing appropriate sizes for your buttons.

You can also add interaction to your buttons by providing different variations of your images so that they look lit up or pushed in when your customers click them or move over them with their mice. This visual feedback and interactivity makes your buttons look and act more clickable, and it is a good way to get more customers to click them. To give your image a slightly different appearance on mouseover or when clicked, you need to have two button images: one to act as the normal, unactivated state and another to replace the original image with activated. Figure 4-2 shows two such images.

Figure 4-2. Normal and activated images for one button

The images in Figure 4-2 are identical, except that the activated image has been tinted gray. You might prefer a little more color or perhaps a highlighted border; to make the image look pushed in, replace the shadow pixels with the button foreground color (in this case, white).

Simply include this JavaScript code to swap one image for another upon mouseover:

```
<input type="image" name="submit" src="yourbutton_up.gif" onmouseover=
    "this.src='yourbutton_over.gif'" onmouseout=
    "this.src='yourbutton_up.gif'">
```

The two images for normal and activated states are yourbutton_up.gif and yourbutton_over.gif, respectively, in the preceding code. To have the button change when it is clicked (as opposed to responding to a mouseover), use this code instead:

```
<input type="image" name="submit" src="yourbutton_up.gif" onMouseDown=
    "this.src='yourbutton_over.gif'">
```

This just scratches the surface of what you can do. The more you do to polish the appearance and behavior of your buttons, the more customized (and hopefully professional) your site will appear to your customers.

Create a Purchase Button for Services

#30 Streamline your purchase buttons for selling intangible goods and services by removing unnecessary fields. By removing certain shipping requirements, you can accept payments from all buyers, regardless of whether they can provide confirmed addresses.

PayPal allows you to accept payment for almost any kind of tangible product or intangible service. When you're selling services, much of the information PayPal gathers is superfluous. You might not always need the customer's address, for instance, and you most likely will not need to charge any shipping or handling fees. By eliminating these options in your purchase buttons, you can simplify the checkout process for your customers, thus making it easier to sell your services.

Here's the code for a service button, adapted from "Create a Buy Now Button" [Hack #28]:

```
<form action="https://www.paypal.com/cgi-bin/webscr" method="post">
<input type="hidden" name="cmd" value="_xclick">
<input type="hidden" name="business" value="sales@payloadz.com">
<input type="hidden" name="item_name" value="Service">
<input type="hidden" name="item_number" value="Serv-001">
<input type="hidden" name="amount" value="1.00">
<input type="hidden" name="shipping" value="0.00">
<input type="hidden" name="handling" value="0.00">
<input type="hidden" name="no_shipping" value="1">
<input type="hidden" name="no_note" value="1">
<input type="hidden" name="currency_code" value="USD">
<input type="image" src=
    "https://www.paypal.com/en_US/i/btn/x-click-but23.gif"
    border="0" name="submit">
</form>
```

The difference between this code and an ordinary Buy Now button is the addition of two variables, shipping and handling (lines ❶ and ❷, respectively), both of which are set to 0.00. This trumps any shipping charges you might have in your PayPal profile. Also, the no_shipping variable (line ❸) instructs PayPal not to ask for a shipping address, and the no_note variable (line ❹) turns off the note field during checkout. All of this makes a simple and streamlined checkout process.

Create an Auction Payment Button

#31 Create payment buttons for auctions, such that the completed transaction updates the payment status on the auction web site automatically.

Merchants that sell using auction sites such as eBay often have to collect payment for their goods after the auction has ended. Sometimes, it can be confusing to the winning bidder how to complete payment, and you'll want to make it as easy as possible for your customers to send you money. Using some simple HTML, you can construct a payment button much like the payment buttons generated by PayPal for Shopping Cart and Web Accept purchases. You then present this button to the winning bidder in an email or on your web site to supplement the payment buttons already on the auction site.

The Easy Way

Since PayPal is an eBay company, it shouldn't be surprising that PayPal is well integrated with the eBay web site. For instance, if you indicate that you accept PayPal payments when constructing an eBay listing, a PayPal button will automatically appear for the winning bidder when the listing ends. Here's how to build the link between your eBay account and your PayPal account:

1. Go to the eBay web site and log into your eBay account.
2. Go to My eBay and click the eBay Preferences link under the My Account heading.
3. Click the Change link next to the Payment Preferences heading, and turn on all the PayPal-related settings here.
4. When you sell your next item, check the PayPal option in the "Seller-accepted payment methods" section and enter the email address of the PayPal account to which you'd like auction payments to be sent.

That's it! When your auction ends, a PayPal payment button will automatically appear at the top of the auction page, but for the winning bidder only.

Furthermore, you can configure PayPal to automatically insert a Pay Now button into each of your running auctions:

1. Log into your PayPal account.
2. Click the Profile tab and then click Auctions.
3. If your eBay account isn't listed here, click Add, and then enter your eBay user ID and password.
4. Otherwise, simply turn on the features you'd like to employ. The changes will take effect immediately.

The PayPal Auction options include the following:

Automatic Logo Insertion
PayPal automatically inserts a PayPal logo into the description of each of your running auctions (using eBay's Add to Description feature). This not only advertises the fact that you accept PayPal, it also gives your winning bidder a shortcut to the payment process.

Winning Buyer Notification

> This instructs PayPal to automatically send an email to all your winning bidders, complete with payment instructions and a Pay Now button. This email is sent independently of eBay's "Congratulations! You are the buyer for..." email.

PayPal Preferred on eBay

> This inserts the PayPal logo into the "Payment methods accepted" section of your auction page, as shown in Figure 4-3. The PayPal logo appears in addition to the logo that might already be there and suggests to your customers that you not only accept PayPal, but you wholeheartedly prefer it as a means of payment.

Figure 4-3. Buttons indicating that you prefer PayPal in an eBay listing

Making Your Own Button

Although eBay provides payment buttons for high bidders, you might want to supplement these buttons with your own. Plus, you might want to add eBay-like functionality to other auction sites, such as Yahoo!, uBid, Amazon.com, MSN, and Bidville auctions.

This code displays a simple Pay Now button that sends your customers to the PayPal web site and guides them through the payment process. The system automatically tracks the payment for this particular auction, so your customer will not have to enter any additional auction-related information. Plus, the auction site, provided that it's linked up with PayPal, will be notified automatically so that it can update the payment status of the auction for you and your bidder.

The goal of providing an extra payment button like this one is to reduce the chances that your customer (bidder) will use PayPal's Send Money function to pay for an auction; in that case, you would receive a payment not linked to its corresponding auction.

Among other difficulties, PayPal's Send Money tab makes it possible for your customer to "forget" to include the shipping charge or sales tax, you might have to process the order manually (or simply refund the payment), and the auction site might not reflect that the customer has paid. To automatically reject all payments sent this way, configure your PayPal account to "Block Payments from users who initiate payments from the Pay Anyone subtab of the Send Money tab," as described in Chapter 3.

Here is the HTML code for an auction payment button, linked to a particular auction:

```
<form method="get" action="https://www.paypal.com/cgi-bin/webscr">
<input type="hidden" name="cmd" value=_cart>
<input type="hidden" name="business" value="youremail@paypalhacks.com">
<input type="hidden" name="item_name_1" value="Widget">
<input type="hidden" name="amount_1" value="1.00">
<input type="hidden" name="quantity_1" value="1">
<input type="hidden" name="site_1" value="eBay">
<input type="hidden" name="ai_1" value="2540252652">
<input type="hidden" name="ab_1" value="your_ebay_id">
<input type="submit" name="upload" value="Pay Now">
</form>
```

This code is similar to the code used in "Integrate a Third-Party Shopping Cart with PayPal" [Hack #50], with the exception of a few new variables: site_n, ai_n, and ab_n, where n is a number representing the item in multiple item payments, starting with 1 (for example, include ab_1, ab_2, and ab_3 if you're requesting payment for three different auctions).

The site_n variable defines the site on which the auction was listed, and it should be set to eBay for eBay auctions or Yahoo for Yahoo! Auctions. This value is case sensitive, so for other auction sites, you'd type uBid, Amazon, MSN, or Bidville. The second variable, ai_n, should be set to the auction (or listing) number at the auction site. Finally, ab_n, is your user ID at the auction site (your_ebay_id in this example). Naturally, you'll need to replace all italicized text in the code with the details of your transaction.

The other variables, such as item_name_n and amount_n, can be modified as described in "Create a Buy Now Button" [Hack #28].

Hacking the Hack

This hack demonstrates how you can create buttons that facilitate auction-specific payments. Naturally, creating a button for each auction manually would be a time-consuming process, but you can use the eBay API to automate this process. Start by sending a query to obtain the information for each of your completed auctions using a GetTransactionDetails call, and then assemble your buttons and email them to the high bidders. The technical procedures involved with implementing this type of system go beyond the scope of this book, but extensive information can be found in David A. Karp's *eBay Hacks* (O'Reilly).

If you use an off-site listing tool or a third-party listing service to build your auctions, you might be able to tie your application into the application's local database. However, you will also need a means of obtaining completed-item details (such as the final price and high-bidder contact information). For an example that shows how to build payment buttons dynamically, see "Create a Dynamic Storefront" [Hack #54].

HACK #32 Provide Purchase Options with Drop-Down Listboxes

Change a few lines of the PayPal Button Factory code to restrict purchase options to a distinct list of choices.

By default, the item_name variable created by the PayPal Button Factory [Hack #28] is a hidden field containing a single string of text, which means that a single payment button corresponds to a single product. So, if you sell three products, you'll need three payment buttons, right?

Not so, thanks to drop-down listboxes.

Since many of the products you're selling probably come in a combination of styles or sizes, you can merge those variations into a single purchase button. For instance, if you're selling clothing, a Size option might contain three choices: Small, Medium, and Large. Fortunately, PayPal doesn't distinguish between text strings sent from text boxes and list elements selected from drop-down listboxes, so you can easily replace any <input> field with a <select> drop-down list. For instance, take:

```
<input type="hidden" name="item_name" value="T-Shirt">
```

and replace it with:

```
<select name="item_name" id="item_name">
  <option>T-Shirt</option>
</select>
```

The problem here is that we still provide the customer with only one option. To add more options, simply insert additional <option> tags, one for each variation, like this:

```
<select name="item_name" id="item_name">
  <option>T-Shirt, Small</option>
  <option>T-Shirt, Medium</option>
  <option>T-Shirt, Large</option>
</select>
```

Figure 4-4 shows the completed drop-down listbox.

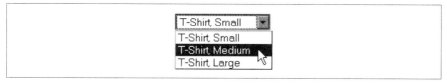

Figure 4-4. Taking advantage of PayPal's option fields with a simple drop-down listbox.

With this simple change, your customers choose a size, click the Buy Now button, and pay for your item. PayPal then sends the customer's selection back to you in the "You've got cash" email.

If you need to provide your customers with more than one option, you can include up to two additional option fields "Include More Than Two Option Fields" [Hack #33] and convert both of them to drop-down lists with this same procedure. Thus, you can have up to three different options with a single payment button.

Hacking the Hack

You can take this hack a step further by changing the values of other fields based on selection. For instance, you can change the price based on the shirt size your customer chooses and send the correct price to PayPal along with the corresponding options. You need to add a few pieces of code to your payment button form for this to work.

First, place this JavaScript code in the section of your page between the <head> and </head> tags:

```
<script type="text/javascript">
<!-- Update Price Change
function UpdateForm (object1) {             // process change selects
var i,item_amt,object,position,val;
  item_amt = object1.amount.value;          // default amount
  for (i=0; i<object1.length; i++) {        // check options
    object = object1.elements[i];
    if (object.type == "select-one" &&
        object.name == "cng") {             // must be named cng
      position = object.selectedIndex;      // option selected
      val = object.options[position].value; // selected value
      position  = val.indexOf ("$");        // set new price
      if (position >= 0) item_amt = val.substring (position + 1)*1.0;
    }
  }
  object1.amount.value = item_amt;
  if (object1.item_total) object1.item_total.value = "$" + item_amt;
}
//-->
</script>
```

Next, change the `<form>` tag for your payment button code so the JavaScript function is executed when the form is submitted, like this:

```
<form action="https://www.paypal.com/cgi-bin/webscr" method="post"
onsubmit="this.target='paypal';UpdateForm(this);">
```

Finally, modify the `<select>` tag so that it, too, is linked to the JavaScript code:

```
<select name="cng" onchange="UpdateForm(this.form);">
<option value="Small $1.00">Size: Small $1.00</option>
<option value="Medium $2.00">Size: Medium $2.00</option>
<option value="Large $3.00">Size: Large $3.00</option>
</select>
```

You can edit the amount charged to your customer by changing the `value="Small $1.00"` section of the form field. You can also change the text displayed to your customer by changing the value between the `<option>` and `</option>` sections.

Make sure the amount tag in your form is set to the same value as the *default* value of the drop-down menu. That way, if the form is submitted without changing the values, the amount has the correct default value.

When this code is in place, the price is updated automatically whenever a new size is selected.

> Since this solution relies on JavaScript to update the price according to a customer action, it will fail if the customer has disabled JavaScript. Although PayPal doesn't do price checking, you can effectively prevent this problem by checking for JavaScript before displaying order pages to your customers.

Include More Than Two Option Fields   HACK #33

Give your customers a large selection of options when purchasing their items, despite the limitations of payment buttons.

PayPal buttons enable you to easily offer fixed products to your customers. Although some flexibility is provided in the form of option fields [Hack #32], Pay-Pal currently supports only two such fields. If your product has more than two options (e.g., Size, Color, and Material), you can employ a little JavaScript code and a hidden field to create as many option fields as you need.

Start with the basic Buy Now button code [Hack #28] for a single item, although this works with Shopping Cart, Subscription, and Donation buttons as well:

```
<form action="https://www.paypal.com/cgi-bin/youbscr" method="post">
<input type="hidden" name="cmd" value="_xclick">
```

```
<input type="hidden" name="business" value="sales@payloadz.com">
<input type="hidden" name="item_name" value="Widget One">
<input type="hidden" name="item_number" value="Wid-001">
<input type="hidden" name="amount" value="1.00">
<input type="hidden" name="no_note" value="1">
<input type="hidden" name="currency_code" value="USD">
<input type="image" src=
    "https://www.paypal.com/en_US/i/btn/x-click-but23.gif"
    border="0" name="submit>
</form>
```

Suppose the item you're selling has three options: Color, Size, and Material. You can provide three drop-down lists [Hack #32], one for each option, with which your customers can customize their purchases. To keep things simple, name your drop-down elements custom1, custom2, and custom3.

This code joins all three of the selected options into a single variable, custom, to be passed to PayPal. You'll need to add the custom form element to your button as a hidden variable with no value specified. The value will be populated by the JavaScript code when the form is submitted. Here's an HTML form with form options and the custom field:

```
Color
<select name="custom1">
    <option value="White" selected>White</option>
    <option value="Grey">Grey</option>
    <option value="Black">Black</option>
</select>
<br>
Size
<select name="custom2">
    <option value="Small">Small</option>
    <option value="Medium">Medium</option>
    <option value="Large" selected>Large</option>
    <option value="X-Large">X-Large</option>
</select>
<br>
Material
<select name="custom3">
    <option value="Spandex" selected>Spandex</option>
    <option value="Cotton">Cotton</option>
</select>
<input type="hidden" name="custom" value="">
```

Figure 4-5 shows the additional custom fields in action. You can include as many option fields as you can fit on your page.

You can continue adding as many option fields as you need, provided that you use the same custom# naming format. Just be sure that the total character count for the labels *and* their possible variable values does not exceed 256 characters, the size limit of PayPal's custom variable.

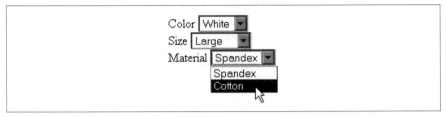

Figure 4-5. Including additional option fields

Add the HTML code to your PayPal button form between the opening and closing <form> tags. Then add the following JavaScript code to the head of the web page:

```
<script language="JavaScript">
<!--
  function joinFields(){
    fmBuy.custom.value = 'Color:' + fmBuy.custom1.value + ' Size:' +
              fmBuy.custom2.value + ' Material:' + fmBuy.custom3.value
  }
// -->
</script>
```

If you add additional fields, you'll need to modify this code to accommodate them.

Finally, add a call to the joinFields routine by inserting the name and onSubmit attributes to the existing <form> tag (the values for the action and method attributes remain unchanged):

```
<form action="https://www.paypal.com/cgi-bin/youbscr" method="post"
name="fmBuy" onSubmit="joinFields()">
```

Here is the final code for the example form:

```
<form action="https://www.paypal.com/cgi-bin/youbscr" method="post"
name="fmBuy" onSubmit="joinFields()">
<input type="hidden" name="cmd" value="_xclick">
<input type="hidden" name="business" value="sales@payloadz.com">
<input type="hidden" name="item_name" value="Widget One">
<input type="hidden" name="item_number" value="Wid-001">
<input type="hidden" name="amount" value="1.00">
<input type="hidden" name="no_note" value="1">
<input type="hidden" name="currency_code" value="USD">
  Color
  <select name="custom1">
    <option value="White" selected>White</option>
    <option value="Grey">Grey</option>
    <option value="Black">Black</option>
  </select>
<br>
Size
<select name="custom2">
```

```
    <option value="Small">Small</option>
    <option value="Medium">Medium</option>
    <option value="Large" selected>Large</option>
    <option value="X-Large">X-Large</option>
  </select>
<br>
Material
<select name="custom3">
    <option value="Spandex" selected>Spandex</option>
    <option value="Cotton">Cotton</option>
  </select>
  <input type="hidden" name="custom" value="">

<input type="image" src="https://www.paypal.com/en_US/i/btn/x-click-but23.gif"
    border="0" name="submit">
</form>
```

When the complete page is loaded (with the button code in the page body and the JavaScript in the page head), the customer-selected option fields will be concatenated into one string and passed through to PayPal in the custom variable. For instance, if the form is submitted with its default values, the custom variable will be set to Color:White Size:Large Material:Spandex. The string will appear in details of the transaction in your PayPal account; your customers will never see it. If necessary, you can also parse this field out in the IPN page [Hack #80].

Override Shipping and Handling Preferences

Modify purchase buttons to override your Profile settings, allowing you to set shipping and handling fees to zero for digital goods.

Certain goods, such as software or other downloadable products, should not incur any shipping charges. By default, PayPal calculates the applicable shipping fees and applies them to every order. To configure your shipping calculation preferences, log into PayPal, click Profile, and then click Shipping Calculations.

The problem is that PayPal applies your shipping preferences to all purchases placed through your PayPal buttons. If you sell both tangible and digital products, you might need to charge different shipping amounts for different products.

To override your shipping and handling preferences, turn on the "Allow transaction-based shipping values to override the profile shipping settings" options in your Shipping Calculations profile page. Then, add two additional variables to applicable buttons and set each of them to zero (or any values you wish) for digital goods purchases, like this:

```
<input type="hidden" name="shipping" value="0.00">
<input type="hidden" name="handling" value="0.00">
```

If you were to omit these two new variables, the shipping fees applied to that product would default to the values in your PayPal profile. You can add these two new form variables anywhere in your button code, as long as they appear between the opening <form> and closing </form> tags.

When you override your Profile's Shipping Preferences for a single item in your PayPal Shopping Cart, the override applies only to that item. All other items are charged shipping according to your Profile's Shipping Preferences.

HACK #35   Build Notification Tracking

Track how your PayPal applications are used by including the Build Notification (BN) tag with all your payment buttons and resulting transactions.

PayPal originally introduced the Build Notification (BN) tag as a way to track developers' projects, allowing them to, for example, include version numbers to gauge application performance. The BN tag is a field for your payment buttons into which you place an identifier string you choose.

An unexpected benefit of the BN tag is that, by demonstrating that your site or application generates a significant amount of transactions, you can receive the benefits of a high-volume merchant. While there is no official disclosure of any specific application rewards, developers can often expect to receive specialized technical support if they ever have problems that affect their applications or sites. High-volume merchants are also invited to participate in testing new features of the PayPal system and receive advance notice of upcoming releases of new product features.

To use the BN system, PayPal suggests assigning a unique, readable value to the BN tag, including the version (and build) number of your application as well as your company name. The suggested format of the BN value is company.product.version, like this:

```
<input type="hidden" name="bn" value="GeekSoft.Cart.1.0">
```

Insert the bn variable into your PayPal form buttons just as you would any other values [Hack #28]:

```
<form action="https://www.paypal.com/cgi-bin/webscr" method="post">
<input type="hidden" name="bn" value="GeekSoft.Cart.1.0">
<input type="hidden" name="cmd" value="_xclick">
<input type="hidden" name="business" value="bn@paypalhacks.com">
<input type="hidden" name="item_name" value="Widget">
<input type="hidden" name="amount" value="1">
<input type="image" src=http://images.paypal.com/images/x-click-butcc.gif
     border="0" name="submit">
</form>
```

Once you deploy the BN tag in your form buttons, make sure you register your application with PayPal so that they can begin tracking your usage. Send an email to *developer@paypal.com* with the BN ID text you use in each of your solutions, along with the name of your company, the title of your application or web site, and your contact information. For further information, see *http://www.paypal.com/pdn-submit.*

Hacking the Hack

The BN tag only allows PayPal to track your sales internally; you won't have access to any usage statistics connected with your use of the BN tag on your web site.

However, you can track your sales by including the custom variable in your purchase buttons. Set the value of the custom variable to some unique identifier for the application or web site in which the button appears:

```
<input type="hidden" name="custom" value="GeekSoft.Cart.1.3">
```

Every time a payment is made with this button, PayPal records the custom value in your transaction history. Next, use the Download My History feature to generate a tab- or comma-delimited text file, as shown in Figure 4-6. Finally, import the file into your spreadsheet or database and use the tools at your disposal to plot sales trends, run reports, or perform statistical analysis.

You can also export your PayPal history into files that Quicken and Quickbooks can understand, allowing you to integrate PayPal sales with your accounting software.

See Also

"Use Mass Pay to Create an Affiliate System" **[Hack #77]** shows another way to track sales through your PayPal payment buttons.

HACK #36 Hack-Proof Your Payment
Prevent code-tampering and price-spoofing with a hidden form post.

When deploying PayPal buttons on your web site, you should consider the risk of spoofed payments. PayPal buttons are normally created in plain HTML, with the variables and their values available for anyone to see (select View → Source in your browser to see for yourself). This means that anyone can view your button source code, copy the HTML to her own system, make changes to the variables (such as the price), and make a payment with the modified button. You can manually review purchases to make sure no

Figure 4-6. Pulling a comma-delimited file from your PayPal history for use in spreadsheets and statistical analysis applications

tampering has taken place, but in high-volume or automated systems, this might be a difficult or even impossible task.

> PayPal offers a button encryption system that allows you to encrypt your purchase buttons, provided that you're not using buttons modified with custom variables. Button encryption is also not supported with Shopping Cart buttons.

This hack uses techniques covered in some of the other hacks in this book to create a hidden form post that sends the button information to PayPal without allowing the customer to see it. To use this technique to its fullest, you should already have deployed "Create a Dynamic Storefront" **[Hack #54]**.

The Code

The hack consists of two pages: *link.asp* and *jump.asp*. First, *link.asp* contains the product and selling information, as well as a link to the second page:

```
<html>
<body>
Widget<br>
```

```
<a href="jump.asp?id=123">Click here to buy</a>
</body>
</html>
```

This first page mimics the Buy Now button, but instead of sending the customer to PayPal, it links to the jump page. Next, *jump.asp* queries your database for the product info and sends the purchase information to PayPal. This code is written in ASP:

```
<%
'Connect to database and create recordset
❶  connStore = "DRIVER={Microsoft Access Driver (*.mdb)};DBQ="C:/InetPub/
   wwwroot/database/dbPayPal.mdb")
   set rsJump= Server.CreateObject("ADODB.Recordset")
   rsJump.ActiveConnection = connStore
❷  rsJump.Source = "SELECT tblProducts FROM tblProducts WHERE Id = " &
   Request("id")
❸  rsJump.Open( )
   %>
   <html>
❹  <body onLoad="document.fmPost.submit( )">
   <form action="https://www.paypal.com/cgi-bin/webscr" method="post"
   name="fmPost">
     <input type="hidden" name="cmd" value="_xclick">
     <input type="hidden" name="business" value="youremail@yourisp.com">
     <input type="hidden" name="item_name" value=
        "<%=(rsJump("ItemName").Value)%>">
     <input type="hidden" name="item_number" value=
        "<%=(rsJump("ItemID").Value)%>">
     <input type="hidden" name="amount" value=
        "<%=(rsJump("ItemPrice").Value)%>">
   </form>
   </body>
   </html>
   <%
   rsJump.Close( )
   %>
```

The jump page queries the database (line ❷) for the requested product information (based on the URL embedded in the link page) and then dynamically builds a PayPal form from this information. Finally, the page uses an onLoad function (line ❹) to automatically submit the form as soon as the page loads, without the customer ever seeing the page.

> Depending on your platform, you might need to change the code that connects to your database (lines ❶ to ❸) and creates the rsJump recordset from the query results. See "Database Coding and Platform Choices" in the Preface for more information.

Hacking the Hack

You don't necessarily have to use the database method described here. Instead, you can simply create a static jump page for each product, complete with all of the product information (name, price, etc.) embedded right in the code. Although this approach wouldn't make any sense for an online store that sells hundreds or thousands of items, it would ultimately be easier to implement than a full database if you sell only one or two products on your site.

Plan B: Obfuscate Your Button Code

If all this seems like too much trouble to guard against a remote possibility, there is an easier way to keep casual observers from seeing exactly what your button code contains and spoofing your button. (Isn't it handy that the word *obfuscate* is, itself, a rather cryptic term?)

1. Create a Buy Now, Add to Cart, Subscription, or Donation button using PayPal's Merchant Tools.

2. Go to *http://www.dynamicdrive.com/dynamicindex9/encrypter.htm*. Copy and paste your button code into the text area window.

3. Click Encrypt. The HTML will be replaced with encoded text that is much harder for mere mortals to read, but the encoded text will easily be parsed and displayed by your customers' browsers.

4. Copy and paste this scrambled code into your web page.

This quick and easy obfuscator makes it harder for casual viewers to see how your button is coded and thus helps protect it from tampering. Additionally, it foils most web spiders looking for fresh email addresses to spam.

 This trick is no substitute for real encryption [Hack #37]. The material is all there, just in a form that is hard for a person to read. Anyone with some time, patience, and an understanding of common encoding methods (or anyone with access to this book) will crack the obfuscation in no time. Also, even if the HTML is not obvious, all the information critical to the consumers' buying decision will be echoed by PayPal once your customer clicks the button.

To illustrate, here's an ordinary payment button:

```
<h1>Plain button</h1>

<form action="https://www.paypal.com/cgi-bin/webscr" method="post">
<input type="hidden" name="cmd" value="_xclick">
<input type="hidden" name="business" value="sales@wwjcd.biz">
```

```
<input type="hidden" name="item_name" value="Jackie Chan bobble head">
<input type="hidden" name="item_number" value="jc-bh">
<input type="hidden" name="amount" value="9.99">
<input type="hidden" name="currency_code" value="USD">
<input type="image" src=
    "https://www.paypal.com/en_US/i/btn/x-click-but23.gif"
    border="0" name="submit" alt="Make payments with PayPal - it's
    fast, free and secure!">
</form>
```

And here's the obfuscated version of the same code:

```
<h1>Button obfuscated</h1>

<script>
<!--
document.write(unescape("%3Cform%20action%3D%22https%3A//www.paypal.com/cgi-
bin/webscr%22%20method%3D%22post%22%3E%0D%0A%3Cinput%20type%3D%22hidden%22%20
name%3D%22cmd%22%20value%3D%22_xclick%22%3E%0D%0A%3Cinput%20type%3D%22hidden
%22%20name%3D%22business%22%20value%3D%22sales@wwjcd.biz%22%3E%0D%0A%3Cinpu
%20type%3D%22hidden%22%20name%3D%22item_name%22%20value%3D%22Jackie%20Chan
%20bobble%20head%22%3E%0D%0A%3Cinput%20type%3D%22hidden%22%20name%3D%22item_
number%22%20value%3D%22jc-bh%22%3E%0D%0A%3Cinput%20type%3D%22hidden%22%20name
%3D%22amount%22%20value%3D%229.99%22%3E%0D%0A%3Cinput%20type%3D%22hidden
%22%20name%3D%22currency_code%22%20value%3D%22USD%22%3E%0D%0A%3Cinput
%20type%3D%22image%22%20src%3D%22https%3A//www.paypal.com/en_US/i/btn/x-click-
but23.gif%22%20border%3D%220%22%20name%3D%22submit%22%20alt%3D%22Make%20
payments%20with%20PayPal%20-%20it%27s%20fast%2C%20free%20and%20secure%21%22%
3E%0D%0A%3C/form%3E"));
//-->
</script>
```

While this hack can indeed be applied to an already-encrypted button (as detailed in [Hack #37], encrypted buttons hardly need the added protection of obfuscation.

HACK #37 Hack-Proof Your Buttons with Encryption

Add yet another layer of security to a Buy Now Button by encrypting its contents with OpenSSL and C/C++.

Now that you've created a complete Buy Now button [Hack #28], how can you prevent potential hackers from seeing (and possibly changing) the information you're passing to PayPal? PayPal's button encryption enables you to hide the exact contents of your HTML form in a PKCS7-encrypted blob.

While it is not necessary to integrate button encryption into every web site, it does allow you to provide another layer of security without affecting your customers' buying experience.

This hack shows how to secure the contents of a button using OpenSSL and C/C++. For a simpler solution, see "Hack-Proof Your Payment" **[Hack #36]**.

OpenSSL and Keys

Button encryption is done using a cryptography library, such as OpenSSL, and a pair of cryptographic keys. OpenSSL is nice, because it allows you to both sign and envelope the message in one action. The first thing to do is install OpenSSL, which is available for download at *http://www.openssl.org*.

Note that some knowledge of compiling programs is required for the installation of OpenSSL on Unix. Instructions for compiling and installation on various platforms can be found in the OpenSSL download. A precompiled Windows version is available at *http://www.slproweb.com/products/ Win32OpenSSL.html*. Simply follow the installation instructions for your particular environment.

Cryptographic keys must be exchanged in order for button encryption to work. You'll need to contact PayPal to obtain PayPal's public key, and you must provide your public key to PayPal. You should generate your keys in PEM format; consult the OpenSSL documentation (*http://www.openssl.org/ docs/HOWTO/keys.txt*) for details.

Basic Button Encryption Using OpenSSL

Start with an unencrypted HTML form tag in your HTML page:

```
<form method="post" action="https://www. paypal.com/cgi-bin/webscr">
<input type="hidden" name="cmd" value="_xclick">
<input type="hidden" name="business" value="sales@company.com">
<input type="hidden" name="amount" value="1.00">
<input type="hidden" name="currency_code" value="USD">
<input type="image" src="https://www.paypal.com/en_US/i/btn/x-click-but23.gif"
    name="submit" alt="Make payments with PayPal - it's fast, free
    and secure!">
</form>
```

The first thing you need to do is convert all the hidden field name/value pairs from this form into a single string, like this:

```
cmd=_xclick
business=sales@company.com
amount=1.00
currency_code=USD
```

Keep in mind that the line feeds required are Unix line feeds (\n), not Windows line feeds (\r\n). Ensure that your program is creating the string correctly or you will get decryption errors when posting your encrypted form.

Next, load the PayPal public key from the *paypal_cert.pem* file:

```
BIO *bio;
X509 *gPPx509;
char* payPalCertPath = "/opt/keys/paypal_cert.pem";
if ((bio = BIO_new_file(payPalCertPath, "rt")) == NULL) {
  printf("Fatal Error: Failed to open (%s)\n", payPalCertPath);
  goto end;
}

if ((gPPx509 = PEM_read_bio_X509(bio, NULL, NULL, NULL)) == NULL) {
  printf("Fatal Error: Failed to read Paypal certificate from
      (%s)\n", payPalCertPath);
  return "";
}

BIO_free(bio);
```

Then, load your public and private keys:

```
X509 *x509 = NULL;
RSA *rsa = NULL;

char* certPath = "/opt/keys/my_cert.pem";
char* keyPath = "/opt/keys/my_key.pem";

if ((bio = BIO_new_file(certPath, "rt")) == NULL) {
  printf("Fatal Error: Failed to open (%s)\n", certPath);
  goto end;
}

if ((x509 = PEM_read_bio_X509(bio, NULL, NULL, NULL)) == NULL) {
  printf("Fatal Error: Failed to read certificate from (%s)\n", certPath);
  goto end;
}

BIO_free(bio);

if ((bio = BIO_new_file(keyPath, "rt")) == NULL) {
  printf("Fatal Error: Failed to open (%s)\n", keyPath);
  goto end;
}

if ((rsa = PEM_read_bio_RSAPrivateKey(bio, NULL, NULL, NULL)) == NULL) {
  printf("Fatal Error: Unable to read RSA key (%s).\n", keyPath);
  goto end;
}
```

```
BIO_free(bio);

' Create an EVP_PKEY instance from the private key you just loaded:
EVP_PKEY *pkey = EVP_PKEY_new( );

if (EVP_PKEY_set1_RSA(pkey, rsa) == 0) {
  printf("Fatal Error: Unable to create EVP_KEY from RSA key\n");
  goto end;
}

' create the PKCS7 instance so you can create the PKCS7 Blob:
PKCS7 *p7 = PKCS7_new( );
PKCS7_set_type(p7, NID_pkcs7_signedAndEnveloped);

PKCS7_SIGNER_INFO* si = PKCS7_add_signature(p7, x509, pkey, EVP_sha1( ));

if (si) {
  if (PKCS7_add_signed_attribute(si, NID_pkcs9_contentType, V_ASN1_OBJECT,
              OBJ_nid2obj(NID_pkcs7_data)) <= 0) {
      printf("OpenSSL Error: %s\n", ERR_error_string(ERR_get_error( ),
NULL));
      goto end;
  }
} else {
  printf("Fatal Error: Failed to sign PKCS7\n");
  goto end;
}

//Encryption
if (PKCS7_set_cipher(p7, EVP_des_ede3_cbc( )) <= 0) {
  printf("OpenSSL Error: %s\n", ERR_error_string(ERR_get_error( ), NULL));
  goto end;
}

if (PKCS7_add_recipient(p7, gPPx509) <= 0) {
  printf("OpenSSL Error: %s\n", ERR_error_string(ERR_get_error( ), NULL));
  goto end;
}

if (PKCS7_add_certificate(p7, x509) <= 0) {
  printf("OpenSSL Error: %s\n", ERR_error_string(ERR_get_error( ), NULL));
  goto end;
}

BIO *p7bio = PKCS7_dataInit(p7, NULL);

if (!p7bio) {
  printf("OpenSSL Error: %s\n", ERR_error_string(ERR_get_error( ), NULL));
  goto end;
}

//Pump data to special PKCS7 BIO. This encrypts and signs it.
```

```
BIO_write(p7bio, data, strlen(data));
BIO_flush(p7bio);
PKCS7_dataFinal(p7, p7bio);

//Write PEM encoded PKCS7
BIO *bio = BIO_new(BIO_s_mem( ));

if (!bio || (PEM_write_bio_PKCS7(bio, p7) == 0)) {
  printf("Fatal Error: Failed to create PKCS7 PEM\n");
}

BIO_flush(bio);

char *str;
int len = BIO_get_mem_data(bio, &str);

char *ret = new char [len + 1];
memcpy(ret, str, len);
ret[len] = 0;

' free the resources:
PKCS7_free(p7);
BIO_free_all(bio);
BIO_free_all(p7bio);
```

The last step to enable button encryption is to change the value of the cmd
form tag to _s-xclick and add the PKCS7 blob as a form value of encrypted..

When you're done, you'll end up with something like this:

```
<form method="post" action="https://www.sandbox.paypal.com/cgi-bin/webscr">
<input type="image" src="https://www.paypal.com/en_US/i/btn/x-click-but23.
gif" name="submit" alt="Make payments with PayPal - it's fast, free and
secure!">
<input type="hidden" name="cmd" value="_s-xclick">
<input type="hidden" id="encrypted" name="encrypted" value="-----BEGIN
PKCS7-----
MIIEvQYJKoZIhvcNAQcEoIIErjCCBKoCAQExggEOMIIBMAIBADCBmDCBkjELMAkG
A1UEBhMCVVMxCzAJBgNVBAgTAkNBMRYwFAYDVQQHEw1Nb3VudGFpbiBWaWV3M3RQw
EgYDVQQKEwtQYXlQYWwgSW5jLjEVMBMGA1UECxQMc3RhZ2UyUyVMlcnRzMRMwEQYD
VQQDFApzdGFnZTJfYXBpMRwwGgYJKoZIhvcNAQkBFg1yZUBwYXlwYWwuY29tAgEA
MAoGCSqGSIb3DQEBAQUABIGACgshgqbB147NFGZlK23kRLaQ3EkGnFmnRWn8euqN
Ecm12daiK57CaU/L36dhc4PtkigXI2TQ/alWglyerZkOhl+qb6ZRTqEq2+7fhvsB
T32Yph/usVQEj5jOnjtFmo9smOyEJuHcNYY5bn3gUsiM6FxIZq8qRlI5W9yh7hTc
1/kxCzAJBgUrDgMCGgUAMGsGCSqGSIb3DQEHATAUBggqhkiG9woDBwQINNLmCVHP
OUWASIMAdhSkOjW5qKb98fpT1yLCByYMjvEOU39fuG3pSOXv8tKzKEz3v1sKDUOR
PRyOekPFI6nEdp+dDJLBy3acM3DGrHk7KdYSLqCCAdIwggHOMIIBN6ADAgECAgEC
MAoGCSqGSIb3DQEBBQUAMBExDzANBgNVBAMTBlBheXBhbDANFwOwNDAzMjkyMTU3
NDdaFwOxNDAzMjcyMTU3NDdaMBExDzANBgNVBAMTBlBheXBhbDCBnzANBgkqhkiG
9wOBAQEFAAOBjQAwgYkCgYEArdX6/kaw/9JWyxedVUBf1hLQOnE3Z8HZTOAb8tTj
tH3anE8lxoA84NBKgsnAfsWSivWZA149NcpNrVgk7aPiCpIlxxLD7dv3OzSqrXUA
kzVZ3xDfxILN42Xe8JZiM7MieixlKL/2RlnqHv6RyfAJyXH7cMlbLQJCBR3g4XnF
7IOCAwEAAaM2MDQwDgYDVROPAQH/BAQDAgGmMA8GA1UdEwEB/wQFMAMBAf8wEQYJ
```

```
YIZIAYb4QgEBBAQDAgIEMAOGCSqGSIb3DQEBBQUAA4GBADOCbksayWCCOyqZSn3c
6J65Yvmi/KrObGX7EzHcB1NO/YbfYkisw5qvZnGUhMjOODL3cvNOnPxXNBIUdHT3
UF108MzLlv8fTAjnS8Zd83vZfSyi6TMSPJlXbx8p+P2IbRNKdQaIHz2tR6tCnUNC
JYYKim3Nkz48skO/jGtjiJPVMYIBGzCCARcCAQEwFjARMQ8wDQYDVQQDEwZQYXlw
YWwCAQIwCQYFKw4DAhoFAKBdMBgGCSqGSIb3DQEJAzELBgkqhkiG9w0BBwEwHAYJ
KoZIhvcNAQkFMQ8XDTAOMDQyMjIxMDkyMVowIwYJKoZIhvcNAQkEMRYEFO10ou9z
6VXvxn6wow7yZXlP6vqeMAOGCSqGSIb3DQEBAQUABIGAoNU5uAeD+pp2bROOfhHh
6oTPZDjhUvKLrhVaHmpHzz1aZTtIdqYcwZ6vEVai6fGG43hqoZYAh97xWDiwW9Ie
X/RtAzc38Yk2vch6ocPF8MjsEMVne3J9iyOrN6AOCby5IgkKFrrYee9eWNIec/6d
3koVvLSCBZvZV+RFYCKhA/O=
-----END PKCS7-----
">
</form>
```

Obviously, this code is nearly impossible to decipher or tamper with, making it sufficiently obfuscated.

—Michael Blanton

Include Payment Buttons in Email Messages
HACK #38

Use the PayPal Payment Request Wizard to send Pay Now buttons from Microsoft Outlook.

Sending invoices via email with PayPal's Request Money feature [Hack #17] is a quick and effective way to ask someone to pay you. The Pay Now buttons PayPal includes in the resulting email make it easy for your customers to pay you; after two clicks and a login, customers with PayPal accounts can send you money in less than a minute.

But the Request Money feature has its limitations. While the email appears to come from you, it's actually sent from PayPal, which means that you won't be able to customize it fully. If you need to include pictures, files, hyperlinks, custom HTML, or multiple purchase buttons, you'll have to send the email yourself.

Creating PayPal Payment Hyperlinks

Adding a PayPal payment hyperlink to your own email involves nothing more than typing a simple URL [Hack #18]. The required parameters to create a basic hyperlink are email address, payment amount, and item name.

However, there are many optional parameters you can include in the hyperlink to help you provide a more complete payment record, such as the currency, item number, quantity, shipping, and request for shipping address. For example:

```
https://www.paypal.com/cgi-bin/webscr?cmd=_xclick&business=
    email%40paypalhacks%2Ecom&amount=10%2E00&currency_code=USD&item_name=
    jersey&item_number=1001&quantity=1&shipping=3%2E00&no_shipping=0
```

As you can see, the hyperlink begins to become unwieldy. Hyperlinks this long or longer cause problems because email programs chop them up into smaller pieces when they wrap the text. More than likely, only the first piece will be hyperlinked and a customer will not think twice about clicking it and attempting to complete the transaction with incomplete information.

The simplest solution is to run the address through TinyURL* (*http://tinyurl. com*), which will convert it to something that looks like this:

```
http://tinyurl.com/2tqz8
```

The resulting link is always short enough to be spared the aforementioned word wrap. Unfortunately, the `https://www.paypal.com/` prefix will be lost, and your more diligent customers might avoid it.

See "Hide Your Email Address from Spammers" [Hack #39] for another, more official way to get shortened payment URLs, and protect your email from spammers in the process.

Using the PayPal Payment Wizard

Want something more professional-looking than a bare URL in your emails? Nearly all modern email programs support HTML (much to the bane of the minimalists among us), which means that you can replace ordinary URLs with hyperlinked, graphical buttons right in your email messages.

Simply use your email software's formatting tools to insert an image and then link it to a payment URL you construct. In fact, URLs in hyperlinks can be as long as 1024 bytes (characters), which is plenty for PayPal's payment URLs. Of course, there's a cost: these payment buttons can be time-consuming to create...until now.

Enter the PayPal Payment Wizard, a free add-in toolbar for Microsoft Outlook and Microsoft Outlook Express that allows you to painlessly insert payment buttons into your emails.

You can create five different types of PayPal payment buttons, each with six different button designs:

Payment Button (Basic)
This type of button is easiest to use, because it requires only your email address and payment amount, but it offers the fewest options.

---

* SnipURL (*http://snipurl.com*) also works and takes it a bit further with tracking features. For a similar, yet far less useful URL-processing tool, try HugeURL (*http://hugeurl.com*).

Product Button

This type allows you to enter product details and request a shipping address [Hack #28].

Service Button

This type allows you to enter a service description [Hack #30].

Auction Payment Button

Use this to request payment for an auction item [Hack #31].

Donate Button

Use this to allow the donor to specify the donation amount [Hack #40].

To use the Payment Wizard toolbar, start by downloading it from *http://www.paypal.com/outlook* and installing it on your computer. You might be asked to close Microsoft Outlook if it's open.

The PayPal Payment Wizard currently supports only Microsoft Outlook and Outlook Express on Windows. If you're using Eudora or some other email software, or if you are using a Mac or Linux, you'll have to create payment buttons manually.

To insert a button with the Payment Wizard, follow these steps:

1. Open Outlook or Outlook Express.

2. Click the Payment Request Wizard icon on the toolbar (shown in Figure 4-7).

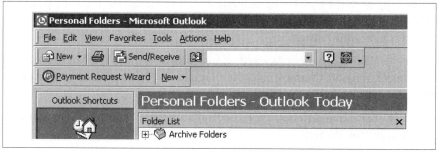

Figure 4-7. Payment Wizard toolbar in Microsoft Outlook Express

3. When you see the first page of the wizard, click Next.

4. On the Payment Button Type screen, choose one of the five aforementioned payment button types. For this example, select the second option, Product Button, and click Next.

5. The Product Button requires only the email address to which payment should be sent, and the payment amount, as shown in Figure 4-8.

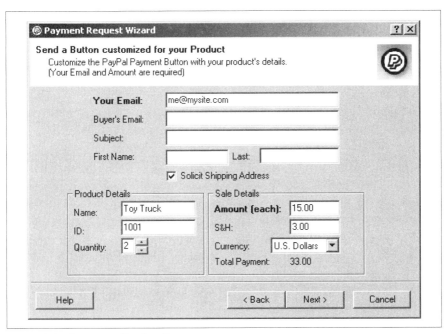

Figure 4-8. Creating a Product Button

There are several optional fields. You can specify the subject of the payment email you'll receive if the recipient pays. The First Name and Last Name fields are not currently used, so you can leave them blank. You can leave the Buyer's Email, Subject, First Name, and Last Name empty, because they are not required.

6. If your product requires shipping, turn on the Solicit Shipping Address option. PayPal will ask the buyer to specify a shipping address.

7. In the Product Details area, enter the name of the product and its ID number, if you have it.

8. In the Sale Details area, enter the price of the product. If you are selling multiple identical products, change the quantity to the reflect the quantity you are going to sell. If you are selling two toy trucks for the same price of $15 each, enter $15 and change the quantity to 2. You will see the Total Payment update to $30.

The Payment Wizard does not support multiple products. If you are collecting payment for more than one product, you will have to summarize the products in the Name field and enter a quantity of 1. See the next section of this hack for another solution.

9. In the S&H field, enter the amount to charge for shipping and handling. If you change this field, you will see the Total Payment update to reflect the new amount.

10. Select the currency, confirm that the Total Payment is correct, and click Next when you're done.

11. On the Button screen, select the button you would like to put into your email. The wizard provides six payment button images, all hosted on the PayPal web site (they might not appear if you or your recipient are not connected to the Internet).

12. If you would like to use another image for your button, select the URL option and enter the URL of your image file (presumably hosted on your own site). The button must be on a web server that can be accessed by anyone via the Internet. You can also choose the Text option to put the PayPal payment URL behind a text link instead of an image.

13. Click Next to view the You're Almost Done screen, where you'll see a summary of the values selected for your Payment Button. Verify that the information is correct and press the Test button to see the button in action.

14. If you are planning on sending many similar buttons, check the Save settings box. The wizard will save your settings for the next time.

15. Click Insert, and the fully configured button will be inserted into a blank email. (You won't be able to click on the button, because you're in edit mode.)

16. At this point, complete the email. Type one or more email addresses into the To field, enter a subject, and include a note or instructions to accompany the button, as illustrated in Figure 4-9.

17. Click Send when you're finished.

When your customer opens the email, he will be able to click the button and pay you after logging into his PayPal account. To test this experience firsthand, send the email to your own email address.

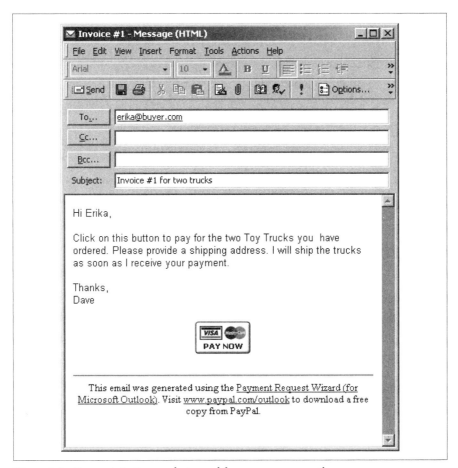

Figure 4-9. Payment Button ready to send from your own email

Including More than One Button in an Email

Since the PayPal Payment Wizard creates a new email message with each button, there is no way to use it to insert more than one button into a single email message. However, overcoming this limitation is easy enough:

1. Insert a payment button with the Payment Wizard, as described in the previous section.

2. Using your mouse, select the area around the new button, making sure to include the lines above and below the new button, as shown in Figure 4-10.

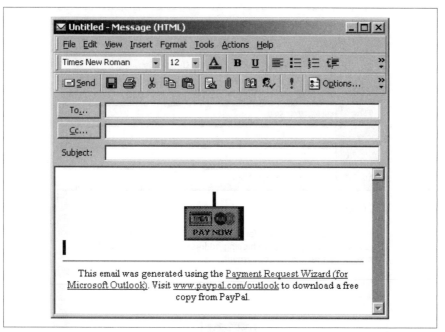

Figure 4-10. Selected Payment Button including line above and below the button

If you select only the button and not the lines above and below, you'll get only the image without the hyperlink.

3. Copy the selection to the clipboard by pressing Ctrl-C or by selecting Copy from Outlook's Edit menu.

4. Click to place the insertion point (text cursor) where you'd like the new button to appear, and paste the button into the existing email by pressing Ctrl-V or by selecting Paste from Outlook's Edit menu. You can paste the button into any email, including one that already contains a payment button.

Repeat the process for each additional payment button you would like to insert. To verify that the image and corresponding hyperlink have been pasted correctly, as well as to make any changes to the URL, right-click the button and select Properties.

Hide Your Email Address from Spammers

Hide Your Email Address from Spammers
Use your PayPal referral ID to prevent your email address from being harvested by spammers.

Spam (unsolicited bulk email) is a growing problem for Internet users, especially for those who have web sites that can be spidered by spambots looking for email addresses. The HTML generated by the PayPal Button Factory contains the email address listed in your PayPal account, making it available to address harvesters. Prevent this potential misuse by replacing your email address with your *referral ID* (also known as the *affiliate ID*).

> This hack does not work with the HTML code generated for the PayPal Shopping Cart [Hack #45]. It also doesn't support encrypted buttons [Hack #37], although buttons protected by encryption are already well-protected from spammers.

To implement this fix, you need to obtain your referral ID from the PayPal web site and then edit your HTML button code, substituting the referral ID for your email address.

To obtain your referral ID from PayPal, click the Referrals link at the bottom of any PayPal page. You will see a text box with a URL in it, which will look something like `https://www.paypal.com/mrb/pal=ABC1DEF2GHIJK`. Your referral ID is the part of the URL after `pal=`; in this case, the referral ID is `ABC1DEF2GHIJK`.

To put the referral ID in place of your email address, open the web page that contains the button in a text or HTML editor and find the all sections of code that look like this:

```
<input type="hidden" name="business" value="youremail@yourisp.com">
```

Replace your email address with your referral ID, like this:

```
<input type="hidden" name="business" value="ABC1DEF2GHIJK">
```

You will need to do this for each button on your site. Your buttons will operate normally, and your customers won't know the difference.

> Keep in mind that this hack does not provide anonymity. Buyers will still see your email address in the process of making a payment.

Accept Donations

#40 Accept PayPal donations to fill your nonprofit's coffers, and tweak the Donate
Now button to suit your needs.

The Internet has long been a tool for bringing together like-minded activists in a common cause. After Howard Dean's campaign for the 2004 Democratic presidential nomination, however, fundraisers working in the mainstream learned that the power of the Net could not only get out the word, but bring in the green as well.

PayPal has long understood the value of making donations quick and easy. The Make a Donation button lets you start accepting contributions immediately. To create a button follow these steps:

1. Log into your PayPal account.

2. Click the Merchant Tools tab, and then click Donations (under Website Payments).

3. Fill in a name and ID number, if you wish. A Donate Now button's name and ID number, like the Item Name/Service and Item ID/Number in a Buy Now button, let you and your contributors identify payments. By using different numbers and descriptions, you can place a number of buttons on your site, each soliciting donations to different programs.

4. Enter an amount or leave blank if you want your donors to enter an amount themselves. Either way, you'll need to select a currency in which donations will be made.

5. Choose from the selection of PayPal donation buttons, or specify the URL of your own button image.

6. Choose the encrypted or unencrypted version of the button. If you're not sure which one to use, choose the unencrypted version; you can replace it later with an encrypted one once your button is functioning. Unencrypted buttons are plain HTML forms—easy to read, understand, and modify. An encrypted button, on the other hand, is inscrutable to anyone but the PayPal system and impossible to modify or customize. While unencrypted buttons can be created with any software tool, encrypted buttons can, at the time of this writing, be created only with the PayPal system's Merchant Tools. Encrypted buttons can be useful in some situations, such as to protect your email address from spammers. Openness, however, is usually best. See "Hack-Proof Your Payment" [Hack #36] to learn more about button encryption.

The encryption of buttons is a relatively new feature to the PayPal system. The unencrypted button, open to be read and understood by all, might have its roots in PayPal's corporate culture, which holds "open and honest communication" as a core value.

7. Click Create Button Now when you're done.

The HTML code generated for your button is found in a `textarea` box on the next page. Just select its contents, press Ctrl-C to copy the text to the clipboard, and then paste the text into your web page.

Establishing Suggested Giving Levels

Your donors might be more comfortable giving at one of several suggested donation *levels* than having to fill in a blank box with a dollar amount.

Include a catchy name for each donation level. For instance, the California State Railroad Museum Foundation (*http://www.csrmf.org*) offers six suggested donation levels: become a Brakeman for $25, a Fireman for $35, a Conductor for $50, an Engineer for $100, a Trainmaster for $250, or a Silver Spike/Railroad Patron for $1,000.

Provide a drop-down list (shown here) or a radio button group to allow your donors to easily choose an amount:

```
<blockquote>
<form action="https://www.paypal.com/cgi-bin/webscr" method="post">
  <p>Please contribute to XHTML Promotion Society, "Diamond" Dave Burchell,
  DocBook Outreach Officer.</p>
<input type="hidden" name="cmd" value="_xclick"/>
<input type="hidden" name="business" value="burchell@inebraska.com"/>
<input type="hidden" name="item_name" value="General Fund Contribution"/>
<input type="hidden" name="item_number" value="GF-1"/>
<!-- <input type="hidden" name="amount" value="3.00"/> -->
<p>Contribution amount:
<select name="amount">
  <option value="200"/>$200
  <option selected value="100"/>$100
  <option value="75"/>$75
  <option value="50"/>$50
  <option value="25"/>$25
</select>
</p>
<input type="hidden" name="no_note" value="1"/>
<input type="hidden" name="currency_code" value="USD"/>
<input type="hidden" name="tax" value="0"/>
```

```
<input type="image" src="https://www.paypal.com/en_US/i/btn/x-click-but21.gif"
    border="0" name="submit" alt="Make payments with PayPal - it's fast,
    free and secure!"/>
</form>
</blockquote>
```

Among other things, a page like the one shown in Figure 4-11 will give your donors some idea how much others might be donating.

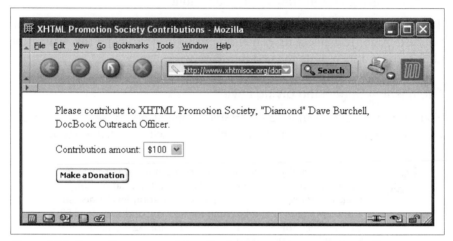

Figure 4-11. Suggesting a range of donation levels to encourage your contributors to donate fistfuls of cash

 You'll collect more money by setting the default donation level (marked with the selected parameter in the code)one notch *higher* than the amount most donors actually give. This will encourage your more generous supporters to stretch just a bit, while raising the bar for those who might otherwise choose the lowest level.

Requiring Information from Your Donors

In some situations, such as the collecting of contributions to a political campaign, you'll require information about your donors. For example, your local election laws might require you to record the occupation and employer of each contributor.

You could simply ask contributors to include this information in the note field (answer Yes to the Collect Additional Information From Your Customers question on the Add More Options page), but when was the last time you saw a customer ever follow directions? Instead, include a little JavaScript to virtually insure that your donors provide the information you need:

```
<script language="javascript">
<!--
function noEntry() {
if (document.contribution_form.os0.value.length<1) {
  alert("Please fill in your Employer.");
  return false; }
else if (document.contribution_form.os1.value.length<1) {
  alert("Please fill in your Occupation.");
  return false; }
if (document.contribution_form.amount.value.length<1) {
  alert("Please fill in the amount to donate.");
  return false; }
else if (document.contribution_form.amount.value<1) {
  alert("No pennies please.");
  return false; }
else if ((document.contribution_form.q1.checked==false) ||
  (document.contribution_form.q2.checked==false) ||
  (document.contribution_form.q3.checked==false) ||
  (document.contribution_form.q4.checked==false)) {
  alert("You must agree to all four certifications.");
  return false; }
else { return true; }
}
// -->
</script>

<blockquote>
  <h4 align="center">Please show your support for "Diamond" Dave Burchell's
      run for the position of city dogcatcher with a generous donation.</h4>

<form name="contribution_form" onsubmit="return noEntry()" action=
      "https://www.paypal.com/cgi-bin/webscr" method="post" target="_blank">
  <input type="hidden" value="Occupation" name="on1"/>
  <input type="hidden" value="Employer" name="on0"/>
  <input type="hidden" value="Dogcatcher Campaign Contribution" name=
      "item_name"/>
  <input type="hidden" value="PayPalTech" name="bn"/>
  <!-- enter the email address on your PayPal account below -->
  <input type="hidden" value="burchell@paypalhacks.com" name="business"/>
  <input type="hidden" value="_xclick" name="redirect_cmd"/>
  <input type="hidden" value="_ext-enter" name="cmd"/>
  <center>
        <table border="0" width="100%">
          <tbody>
            <tr>
              <td width="37%" align="right">First Name: </td>
              <td width="63%"><input name="first_name" size="15"/> </td>
            </tr>
            <tr>
              <td width="37%" align="right">Last Name: </td>
              <td width="63%"><input name="last_name" size="15"/> </td>
            </tr>
            <tr>
```

```
          <td width="37%" align="right">Employer:</td>
          <td width="63%"><input name="os0"/> (required)</td>
        </tr>
        <tr>
          <td width="37%" align="right">Occupation: </td>
          <td width="63%"><input name="os1"/> (required)</td>
        </tr>
        <tr>
          <td width="37%" align="right">Phone Number: </td>
          <td width="63%"><input name="item_number" size="12"/> </td>
        </tr>
        <tr>
          <td width="37%" align="right">Amount: </td>
          <td width="63%">$ <input name="amount" size="7"/> (limit
$1000)</td>
        </tr>
      </tbody>
    </table>
    <table border="0" width="90%">
      <tbody>
        <tr>
          <td width="305"><br/>
You must check each of the boxes below to meet federal contribution
requirements:<br/>
          <br/>
          <input type="checkbox" value="1" name="q1"/>This
contribution is made from my own funds, and not from those of another.<br/>
          <br/>
          <input type="checkbox" value="1" name="q2"/>
This contribution is not made from general treasury fund of a
corporation, labor organization, or national bank.<br/>
          <br/>
          <input type="checkbox" value="1" name="q3"/>
I am not a Federal Government Contractor, nor am I a Foreign National
who lacks permanent resident status in the United States.<br/>
          <br/>
          <input type="checkbox" value="1" name="q4"/>
This contribution is made on a personal credit card or debit card for
which I have a legal obligation to pay, and is made neither on a
corporate or business entity card nor on the card of another.
          </td>
        </tr>
      </tbody>
    </table>
    <p align="center"><input type="submit" value="Contribute"
name="button"/></p>
    </center>
</form>
```

Here, the noEntry( ) JavaScript routine, executed when the contributor submits the form, displays an error if the Employer or Occupation fields are
blank, or if the donor enters a donation that's too low, as shown in
Figure 4-12.

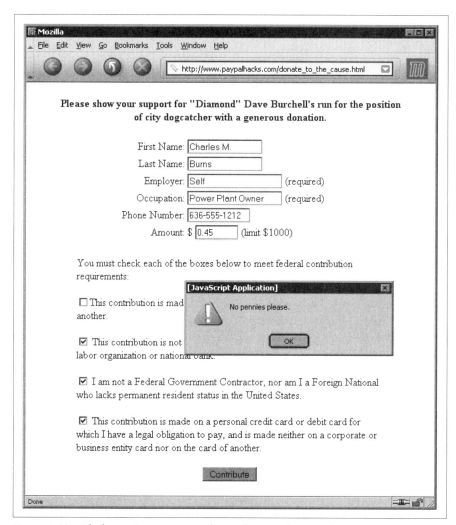

Figure 4-12. A little JavaScript prevents donors from sending you donations you can't use

This client-side validation script will fail if the contributor's JavaScript option is disabled in the browser settings. You should always supplement this script with server-side validation to ensure that improper submissions aren't let through.

PayPal-Enable Your Flash

Add PayPal Buy Now or Subscription functionality to your Flash-powered online store using the WebAssist PayPal eCommerce Snap-ins.

Increasingly, Flash has been putting the sizzle in the online shopping experience by adding cool interactivity and fancy special effects to otherwise bland web pages. Over the last couple years, Macromedia has added several full-fledged software architectures to support Flash-based transactions. Flash forms take advantage of the enhanced interactive capabilities of the vector-based client and allow all manner of special effects, including visual sorting and drag-and-drop shopping options. The latest versions of Flash also provide standard components for commonly used form elements, such as text fields, checkboxes, radio buttons, and lists, which means that you can accept PayPal payments from within Flash elements on your web site.

Snap in the PayPal Connection

So, what does it take to make the Flash connection to PayPal? In truth, the back-end ActionScript required to make the necessary PayPal connection is extremely complex. The good news, however, is that a Flash extension, developed by PayPal and WebAssist, provides the core functionality while leaving a great deal of room for programmatic customization.

Get the extension—known as the WA PayPal eCommerce Snap-ins for Flash MX—from *http://webassist.com/Products/ProductDetails. asp?PID=24*. The extension is free; you just need to register with WebAssist. Install the extension into Flash MX by double-clicking the downloaded file, or into Flash MX 2004 via Macromedia's Extension Manager. If you have Flash open, you'll need to quit and relaunch the program for the snap-in to appear.

Once the extension is installed, you can straightforwardly handle the basics for adding a Buy Now or Subscription button to your page. If the item you're selling has no options or other complications, you don't even have to touch the ActionScript.

Start by building your basic product page. Make sure there is at least one clickable element (such as a button) on the Flash stage, and give it a name in the Property inspector.

Typically, Flash buttons are used for such an interactive event. If you're design-challenged, the installed extension includes a number of Buy Now or Subscription buttons, located in the PayPal Buttons folder of the Common Libraries window. You can drag these to any location on the stage.

Open the Components panel and look in the WA PayPal eCommerce category. Drag either the Buy Now or Subscription object (these are the actual snap-ins) anywhere onto the stage.

Although the snap-in appears as a visual element at design-time, you won't see it when the movie is published. All of its power is behind the scenes.

To complete the simple Flash PayPal configuration, you'll need to establish the details to be sent. While you can set these values in ActionScript, as explained later in this hack, you can also use the snap-in's Component inspector. Select the snap-in and, in the Property inspector, click the Launch Component Inspector button.

In the Parameters tab of the Component Inspector panel, you'll see a custom dialog box for the snap-ins, as shown in Figure 4-13. Each of the snap-in parameter dialogs is a specialized multitabbed affair.

Figure 4-13. Setting the properties of the PayPal extension in Macromedia's Component Inspector

Take a look at the Component Inspector for the Buy Now snap-in, in which the following parameters are separated into three tabs (General, Item Details, and Shipping):

General tab

PayPal Account

The PayPal recipient's email address (required)

Company Logo

The web address (URL) of your logo graphic (such as a *.jpg* file), which will be incorporated into the PayPal page

Success URL

A fully formed URL to the web page you want your customers to see after a successful PayPal transaction

Cancel URL

The web address of the page to which customers who cancel are sent

Item Details tab

Item Name/Service

The name of the item being sold

Item ID Number

The product SKU or other ID number passed through to you (not seen by the customer)

Price

The base price of the item

Currency

The type of currency to be used (choices are U.S. dollars, Canadian dollars, euros, British pounds and Japanese yen)

Multiple Units Option

A checkbox that controls whether customers can order a quantity of more than one

Shipping tab

Base Shipping

The shipping cost for a single item

Extra Shipping

Shipping charges added, per additional item, if more than one unit is ordered

Handling

The handling charge, over and above the aforementioned shipping charges, applied to the entire order

Shipping Information Option

A checkbox that determines whether PayPal will request the customer's shipping information

Note Option

An option that allows customers to add a note with their PayPal order

The Subscription Component Inspector parameter dialog is similar to the one for the Buy Now snap-in, but it offers special fields for specifying one-time or recurring billing, as well as trial offers.

For items with properties that are completely covered by the options in the Component Inspector panel, no additional ActionScript is required to complete the PayPal order. All you need do is publish the *.swf* file and put it in an HTML page on the Web; the rest is automatic. But, of course, you want more, don't you?

Hacking the Hack

So, what's underneath the hood of the WebAssist PayPal eCommerce Snapins for Flash MX? Quite a bit, as it turns out. There are 31 different methods embedded in the Buy Now snap-in and 38 in the Subscribe snap-in. Of these, about half are used to set values, and the other half are used to pass those values to PayPal. The setting methods are of prime interest to the Flash/PayPal hacker.

Take a look at a typical example that ties additional options (and their related prices) to a PayPal item. Imagine a fictional online T-shirt emporium that offers a fancy-dancy item available in five different colors and four different sizes. There's no difference in price for the various colors available. However, Flash can represent the different colors quite easily, thus adding a nice visual flair to our product page. T-shirt size, on the other hand, goes up with price: $10.99 for small, $13.99 for medium, $15.99 for large, and $18.99 for extra large.

Again, representing this in the *.swf* is trivial for Flash MX or Flash MX 2004. The values in the drop-down size list are displayed in a dynamic text variable as the current price. But how do you send the correct item cost and order details to PayPal? Short answer: use the set methods. Here's the longer, code-oriented answer—just place this ActionScript code into your project:

```
function setPrice( )  {
  // Get the price (based on size list)
  var newPrice = sizeList.getValue( );
❶  BN.setAmount(newPrice);
❷  BN.setItemName(sizeList.getSelectedItem( ).label+" "+colorList.
getSelectedItem( ).label+" WebAssist.com T-Shirt");
❸  BN.setItemNumber(String(sizeList.getSelectedIndex( )) + String(colorList.
getSelectedIndex( )));
}
```

The function setPrice( ) is called when the page is first loaded and each time any option changes. Both options (color and size) are selected from drop-down lists, colorList and sizeList, respectively. The first line of the code picks up the price from the sizeList. The user sees the labels in the list (Small, Medium, Large, and X-Large), but the values are set to prices of 10.99, 13.99, 15.99, and 18.99. The current item price is established as amount to send to PayPal on line ❶.

The Buy Now snap-in instance placed on the stage is named BN, and any methods that relate to that instance are named with the BN prefix. Two more functions are used to set the item name (which is what the customer sees on the Payment For line of the PayPal page) and the item number (a SKU number that is sent to the online store owner for order processing) on lines ❷ and ❸, respectively.

Any value that you can set in the Component Parameter dialog can be set programmatically in ActionScript. Table 4-1 shows all Buy Now methods that set values.

Table 4-1. Buy Now Button methods that set values

Buy Now method	Argument	Description
setAllowNote("*allow*")	Boolean; true or false	Sets whether the buyer can include a note with the payment. If set to false, your customer will not be prompted to include a note.
setAmount("*amount*")	String	Sets the base amount of the item.
setBusinessID("*business*")	String	Specifies the PayPal ID, or email address, where payments will be sent. This email address must be confirmed and linked to your verified Business or Premier account.
setCancelURL("*url*")	String; fully formed URL	Sets the URL of the page viewed when the Cancel button is clicked. This item is optional; if omitted, users will be taken to the PayPal site.
setCurrency("*currency*")	String; valid values are USD, GBP, EUR, CAD, or JPY	Sets the currency to be used for payment. For example, to use the euro instead of the U.S. dollar, change the currency from USD to EUR. Other available currencies include pounds sterling (GBP), the Canadian dollar (CAD), and Japanese yen (JPY).
setExtraShipping("*amount*")	String	Sets the extra shipping cost per item after the first item. If this optional value is omitted, and your Profile-based shipping is enabled, your customer will be charged the amount or percentage defined in your Profile.

Table 4-1. Buy Now Button methods that set values (continued)

Buy Now method	Argument	Description
setHandling("*amount*")	String	Sets the handling charge. This is not quantity-specific. The same handling will be charged regardless of the number of items purchased.
setItemName("*name*")	String	Specifies the name or description of the item (maximum 127 characters).
setItemNumber("*itemNumber*")	String	Sets the item number, SKU, or unique key; this is the pass-through variable with which you can track payments. It will not be displayed to your customer but will get passed back to you at the completion of payment (maximum 127 characters).
setLogoURL("*url*")	String; fully formed URL	Sets the URL to your company logo, an image up to 150 by 50 pixels. This is optional; if omitted, your customer will see your business name (if you have a Business account) or email address (if you have a Premier account).
setNoShipping("*bNoShipping*")	Boolean; true or false	Sets whether shipping information is necessary for checkout. If set to true, your customer will not be asked for a shipping address.
setShipping("*amount*")	String	Sets the shipping charge. If shipping is used and shipping_extra is not defined, this flat amount will be charged regardless of the quantity of items purchased. If you are using item-based shipping, make sure the Override checkbox is checked in your Profile.
setReturnURL("*url*")	String; fully formed URL	Sets the URL of the page to which the customer is sent when the order is complete. This item is optional, if omitted, customers will be taken to the PayPal site.
setTarget("*window*")	String; default value is _self	Sets the target window where the payment processing information will be displayed. The constant _self can be used for the current window, _blank will always open a new window, and _parent will replace the parent frameset. You can also specify another frame in your frameset, such as content.
setUpdateableQuantity ("*updateable*")	Boolean; true or false	Sets whether the buyer can change the quantity on the PayPal site. If set to true, the customer will be able to edit the quantity. If this optional value is omitted or set to false, the quantity will default to 1.

The Subscription methods are, for the most part, the same as the methods that set values; all methods listed in Table 4-1, with the exception of setAmount, setExtraShipping, setHandling, setShipping, and setUpdateableQuery, can also be used with an instance of a Subscription snap-in. Table 4-2 lists the additional Subscription set methods available.

Table 4-2. Subscription Button methods that set values

Subscription method	Argument	Description
setBillContinuous ("billContinuously")	Boolean; true or false	Specifies whether this is a recurring payment. If set to true, the payment will recur unless your customer cancels the subscription before the end of the billing cycle. If omitted, the subscription payment will not recur at the end of the billing cycle.
setBillingAmount("amount")	String	Sets the price of the purchase at the standard rate.
setBillingPeriod("period")	String	Specifies the length of the billing cycle. The number is modified by the regular billing cycle units, set by setBillingTime("timeUnit").
setBillingTime("timeUnit"	String; valid values are D, W, M or Y	Sets the unit of time that the billing period is measured in (D=days, W=weeks, M=months, Y=years).
setReattempt("reattempt")	Boolean; either true or false	Sets whether to reattempt billing if the payment is declined. If set to true and the payment fails, the payment will be reattempted two more times. After the third failure, the subscription will be canceled. If omitted and the payment fails, payment will not be reattempted and the subscription will be immediately canceled.
setStopAfterBilling("number")	String	Specifies the number of payments to occur at the regular rate. If omitted, payment will recur at the regular rate until the subscription is cancelled.
setTrialAmount("amount")	String	Sets the trial price. For a free trial, use a value of 0.
getTrialPeriod("period")	String	Sets the length of the trial period. This number is modified by the trial period units, set by setTrialTime("timeUnit").
getTrialTime("timeUnit ")	String: valid values are D, W, M or Y	Sets the unit of time in which the trial is measured (D=days, W=weeks, M=months, Y=years).

Combine Flash's interactive flair with the ActionScript methods to put your customers in the driver's seat and still get all the information you need to process your PayPal order correctly.

—*Joe Lowery*

HACK #42 Get More Out of Dreamweaver and PayPal

Use the WebAssist PayPal eCommerce Toolkit to enable fast, easy, and flexible PayPal transactions with Dreamweaver.

If you use Macromedia Dreamweaver to design and produce web pages, you can use the WebAssist PayPal eCommerce Toolkit (an extension to Dreamweaver) to integrate PayPal with your web site. Naturally, you can use Dreamweaver's code editor to insert any PayPal transaction you want, but why hand-code when you can point and click? The results are the same as hand-coding; it's just quicker, less error prone, and requires almost no technical savvy: what's not to love?

Drag and Drop eCommerce

With WebAssist PayPal eCommerce Toolkit (available for free at *http://www.webassist.com*), you can insert Add to Cart, View Cart, Subscription, and Buy Now buttons. Insert any of these objects and a multistep wizard walks you through the particulars of the process. Each wizard offers a nice library of button designs to choose from, so you don't have to create any artwork from scratch. However, if you do have your own button, you can enter the URL of its web-based location and that button will be used.

Other available options depend on which button type is being inserted. The Buy Now button, for example, lets you specify the base shipping, any extra shipping to be added for each additional item ordered, and overall handling charges. If you enter these additional values, they override your general account settings on a per-item basis. Adding a Subscription button, on the other hand, gives you the ability to establish periodic billing values (i.e., how much for how long) and trial-offer settings, such as the length of the trial offer. You can even determine a setup fee for a subscription.

Hacking the Hack

By itself, the WebAssist PayPal eCommerce Toolkit is great for items with no options or variations. However, by doing a little work on the form that contains the PayPal buttons, you can greatly extend the toolkit's functionality. Most of the following techniques center on two concepts: naming form elements properly and using hidden form fields. These concepts work together to pass the correct information to PayPal when the transaction is initiated.

Say your your item is available in several sizes or configurations at varying prices. You can pass the right price to PayPal in two ways: using drop-down lists or radio buttons. To offer multiple prices with a list, follow these steps:

1. Insert a list/menu form element from Dreamweaver's Insert bar, found in the Forms category.

2. Select the list element and, in the Property inspector, enter amount in the (ironically unlabeled) name field on the top left.

3. Choose List Values to open the List Values dialog box.

4. In the dialog, enter the first item you want the user to see in the Label column.

5. Press Tab and, in the Value column, enter the corresponding amount you want passed to PayPal when this item is chosen. Enter just the raw number without dollar signs. For the first item, it's common to use a directive like "Choose From This List" rather than an item. If you use basic text like this, be sure to leave the corresponding Value empty.

6. Press Tab again to enter another Label/Value pair.

7. When you're done, click OK.

When the user makes a selection from the list, the related value is assigned as the amount and sent to PayPal at transaction time. If you'd prefer to display all options on-screen rather than contain them in a list, use radio buttons to vary the price. Here's how:

1. Insert a radio button from the Insert bar, in the Forms category.

2. In the Property inspector, enter amount in the name field.

3. In the Checked Value field, enter the number value you want to send to PayPal when this option is selected.

4. Repeat steps 1–3 for each additional option and price point you'd like.

Keep the name of each button in the radio group the same (amount) and vary the Checked Value numbers. You can use as many radio buttons as needed.

What about other types of options? PayPal allows two additional options per item. Using the following technique, you can pass two pairs of name and associated information to be included in the order sent to the store owner for fulfillment. If this technique is used to pass color choices, for example, the string passed to PayPal (and on to the owner) might be color="Cream".

Let's say that you have a list of colors for the customer to choose from in your product page. Set up the color list with name/value pairs as described in the previous steps for establishing the amount. This time, however, name the list/menu form object os0, which stands for *Object String 0*, the first of the two PayPal option values allowed.

Of course, you can't send a value without identifying it. To tell PayPal and, eventually, the fulfillment folks, what this value is for, insert a hidden form field from Dreamweaver's Insert bar, in the Forms category. With the hidden form field selected, enter its name in the Property inspector: on0 (short for *Object Name 0*). Complete the operation by entering color in the Value field of the Property inspector. Your first option is ready to go. You can enter another option (perhaps setting the item's size) by following same procedure and substituting os1 and on1 for the new option's value and name, respectively.

—Joe Lowery

Provide Options with ASP.NET Web Controls

Create custom web controls in ASP.NET to allow customers to specify product options with their orders.

As described in "Create a Buy Now Button" [Hack #28], you can send option information to PayPal so that it appears as part of the transaction along with other item details, such as quantity and price. This information is vital to order fulfillment and also allows customers to review fully what they are buying.

Sending this information to PayPal is simple. You can do it in one of two ways:

- Send the information through the URL as parameters.
- Send the information through form submission using HTTP POST.

PayPal looks for four parameters when information is passed to it by its payment controls: option name one, option value one, option name two, and option value two. Geeks came up with the naming here, and to us geeks (you might be one and find comfort in this), traditional base-10 numeric series start with the number 0 and end with the number 9.[*] So, the first option is called option 0 and the second is called option 1, and when you pass this information to PayPal, it looks something like this:

```
on0="Size"
os0="Large"
on1="Color"
os1="Blue"
```

This information can be passed to PayPal through a URL, like this:

```
http://please.include.a/complete/url?on0=Size&os0=Large
```

or through an HTTP form POST:

```
<input type=hidden name="on0" value="Size">
```

---

[*] Actually, there are many numeric patterns that start at zero, such as the way we track the minutes in an hour.

```
<input type=hidden name="os0" value="Large">
```

PayPal will include this information in the description section of the item, so your user can view it at the time of the sale.

Using the .NET Payment Controls

Collecting order details is fairly straightforward with traditional scripting languages (e.g., ASP or PERL). Simply display the information for each product, with relevant options, in a single form for each product (this example uses Active Server Pages with VBScript):

```
<% while not rs.eof%>
<form action="https://www.paypal.com/cgi-bin/webscr" method=POST>

<!-- The product name and description go here -->

<input type=hidden name="on0" value="Size">
<select name=os0>
  <option value="Large">Large</option>
  <option value="Medium"> Medium </option>
  <option value="Small">Small </option>
</select>
<input type=hidden name="on1" value="Color">
<select name=os1>
  <option value="Yellow"> Yellow </option>
  <option value="Blue"> Blue </option>
  <option value="Gold"> Gold </option>
</select>

<input type=submit value="Add To Basket">

<form>
<%
rs.movenext
wend
%>
```

This code provides purchase options with drop-down list-boxes [Hack #32] to restrict the inputs on the form.

Using product options with the .NET payment controls, however, offers a bit of a challenge, given that an ASP.NET page only lets you have one <form> tag per ASP.NET web page, thus allowing it to maintain page state properly.

To get around the single-form limitation, you can use the Click event of the Payment Controls to add the option controls at runtime. The first thing you must do is set the control to use the postback routine (UseFormGet=false) and disallow the pop-up command (UsePopUp=false), so that PayPal can glean the options from the postback.

This is a delicate process, especially when using the .NET-native data controls (e.g., DataList, Repeater, or DataGrid). You need to understand which events fire and in what order, because this can affect how your option controls are populated. You will be dealing with the Click event of the PayPal control, not one of the events of the data controls, which can get a little confusing. Thus, it's best to skip ahead to the good part: how to do it!

Creating Your Own PayPal Control

If you are a serious geek, you've probably already created your own Custom Server Control to handle the intricacies of gathering option information from the ViewState. Or, at the very least, you have something mapped out in your head. However, there might be something simpler in the following approach, and I appeal to you to quell your ADD for another five minutes. Custom Server Controls can be useful, but they can also (and often do) add a layer of complication (a.k.a. lots of code) to an otherwise simple task.

This approach starts with a user control and then populates its options from the product information you pass to it. User controls allow you to encapsulate functionality for individual UI components, which this is, so you don't need to write the same code twice or create spaghetti code in order to find the control you want hidden within your page.

 This example uses PayPal's Shopping Cart and the Add to Cart Button, and it is written in C# using ASP.NET.

Create a user control called *AddToCartOptions.ascx*, and add the PayPal AddToCart server control, along with a RadioButtonList called radColors and a DropDownList called ddSize:

```
<table>
  <tr>
    <td><asp:dropdownlist id="ddSize" runat="server">
      <asp:ListItem Value="Small" Selected="True">Small</asp:ListItem>
      <asp:ListItem Value="Medium">Medium</asp:ListItem>
      <asp:ListItem Value="Large">Large</asp:ListItem>
      </asp:dropdownlist>
    </td>
    <td width="290">
      <asp:radiobuttonlist id="radColors"
              runat="server" RepeatDirection="Horizontal" Width="280px"
                Height="24px">
      <asp:ListItem Value="Black">Black</asp:ListItem>
      <asp:ListItem Value="Blue">Blue</asp:ListItem>
      <asp:ListItem Value="Paisley">Paisley</asp:ListItem>
      <asp:ListItem Value="Polka Dots">Polka Dots</asp:ListItem>
      </asp:radiobuttonlist>
```

```
          </td>
          <td>
            <cc1:addtocartbutton id="AddToCartButton1" runat="server"
                  BusinessEmail="mybusinessemail" ItemNumber="xxxx"
      ItemName="Small Army Men"
                  Amount="1.02" ReturnUrl="http://myserver/myhandler.aspx"
                  CancelPurchaseUrl="http://myserver/mycancelhandler.aspx"
                  Shipping=".01" Tax=".01" UsePopup="false" UseFormGet="false"
            </cc1:addtocartbutton>
          </td>
        </tr>
      </table>
```

Make sure to set the UseFormGet and UsePopup values to false, which will force a postback to the server. Next, in the code behind the page, add the properties or fields that will be set by the calling page:

```
    public string ItemName;
    public string ItemNumber;
    public string Amount;
```

In the Page_Load event of the ASP.NET page, populate these values, as well as those of your options (in case you need to populate the option controls from the database):

```
    //expose the properties as needed
    AddToCartButton1.ItemName=ItemName;
    AddToCartButton1.ItemNumber=ItemNumber;
    try{
      AddToCartButton1.Amount=Convert.ToDouble(Amount);
    }catch{
      throw new Exception("Invalid value for a double: "   +Amount.ToString());
    }
```

Add the event handler for the button Click event in the InitializeComponent( ) method:

```
    this.AddToCartButton1.Click+=new System.EventHandler(this.AddClicked);
```

Finally, add the method to handle the PayPal button Click event, which reads the values of the controls and populates the AddToCartButton1 options accordingly:

```
    private void AddClicked(object sender, System.EventArgs e) {
      AddToCartButton1.Option1FieldName="Size";
      AddToCartButton1.Option1Values=ddSize.SelectedValue;
      AddToCartButton1.Option2FieldName="Color";
      AddToCartButton1.Option2Values=radColors.SelectedValue;
    }
```

This method populates the control just before the output is rendered to the browser, which redirects the user to PayPal for the purchase.

It should be noted at this point that the geeks who created this control appear not to be the same geeks who created the aforementioned naming convention at PayPal: the geeks who created this control are not Zeroians but nonbelievers in the primary status of the Almighty Zero. Thus, Option1FieldName represents option number 1, which, in turn, corresponds to on0.

To reward those of you who are patient enough to have made it this far, here is a final piece of wisdom: .NET is notoriously tricky when it comes to marrying the concept of events to a stateless medium such as a web page. There is a mess of events that goes into every request and every object; adding more objects to a page only complicates matters, especially when those objects have event sets of their own.

If you have ever tried to run logic using the events in a user control—which is, itself, part of a DataList or Repeater—you have undoubtedly run into the Event Freak Show™, wherein you cannot get your events to work properly or fire in the correct order, despite using all the Page.Postback tests in existence. If not done properly, the options selected by your customer will be overwritten by the initialization routine of the page, and the same meaningless information will be passed to PayPal.

The solution to this problem lies in setting the DataSource property, not the DataBind() method, of your Repeater or DataList. Consider that the user control, discussed earlier in this hack, is in a Repeater called MyRepeater:

```
<asp:Repeater id=MyRepeater Runat="server">
  <ItemTemplate>
  <uc1:_AddToCartOptions'
  id=_AddToCartOptions1
  runat="server"    ItemName='<%#DataBinder.Eval(Container.DataItem,
"ModelName")%>'   ItemNumber='<%#DataBinder.Eval(Container.DataItem,
"ModelNumber")%>'    Amount='<%#DataBinder.Eval(Container.DataItem,
"UnitCost")%>'   >
  </uc1:_AddToCartOptions>
  </ItemTemplate>
</asp:Repeater>
```

To preserve the ViewState of the user control, be sure to DataBind the Repeater:

```
MyRepeater.DataSource = MyDataSource;
if(!Page.IsPostBack){
  MyRepeater.DataBind();
}
```

The DataBind() method overwrites whatever state the user control was in when submitted by the customer, so you need to handle the population of this control and test for the postback. Setting the DataSource at runtime apparently helps the control remember the ViewState of its child controls.

Thus, your Repeater (or DataList) and all of its controls will maintain their ViewState, and your customer's option selections will be passed properly.

—*Rob Conery*

Try Accepting Payments in a Bogus Currency
#44

Weird out your pals and amuse your customers with PayPal's devilishly clever error message.

PayPal allows you to send and receive payments in five currencies: U.S. dollars (USD), Canadian dollars (CAD), pounds sterling (GBP), euros (EUR), and Japanese yen (JPY). If you are creating your own PayPal buttons, you'll need to indicate one of these five currencies in the button's markup. If you make a mistake here, your prospective buyers will be greeted with a confusing error message.

However, you might want to turn this error on its ear by working it into the storyline of your web site. If you offer products to Harry Potter fans, for example, you might want to put up a button like this:

```
<form action="https://www.paypal.com/cgi-bin/webscr" method="post">
<input type="hidden" name="cmd" value="_xclick">
<input type="hidden" name="business" value="burchell@inebraska.com">
<input type="hidden" name="item_name" value="The Monster Book of Monsters">
<input type="hidden" name="item_number" value="MboM">
<input type="hidden" name="amount" value="49.00">
<input type="hidden" name="no_note" value="1">
<input type="hidden" name="currency_code" value="sickles">
<input type="image" src="https://www.paypal.com/en_US/i/btn/x-click-but23.
gif" border="0" name="submit" alt="Make payments with PayPal - it's fast,
free and secure!">
</form>
```

Your customers will see this message:

> This recipient does not accept payments denominated in sickles. Please contact the seller and ask him to update his payment receiving preferences to accept this currency.

The useful lesson: if your customers contact you asking you to change your payment preferences to accept CAN, CND, or YEN (none of which are valid), check your button code.

Storefronts and Shopping Carts

Hacks 45–60

Payment buttons are the means by which you can connect PayPal to your site and start collecting payments for your products in minutes. If you expect customers to come along and purchase only single products from your site, single payment buttons (discussed in Chapter 4) are perfectly adequate.

As your online business grows, however, your product offering will begin to increase and diversify and you'll have to start thinking about ways to increase sales. A good place to start is with some sort of system to allow customers to purchase more than one product at a time, a system commonly known as a *shopping cart*.

PayPal provides a complete Shopping Cart system, built with the same PayPal buttons you've come to know and love. All you need to do to get started is place Add to Cart and View Cart buttons on your product pages [Hack #45], and PayPal does the rest.

The hacks in this chapter help you manage your online inventory, fulfill orders, customize your customers' experience, promote your online store, and sell more products with the PayPal Shopping Cart system.

Hack Shopping Cart Buttons

#45 Change code from the PayPal Button Factory to provide flexibility for your Shopping Cart.

PayPal's Shopping Cart allows merchants to provide the ability for customers to purchase a basket of goods rather than buy one item at a time with Buy Now buttons. The Shopping Cart system is ideal for stores with many items, but it doesn't make sense to use the PayPal Button Factory to create each and every button for your store. Instead, you can create a single generic Shopping Cart button and then use the HTML code as a template for all your items.

To generate the code for a simple Shopping Cart button, follow these steps:

1. Go to *http://www.paypal.com*, log into your account, and click the Merchant Tools tab.

2. Click on the Shopping Cart link under the Website Payments section to open the PayPal Shopping Cart Button Factory, as shown in Figure 5-1.

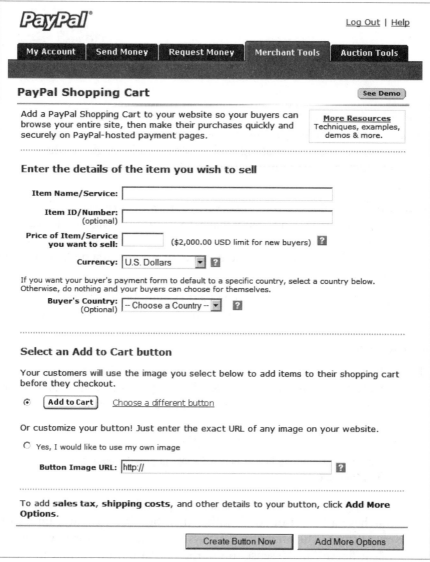

Figure 5-1. Using the PayPal Button Factory to create Shopping Cart buttons

3. Create a basic Shopping Cart button by entering any information for the item name and item number.

4. When you're done, click Create Button Now to generate the code.

The resulting code for the Add to Cart button should look like this:

```
<form target="paypal" action="https://www.paypal.com/cgi-bin/webscr"
method="post">
<input type="image" src="https://www.paypal.com/en_US/i/btn/x-click-but22.gif"
      border="0" name="submit" alt="Make payments with PayPal - it's
      fast, free and secure!">
<input type="hidden" name="add" value="1">
<input type="hidden" name="cmd" value="_cart">
<input type="hidden" name="business" value="sales@paypalhacks.com">
<input type="hidden" name="item_name" value="Widget">
<input type="hidden" name="item_number" value="Wid-001">
<input type="hidden" name="amount" value="1.00">
<input type="hidden" name="no_note" value="1">
<input type="hidden" name="currency_code" value="USD">
</form>
```

Lines ❷–❹ contain the three variables that define the details of the individual product, such as the product name, item number, and price. All the other variables remain the same for all of your products. Make sure to specify the email address for the account you want to use on line ❶, although any button you create with the PayPal Button Factory includes your email address by default.

The Button Factory also provides code for a View Cart button:

```
<form target="paypal" action=
      "https://www.paypal.com/cgi-bin/webscr" method="post">
<input type="hidden" name="cmd" value="_cart">
<input type="hidden" name="business" value="sales@paypalhacks.com">
<input type="image" src="https://www.paypal.com/en_US/i/btn/view_cart_02.gif"
      border="0" name="submit" alt="Make payments with PayPal - it's
      fast, free and secure!">
<input type="hidden" name="display" value="1">
</form>
```

Place this second block of code, as is, on all the pages of your web store to allow your customers to display the items they have added to their cart, as well as initiate the checkout process when they have finished shopping. The only variable you'll need to customize in this example is business, in which you specify your email address. Figure 5-2 shows the resulting page.

Hacking the Hack

The PayPal Shopping Cart allows extensive customization using the additional variables supported by regular Buy Now buttons [Hack #28]. For exam-

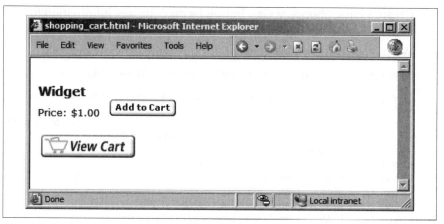

Figure 5-2. The Add to Cart and View Cart buttons: all you need to implement PayPal's Shopping Cart interface on your web site

ple, the `handling_cart` variable allows you to define a cart-wide handling charge to be applied to the entire order, regardless of any individual handling charges you might have specified:

```
<input type="hidden" name="handling_cart" value="4.00">
```

The `handling_cart` charge takes effect when the first item is added to the cart.

Create Shopping Cart Links
HACK #46

Convert Shopping Cart button code to single-line URLs that can be emailed or linked to images.

Although you can create Shopping Cart buttons [Hack #45] at the PayPal web site, you can also create buttons off-site. This gives web page designers more flexibility and gives programmers the ability to create buttons dynamically with programming code. One of the simplest and most flexible approaches involves creating URLs instead of HTML forms.

The Code

The HTML code for a simple Add to Cart button looks like this:

```
<form method="post" action="https://www.paypal.com/cgi-bin/webscr"
      target="paypal">
<input type="hidden" name="cmd" value="_cart">
<input type="hidden" name="business" value="pay@paypalhacks.com">
<input type="hidden" name="item_name" value="PayPal Hacks">
<input type="hidden" name="amount" value="24.95">
<input type="submit" name="add" value="Add to Cart">
</form>
```

The equivalent button in the form of an Add to Cart hyperlink looks like this:

```
<a href=https://www.paypal.com/cgi-bin/webscr?cmd=_cart&add=1&business=
    pay@paypalhacks.com&item_name=PayPal+Hacks&amount=24.95
    target="paypal">Add to Cart</a>
```

This link opens a window and displays the PayPal Shopping Cart with one item in it: *PayPal Hacks* for $24.95.

In both examples, note the presence of the important `target="paypal"` attribute, which causes the Shopping Cart to open in a new browser window. Without it, the cart will not display a Continue Shopping button. Always include this attribute in your Add to Cart buttons and also make sure paypal is all in lowercase.

Shortening the Link

Many PayPal URLs can be shortened, which can be useful (and sometimes necessary) when sending links in emails, because it prevents them from getting cut at the end of a line. The short link for the Shopping Cart begins with *https://www.paypal.com/cart/*. Just append all the fields you want to use to the end, as in this payment link:

```
https://www.paypal.com/cart/add=1&business=pay@paypalhacks.com&amount=20
```

This works for displaying the Shopping Cart as well:

```
https://www.paypal.com/cart/display=1&business=pay@paypalhacks.com
```

—Patrick Breitenbach

Specify the Size of the Shopping Cart Window

#47 Control the size and other aspects of PayPal Shopping Cart pop-up window.

PayPal's Button Factory generates Buy Now and Shopping Cart button code based on form inputs. In the case of the Shopping Cart, the target for the form defaults to a new window named paypal. Because this is submitted by a form, the size of the window defaults to the customer's browser's default. This default size can be too large and take up the customer's entire screen, obscuring your store's pages. Or, even worse, the window can be too small, forcing your customer to scroll around to see all the information for his cart.

With some simple HTML and JavaScript, you can specify the size of the Shopping Cart window PayPal opens.

The Code

Here's the code for form buttons:

```
<form method="post" action=
    https://www.paypal.com/cgi-bin/webscr target="paypal">
<input type="hidden" name="cmd" value="_cart">
<input type="hidden" name="business" value="pay@paypalhacks.com">
<input type="hidden" name="item_name" value="PayPal Hacks">
<input type="hidden" name="amount" value="19.95">
<input type="submit" name="add" value="Add to Cart" onClick=
    "window.open('','paypal','width=780,height=500,scrollbars=yes,
    resizable=yes,status=yes')">
</form>
```

And here's the equivalent as a hyperlink [Hack #46]:

```
<a href=# onClick="window.open('https://www.paypal.com/cgi-bin/webscr?cmd=
    _cart&add=1&business=pay@paypalhacks.com&item_name=PayPal+Hacks&
    amount=19.95','paypal','width=780,height=500,scrollbars=yes,
    resizable=yes,status=yes')">Add to Cart</a>
```

Hacking the Hack

While you can experiment with the height and width to get the window size that works best for you, 780x500 is a good size, because it accommodates the size of PayPal's web pages fairly well and works with most customers' screens. Note some of the other attributes in this code:

resizable

> No preset window size will be right for all your customers, so you'll most likely want to allow them to resize the window. Set the resizable attribute to no only if you want the window to be a static size. This option can be useful if the window is to accompany a static-sized web site or if it will be used with some sort of kiosk system.

scrollbars

> Set this attribute to yes if you want scrollbars to be displayed in the window (when appropriate), or set it to no to disable scrolling and really frustrate your customers. Be careful not to disable scrollbars if the window is not resizable.

status

> Use this setting to turn on or off the window's status bar. Turn it off for a more tidy look, or enable it if you want your customers to see the little yellow padlock that tells them the site is secure.

Deal with Design and Layout Issues

#48 Embed the Button Factory code in a table to maintain the appearance of your web page's layout.

Browsers interpret HTML forms in different ways that can affect the appearance of your web page. Most browsers create unwanted spacing where HTML forms are inserted, similar to the effect of a line break tag (<br>). If your web page's design and layout is very precise, it can be negatively affected by PayPal's code, throwing your layout off by a few pixels. Avoid this effect by embedding the button code in an otherwise empty table.

 Make a backup of your original file before trying this hack. It is easier to start from the original if you make a mistake.

Here is the familiar button code, generated at the PayPal site, surrounded by the table markup. The width, border, cellspacing, and cellpadding variables are all set to zero:

```
<table width="0" border="0" cellspacing="0" cellpadding="0">
  <tr>
    <td>
<form action="https://www.paypal.com/cgi-bin/webscr" method="post">
<input type="hidden" name="cmd" value="_xclick">
<input type="hidden" name="business" value="youremail@yourisp.com">
<!-- Other input elements here -->
</form>
    </td>
  </tr>
</table>
```

However, this code will still cause shifting in the design. Avoid this shift by moving the opening and closing form tags outside of the opening and closing table data tags:

```
<form action="https://www.paypal.com/cgi-bin/webscr" method="post">
<table width="0" border="0" cellspacing="0" cellpadding="0">
  <tr>
①    <td>
②<input type="hidden" name="cmd" value="_xclick">
③<input type="hidden" name="business" value="youremail@yourisp.com">
④<!-- Other input elements here -->
⑤    </td>
  </tr>
</table>
</form>
```

Now, when the page is viewed in a browser, no shifting appears where the form has been inserted, as shown in Figure 5-3.

Figure 5-3. Cleaning up alignment problems

To perfect your table spacing, make sure to eliminate any extraneous spaces or line breaks between the <td> and </td> tags. For instance, if you put lines ❶ through ❺ all on one line, removing all spaces between the tags, you'll remove the last of the unsightly gaps from your tables.

Put Both Cart Buttons in One Form

HACK #49

Overcome the limitations of some web development tools by combining the Add to Cart and View Cart buttons into a single HTML form.

If you're using a web page editor that prefers or allows pages to contain only one form (such as some versions of Dreamweaver), or if you're a Microsoft .NET programmer, you might need to combine both Shopping Cart buttons into a single web form.

Fortunately, PayPal relies on the names of the buttons, not on the post URL or other details of the HTML form, to correctly interpret the buttons.

The Code

To implement this single-form design, simply include two submit buttons in the PayPal cart form. Name one button add and the other button display, like this:

```
<form method="post" action="https://www.paypal.com/cgi-bin/webscr"
    target="paypal">
<input type="hidden" name="cmd" value="_cart">
<input type="hidden" name="business" value="pay@biz.com">
<input type="hidden" name="item_name" value="Teddy Bear">
<input type="hidden" name="amount" value="19.95">
<input type="submit" name="add" value="Add to Cart">
<input type="submit" name="display" value="Display Cart">
</form>
```

Naturally, this form accepts the additional fields and other customization afforded by the other hacks in this chapter.

The Right Tools for the Right Job

If you use an HTML editor such as Microsoft FrontPage or Macromedia Dreamweaver to create your web pages, you should consider trying out one of the PayPal plug-ins available for those tools. These plug-ins integrate right into the tool and can be called up while you're editing your pages. They step you through creating the button and then automatically insert the HTML into your web page.

Here are some links to plug-ins for popular page editors. Most of them are offered by third parties who have worked closely with PayPal to make sure they work properly:

Macromedia Dreamweaver
> *http://www.webassist.com/Products/ProductDetails.asp?PID=18*

Microsoft FrontPage
> *http://www.auctionmessenger.net/paypal*

Adobe GoLive
> *http://www.transmitmedia.com/golive/paypal*

NetObjects Fusion 7.0 and higher (with built-in PayPal module)
> *http://www.netobjects.com*

Integrate a Third-Party Shopping Cart with PayPal
HACK #50

> Pass the contents of a non-PayPal shopping cart to PayPal using the Aggregate Cart and Upload Complete Cart features.

Shopping carts have proven to be effective online selling tools and have become a standard on many eCommerce web sites. PayPal makes it extremely easy to add a shopping cart to your web site, because PayPal hosts all the functionality. All you need to do is add the Add to Cart button code to your pages [Hack #45].

In many cases, however, the PayPal Shopping Cart is insufficient for merchants who might need a more customized design, more sophisticated tax and shipping calculations, or other features that the PayPal Shopping Cart system doesn't offer. Fortunately, using a non-PayPal shopping cart system doesn't mean that you can't still accept PayPal as a payment option.

PayPal offers two ways to integrate your shopping cart: Aggregate Cart and Upload Complete Cart.

Aggregating Your Cart

Of the two systems, PayPal's Aggregate Cart has the advantage of being easier to integrate. Although your shopping cart system might save your customers' cart contents into a database, you don't need to send all this information to PayPal. All you need to do is send PayPal the order ID associated with your customer's shopping cart, along with the total dollar amount for your customer to pay in the amount field.

Since there is no dedicated order_ID parameter, pass the order ID to PayPal in the item_name field for the purpose of Aggregate Cart payments.

You can also add shipping, handling, and tax parameters. Here is the most basic code to do all this:

```
<form action="https://www.paypal.com/cgi-bin/webscr" method="post"
    name="form1"> <input type="hidden" name="cmd" value="_xclick">
❶  <input type="hidden" name="business" value="you@paypalhacks.com">
❷  <input type="hidden" name="item_name" value="Order#21874">
❸  <input type="hidden" name="amount" value="151.80">
    <input type="image" src="http://images.paypal.com/images/x-click- but01.gif"
        name="submit" alt="Pay Now with PayPal">
</form>
```

Specify the email address to which the payment should be sent on line ❶, a reference to your order on line ❷, and the total amount of the items in the customer's cart on line ❸.

There are plenty of optional parameters you can include here, all of which are documented in "Create a Buy Now Button" [Hack #28]. Here are some of the most useful:

```
<input type="hidden" name="shipping" value="9.00">
<input type="hidden" name="handling" value="3.00">
<input type="hidden" name="tax" value="21.92">
<input type="hidden" name="invoice" value="442">
<input type="hidden" name="custom" value="paypalhacks">
```

PayPal hides the invoice and custom fields from the buyer, so make sure not to use them to pass your order ID or any other information you want your customers to see during the checkout process. Instead, use item_name for this purpose. Also, don't use any parameters normally used to specify quantity with Aggregate Cart, because there will likely be multiple items in the cart and the quantity parameter would apply to only one of them.

You might have noticed that these parameters are the same as those used in a regular Buy Now button. The Aggregate Cart feature is essentially a glorified Buy Now button that processes the data for your entire Shopping Cart. It's not terribly sophisticated, but if that's all the functionality you need, this is all the code you need.

Uploading Shopping Cart Details to PayPal

Although Aggregate Cart is easy to implement, it sends only a total dollar amount to PayPal. By contrast, the Upload Complete Cart feature has the distinct ability to send a listing of all the items in the customer's shopping cart to PayPal. This means that PayPal will display a summary of the cart contents on the PayPal site (as shown in Figure 5-4) and record those details within the customer's payment history and in your seller history logs and notifications.

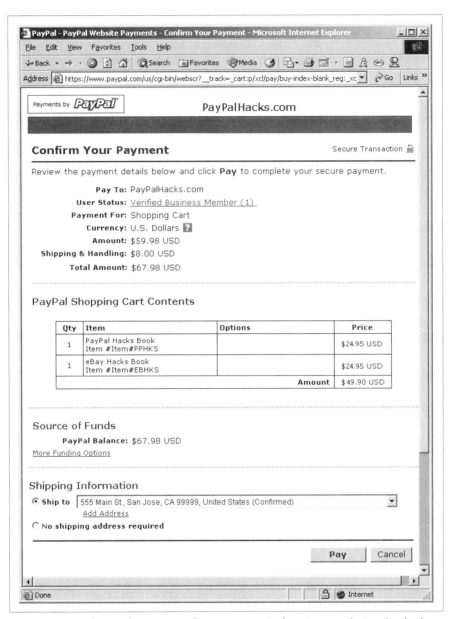

Figure 5-4. Displaying the contents of your customer's shopping cart during the checkout process

To create an Upload Complete Cart button, start with the same HTML code used earlier in this hack with the Aggregate Cart button. Then, for the cmd input value, replace _xclick with _cart, and add a new hidden field called upload and set its value to 1. (You can remove the item_name and amount fields, because they aren't needed for Update Complete Cart.) You'll then end up with something like this:

```
<form action="https://www.paypal.com/cgi-bin/webscr" method="post"
    name="form1">
<input type="hidden" name="cmd" value="_cart">
<input type="hidden" name="upload" value="1">
<input type="hidden" name="business" value="you@paypalhacks.com">
<input type="image" src="http://images.paypal.com/images/x-click-but01.gif"
    name="submit" alt="Pay Now with PayPal">
</form>
```

Next, insert the details of the contents of the shopping cart. To add the first item, insert the following code somewhere inside the `<form></form>` structure:

```
❶   <input type="hidden" name="item_name_1" value="PayPal Hacks Book">
❷   <input type="hidden" name="item_number_1" value="Item#PPHKS">
❸   <input type="hidden" name="quantity_1" value="1">
❹   <input type="hidden" name="amount_1" value="24.95">
❺   <input type="hidden" name="shipping_1" value="3.00">
❻   <input type="hidden" name="shipping2_1" value="2.00">
❼   <input type="hidden" name="handling_1" value="1.00">
```

The _1 suffix after each variable name gives every tag an item reference. So, these parameters describe the first item as a single copy of the *PayPal Hacks* book (line ❶) with a product code set to PPHKS (line ❷) and a per-item price of $24.95 (line ❹).

The cost of shipping, $3.00, is specified on line ❺. This is a per-quantity charge: if the quantity (line ❸) is more than one, the same $3.00 shipping charge will be applied to each copy of the book ordered. The exception to this rule is when you specify a shipping2 amount (as line ❻ does in this example), this shipping amount will be used only for the first item and the shipping2 amount will be charged for each additional book ordered (e.g., three books would cost $3.00 + $2.00 + $2.00, or $7.00, to ship).

The handling cost, $1.00, is specified on line ❼ and is applied only once, regardless of the number of items ordered.

Notice that the form method is POST (as opposed to GET). This allows you to post your data to PayPal without the size limit imposed by the fact that GET places all the form data in the URL.

Adding Additional Items

For every additional item you have in your shopping cart, add another set of parameters. For each parameter, append _n to the variable name, where n is the item number, starting with 1. Here's a second book thrown into the shopping cart:

```
<input type="hidden" name="item_name_2" value="eBay Hacks Book">
<input type="hidden" name="item_number_2" value="Item#EBHKS">
<input type="hidden" name="quantity_2" value="1">
<input type="hidden" name="amount_2" value="24.95">
<input type="hidden" name="shipping_2" value="3.00">
<input type="hidden" name="shipping2_2" value="2.00">
<input type="hidden" name="handling_2" value="1.00">
```

You should always verify that the amount paid matches the order total. You can automate this verification by using IPN [Hack #73] and by using the item_name and amount fields to verify that the amount paid to your PayPal account was the same as the total order amount.

Hacking the Hack

Presumably, you'll need to store the contents of a customer's shopping cart in your database before sending the data (and the customer) to PayPal. This means that the Add to Cart buttons on your site will need to submit data to your own server, and then, at checkout, your server will generate the HTML code for the Upload Complete Cart feature. Unfortunately, this means that you have to include an intermediate page, on which your customer will have to click another button to submit the cart to PayPal.

The solution is to add a little JavaScript to the <body> tag, so that the customer's browser submits the form automatically when the form loads:

```
<body onload="document.form1.submit();">
```

Here is a complete example of the code:

```
<html>
<body onload="document.form1.submit();">

<form name="form1" action="https://www.paypal.com/cgi-bin/webscr"
      method="post">
<input type="hidden" name="cmd" value="_cart">
<input type="hidden" name="upload" value="1">
<input type="hidden" name="business" value="you@paypalhacks.com">

<input type="hidden" name="item_name_1" value="PayPal Hacks Book">
<input type="hidden" name="item_number_1" value="Item#PPHKS">
<input type="hidden" name="quantity_1" value="1">
<input type="hidden" name="amount_1" value="24.95">
<input type="hidden" name="shipping_1" value="3.00">
<input type="hidden" name="shipping2_1" value="2.00">
<input type="hidden" name="handling_1" value="1.00">

<input type="hidden" name="item_name_2" value="eBay Hacks Book">
<input type="hidden" name="item_number_2" value="Item#EBHKS">
<input type="hidden" name="quantity_2" value="1">
<input type="hidden" name="amount_2" value="24.95">
```

```
<input type="hidden" name="shipping_2" value="3.00">
<input type="hidden" name="shipping2_2" value="2.00">
<input type="hidden" name="handling_2" value="1.00">

<input type="image" src="http://images.paypal.com/images/x-click-but01.gif"
    name="submit" alt="Pay Now with PayPal">
</form>
</body>
</html>
```

Depending on the speed of your customer's Internet connection and the traffic at the PayPal server, the page might redirect almost instantly or it might display momentarily for a second or two before the next page is displayed. For this reason, you might want to include some kind of "Please wait..." message on the page so that your customers don't interrupt the process out of confusion. Plus, you still need to include a real Submit button and a sentence of instruction just in case your customer has disabled the browser's support for JavaScript.

HACK #51   Customize Checkout Pages

Give your customers a smooth buying experience by changing the look and feel of PayPal payment pages to match your web site.

When you sell online using PayPal, you are selling to PayPal veterans and newbies alike. While PayPal represents online transaction safety to tens of millions of satisfied users, some less experienced buyers might find being sent off to another site to pay for their purchases rather jarring. And since you have gone to the trouble of creating your beautiful web site, why send people away from it when they are ready to buy?

Well, you send customers to PayPal so that Paypal can run the secure transaction and you don't have to. But your customers don't have to feel like they are being sent off to a foreign country when they go to the PayPal payment flow. By customizing the PayPal pages so they function more like your own web site, you can make all your customers happy.

PayPal's Custom Payment Pages feature lets you control key parts of the user experience on PayPal's web site. You can place a 750x90–pixel banner at the top of PayPal's pages and carry your site's color scheme through the payment process. Did you know PayPal could look like Figure 5-5?

Here's how to get started:

1. Log into your PayPal account.
2. Click the Profile link and select Custom Payment Pages from the right column.

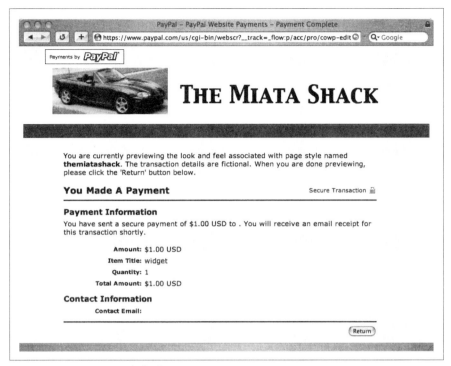

Figure 5-5. A customized checkout page

3. Click on the Add button to add a page style. Give the style a name (you can store up to five named styles), add the URL to your banner, and select appropriate colors for the page background and the header, as shown in Figure 5-6.

4. Press the Preview button to see what PayPal's pages will look like for your buyers. When you like the result, save the style.

5. Press the Make Primary button, and all your customers will be treated to this new style.

Presto! You're done.

Using Multiple Custom Page Styles

Setting a *primary* style makes that style the default for all the existing payment buttons on your web site. However, you can save up to five different custom page styles on your PayPal account and apply any of those page styles to a particular payment flow. This is particularly helpful if you have more than one web site or if you use visual cues to distinguish particular areas of your web site.

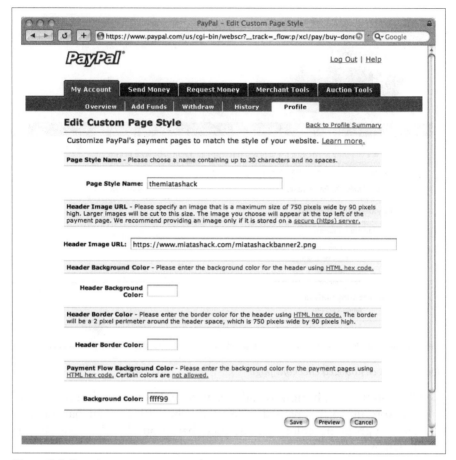

Figure 5-6. Creating a custom page style

Simply name your styles appropriately (e.g., electronics or marys_crafts) and then select which page style to associate with each button on your site by including the style's name in the button HTML, like this:

```
<input type=hidden name="page_style" value="marys_crafts">
```

Specifying a page style in a GET link is easier; add &page_style=marys_crafts to the end of the PayPal URL.

Getting the Most from Custom Page Style Banners

Header banners allow you to continue your site's look and feel through the payment process, so PayPal has ceded you a 750x90–pixel area at the top of all their payment pages. That's great for brand awareness and all, but what else could you do with 67,500 pixels?

How about presenting your site's message of the day? Or advertising your best-selling accessories? No problem. Create a custom page style and point the image URL to a location on your site (e.g., *https://www.mysite.com/motd.jpg*). Then, you can put any image (as long as it fits in the banner space; Pay-Pal clips oversized images) in that location. In today's banner, you can push overstocked product: "scratching posts—Frisky loves them!" When the posts are sold out, you can fire up Photoshop and replace the banner with an advertisement for catnip mice.

Change as often as you like without logging into PayPal at all. If you want to get fancy, you can write a script that rotates through a set of banners so that customers always see a fresh message.

PayPal Etiquette

PayPal has the ability to review the contents of custom page styles and can remove styles that violate the company's guidelines. Repeated violations might bring other sanctions too. Sorry, no nekkid ladies or gents on your banners. You can't sell already-detonated airbags either.

For a full list of the company's guidelines for appropriate content (not to mention some good laughs), see *http://www.paypal.com/cgi-bin/webscr?cmd=p/gen/ua/use/index_frame-outside*.

Here are a few more tips to remember when you are customizing your payment pages:

- Host your banner image on a secure (*https*) site so that your customers will not see warnings about mixing secure and insecure context.

- Before PayPal offered Custom Payment Pages, it offered more limited functionality in the form of two optional button variables: `image_url` and `cs`. The old and new features are not compatible, so if you are using Custom Payment Pages, do not use the `image_url` or `cs` variables in your buttons.

- PayPal selects white or black foreground text based on your background color. On light backgrounds such as #FFFFFF (pure white) PayPal uses black text. If you select a dark background such as #000033 (dark blue), PayPal uses white foreground text. This ensures that your payment pages have sufficient contrast to be legible, regardless of which background color you select.

- There are a few colors that PayPal does not allow you to select as background colors because they are too similar to the bright red (FF0000) that PayPal uses to alert users to errors. If you run into this restriction, try a similar or complementary color. You might also be able to stay in the desired color family by selecting a color that has a different total brightness.

—Glenn Ellingson

Display the Merchant Transaction ID on Your Return Page

Because the transaction numbers issued to merchants and buyers are different, you need to provide the merchant ID to customers.

As a merchant on PayPal, you will undoubtedly have occasional post-sale questions from your customers. If your customers give you the transaction IDs they see in their PayPal account history, you will quickly realize they don't match the transaction IDs you see. This is because PayPal generates two unique transaction IDs: one for the merchant and one for the customer. This makes it difficult to track orders for your customers because they do not have the transaction ID you are using. Some simple scripting can head off this problem by giving your transaction ID to your customer.

The PayPal Button Code

To enable this hack, you'll need to employ the return variable in your purchase buttons. This variable specifies the URL of the page to which customers should be sent when they complete payment. Insert it into the standard PayPal-generated button code between the opening and closing <form> tags. Set the variable to the URL of the return page on your web site:

```
<form target="paypal" action="https://www.paypal.com/cgi-bin/webscr"
    method="post">
<input type="hidden" name="business" value="youremail@yourisp.com">
<input type="hidden" name="item_name" value="Widget">
<input type="hidden" name="item_number" value="Wid-001">
<input type="hidden" name="amount" value="1.00">
<input type="hidden" name="no_note" value="1">
<input type="hidden" name="currency_code" value="USD">
<input type="image" src="https://www.paypal.com/en_US/i/btn/x-click-but22.gif"
    border="0" name="submit">
<input type="hidden" name="add" value="1">
<input type="hidden" name="return" value=
    "http://yoursite.com/returnpage.asp">
</form>
```

Your customer sees a Continue button on the Payment Sent confirmation page after making the payment. Clicking the button takes the buyer to the return page.

Creating Your Return Page

The return page is where you display the merchant's transaction ID to the customer. You want to display *your* ID; if your customer needs to contact you, he can give you this ID, and you can use it to look up the transaction in your transaction history. This is the easiest way to know for certain which order the customer is talking about.

Your transaction ID is passed as the txn_id variable. Access it in the same way you access the values passed to any CGI. You can do this with whatever method works best with your server's operating system and scripting languages. Here is the ASP way:

```
<body>
Here is your transaction Id. Keep it for all future order questions:
<%=Request.Form("txn_id")%>
</body>
```

And here's the PHP way:

```
<body>
Here is your transaction Id. Keep it for all future order questions:
<?php
echo $_GET['txn_id'];
?>
</body>
```

Remember Your Customers

HACK #53

Track your site visitors, regardless of whether they made a purchase with PayPal.

As your eCommerce site becomes more advanced, you might want to begin tracking visitors as they move through your site. For example, you could create a membership system, encouraging users to register and then log in during each subsequent visit. Once acknowledged, your users might have access to special insider deals or premium content. Or, you could address your customers by name on your site's pages.

However, there's a downside. Designing, building, and maintaining a membership database for customers can be a lot of work, and some customers might balk at being asked for a username and password each time they visit. Using the techniques in this hack, you can identify your users by name and offer buyers-only content in minutes—no login required.

Tracking Buyers with Cookies

A popular way to remember your visitors is by using *cookies*. Cookies are small chunks of information that a user's browser remembers on behalf of your web site. They are handed back to your web site (if it asks) on a subsequent visit. By setting, then reading back, personal information for a visitor, your web site can remember your customers.

This hack sets a cookie when your buyer has returned to your site after making a payment to you with PayPal. Your site will look for this information whenever someone visits and, if found, use it to personalize the site by using the buyer's name and granting access to customer-only content.

You can implement this hack with any web scripting technology; the example code uses ASP with VBScript.

The Return Page

The return page is a page on your site that is activated after a payment has been made, when the buyer clicks the "Click here to continue" link on the You Made A Payment page. Set the return variable in your Buy Now button to the URL you want to use.

Use the return page to create cookies that record the user's name and the fact that the user is a buyer. You should also set the cookies' expiration times; if you don't set the cookies to expire in a set amount of time (such as about an hour, as in the following code), the settings will be lost at the end of the session (such as when your customer closes the browser).

Here's a simple ASP implementation of this:

```
<%
'Set cookie expiration
'If this is a completed payment, set "paid" to "yes"
If Request.Form("payment_status") = "Completed" Then
  Response.Cookies("paid") = "Yes"
  'Set the expiration time of the cookie
  Response.Cookies("paid").Expires = Now() + 0.042 'About 1 hour
End
Response.Cookies("user") = Request.Form("first_name")
'Set the expiration time of the cookie
Response.Cookies("user").Expires = Now() + 0.042 'About 1 hour
%>
```

The user is identified by the first name provided by PayPal via the first_name variable. The paid cookie remembers that this user is a paying customer; user stores the buyer's name.

In addition to the cookie-handling code in this example, you'll want to have links to other portions of your site, such as your home page.

Cookies at Work

You can use the cookies you created on the other pages of your site. For example, you can greet your customer by name:

```
Welcome<br><%= Request.Cookies("user")%><br>
```

Or you can reward your loyal customers with inside information:

```
<%
If Request.Cookies("paid") = "Yes" Then
'They have paid, show secret text
%>
We'll be having a <b>big sale</b> on all our exclusive monkey toys this
Thursday! (Preferred customers only.)
<%
End If
%>
```

This code shows the secret text only to people who have completed a purchase using PayPal.

Hacking the Hack

PayPal provides more information to your return page than just the payment status and the buyer's name. For example, you can also get the name of the item purchased. Try this addition to your return page to record the item name:

```
<%
'Set cookie expiration
'If this is a completed payment, set "paid" to "yes"
If Request.Form("payment_status") = "Completed" Then
  Response.Cookies("paid") = "Yes"
  'Set the expiration time of the cookie
  Response.Cookies("paid").Expires = Now( ) + 0.042 'About 1 hour
  Response.Cookies("item_name") = Request.Form("item_name")
  Response.Cookies("item_name").Expires = Now( ) + 0.042 'About 1 hour
End
Response.Cookies("user") = Request.Form("first_name")
'Set the expiration time of the cookie
Response.Cookies("user").Expires = Now( ) + 0.042 'About 1 hour
%>
```

Then, use the item name in your content pages:

```
Welcome<br><%= Request.Cookies("user")%><br>
<%
If Request.Cookies("paid") = "Yes" Then
%>
Thank you for your recent purchase of
<%= Request.Cookies("item_name")%>.
<%
End If
%>
```

You will need to modify this code for shopping cart applications, because there will likely be more than one item name.

Also, remembering your customer for an hour might not be as long as you would like. Try setting the value to a year:

```
Response.Cookies("paid").Expires = Now( ) + 365 'About a year
```

See Also

The "HTML and Hyperlink Variables" section in the PayPal Buy Now Buttons Manual offers important information about using the return and rm parameters.

HACK #54 Create a Dynamic Storefront

Produce a powerful storefront with a simple database and dynamic server scripting.

PayPal's Button Factory makes managing a small web store easy, provided that you have a small number of products. But if your store has hundreds or thousands of products, generating the necessary HTML code through the Button Factory (not to mention later changing that code) would be a daunting task. Therefore, you'll need a method to quickly generate generic shopping cart HTML button code for all your store's products.

This hack provides an ideal situation for a database-driven page that can use a single page as a template for an arbitrary number of products contained in a database. The example illustrates the techniques using Microsoft Active Server Pages written in VBScript with an Access database, though the principles described here can be applied to any server platform/database combination.

Creating the Storefront Database

The first step in building your dynamic site is to create a database table that holds your PayPal button values for all your products. You'll need one column for each unique aspect of the button for each product: item_name, item_number, item_price, and Id. Both item_name and item_number should be text fields, while item_price should be a money (or currency) field. Finally, include the Id field as the primary key and set it to increment automatically.

Save this new database table as tblProducts, as shown in Figure 5-7. Your table can have more rows, including shipping information, return URLs, or tax data, depending on the variables you are using for your buttons.

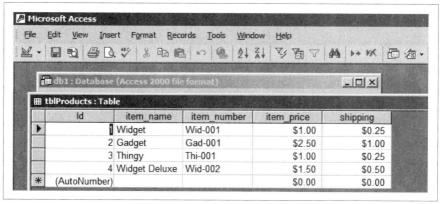

Figure 5-7. The database table containing your product information

   See the "Database Coding and Platform Choices" section of the Preface for database considerations.

Once the table is built and saved, populate it with your product data. You can enter the information into the table like a spreadsheet or import the data from another source. After the data is entered, your database is ready for use in your dynamic page.

Building the Template

The second step in creating your storefront is to generate generic HTML Button Factory code [Hack #28] to serve as your template for your database-driven store. Your button code should look something like this:

```
<form target="paypal" action=
     "https://www.paypal.com/cgi-bin/webscr" method="post">
<input type="hidden" name="business" value="yyouremail@yyourisp.com">
<input type="hidden" name="item_name" value="Widget">
<input type="hidden" name="item_number" value="Wid-001">
<input type="hidden" name="amount" value="1.00">
<input type="hidden" name="no_note" value="1">
<input type="hidden" name="currency_code" value="USD">
<input type="image" src=
     "https://www.paypal.com/en_US/i/btn/x-click-but22.gif" border="0"
     name="submit">
<input type="hidden" name="add" value="1">
</form>
```

The storefront page displays all the items for sale by taking the information in your tblProducts database table and dynamically inserting it into the generic PayPal Button Factory code you just created. To get started, use a

SQL query to retrieve the product information. Depending on the server platform, languages supported, and database technology used, the syntax to connect to the database and return the data will vary. The SQL query to create your recordset should look like this:

```
SELECT item_name, item_number, item_price, Id FROM tblProducts
```

See the "Database Coding and Platform Choices" section of the Preface for the additional information needed to put this SQL statement to work with this and the other hacks in this book.

Your database then returns all of the products in the table, which you'll need to place into a recordset called rsProducts.

Next, take the generic button code from the previous step and replace the field values with references to fields in your database. For instance, change this line:

```
<input type="hidden" name="item_name" value="Widget">
```

to this (assuming you're using VBScript for ASP, as discussed in the Preface):

```
<input type="hidden" name="item_name" value="<%=rsProducts("item_name")%>">
```

Your final code should look something like this:

```
<form target="paypal" action="https://www.paypal.com/cgi-bin/webscr"
      method="post">
<input type="hidden" name="business" value="yyouremail@yyourisp.com">
<input type="hidden" name="item_name" value="<%=rsProducts("item_name")%>">
<input type="hidden" name="item_number" value="<%=rsProducts
      ("item_number")%>">
<input type="hidden" name="amount" value="<%=rsProducts("item_price")%>">
<input type="hidden" name="no_note" value="1">
<input type="hidden" name="currency_code" value="USD">
<input type="image" src="https://www.paypal.com/en_US/i/btn/x-click-but22.gif"
      border="0" name="submit">
<input type="hidden" name="add" value="1">
</form>
```

When this page is loaded into a web browser, your server executes the SQL query before it is presented to the customer. The code then pulls the first item from the recordset and generates the button code for the corresponding product dynamically. The next step is to generate a whole page of buttons, one for each item in your database:

```
'While recordset still has products, loop code
While NOT rsProducts.EOF

<form target="paypal" action="https://www.paypal.com/cgi-bin/webscr"
      method="post">
```

```
<input type="hidden" name="business" value="yyouremail@yyourisp.com">
<input type="hidden" name="item_name" value="<%=rsProducts("item_name")%>">
<input type="hidden" name="item_number"
    value="<%=rsProducts("item_number")%>">
<input type="hidden" name="amount" value="<%=rsProducts("item_price")%>">
<input type="hidden" name="no_note" value="1">
<input type="hidden" name="currency_code" value="USD">
<input type="image" src="https://www.paypal.com/en_US/i/btn/x-click-but22.gif"
    border="0" name="submit">
<input type="hidden" name="add" value="1">
</form>

'Move to next record
rsProducts.MoveNext()
Wend
```

Figure 5-8 shows the finished product listing, complete with multiple dynamically generated payment buttons.

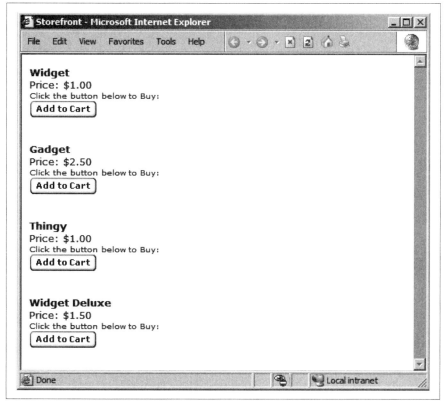

Figure 5-8. The finished web page, loaded into a browser

Including Product Details

Not only can you use the values returned from the database to populate your button code, you can also display the item name and price (and perhaps a photo) of the product alongside each button. Add a little spacing to the buttons to keep the site organized:

```
'While recordset still has products, loop code
While NOT rsProducts.EOF

Product: <%=rsProduct("item_name"%><br>
Price: <%=rsProduct("item_price"%><br>
Click the button below to Buy<br>
<form target="paypal" action="https://www.paypal.com/cgi-bin/webscr"
     method="post">
<input type="hidden" name="business" value="yyouremail@yyourisp.com">
<input type="hidden" name="item_name" value="<%=rsProducts("item_name")%>">
<input type="hidden" name="item_number"
     value="<%=rsProducts("item_number")%>">
<input type="hidden" name="amount" value="<%=rsProducts("item_price")%>">
<input type="hidden" name="no_note" value="1">
<input type="hidden" name="currency_code" value="USD">
<input type="image" src="https://www.paypal.com/en_US/i/btn/x-click-but22.gif"
     border="0" name="submit">
<input type="hidden" name="add" value="1">
</form>
<br><br>

'Move to next record
rsProducts.MoveNext( )
Yound
```

This simple technique can serve as the foundation for a powerful eCommerce web site. Simply by managing this one template page and a database table, you can build a site that supports an arbitrary number of products, without needing to manually create and edit individual product pages.

H A C K   Add Dynamic Storefront Details
#55   Extend a dynamic storefront by creating a product details page for each product you sell.

The product details page allows you to provide detailed information on a specific product, such as a description, weight, availability, or other tidbits to educate customers and increase sales.

Start with the code from "Create a Dynamic Storefront" **[Hack #54]**, which loops through all the products you have in your database table and displays them on your web page. For each product, the code displays the product name, price, and a corresponding purchase button.

First, add a line to display a link to another web page on which detailed product information for the item is displayed. In the link, pass the unique identifying field for that product to the details page in the id query string parameter, like this:

```
<a href="detail.asp?id=<%=rsProducts("Id")%>>Product details, click here</a>
```

The finished code looks like this:

```
'While recordset still has products, loop code
While NOT rsProducts.EOF

Product: <%=rsProduct("item_name"%><br>
Price: <%=rsProduct("item_price"%><br>
<a href="detail.asp?id=<%=rsProducts("Id")%>>Product details, click here</a>
<br>
Click the button below to Buy<br>
<form target="paypal" action="https://www.paypal.com/cgi-bin/webscr"
      method="post">
<input type="hidden" name="business" value="youremail@yourisp.com">
<input type="hidden" name="item_name" value="<%=rsProducts("item_name")%>">
<input type="hidden" name="item_number"
      value="<%=rsProducts("item_number")%>">
<input type="hidden" name="amount" value="<%=rsProducts("item_price")%>">
<input type="hidden" name="no_note" value="1">
<input type="hidden" name="currency_code" value="USD">
<input type="image" src="https://www.paypal.com/en_US/i/btn/x-click-but22.gif"
      border="0" name="submit">
<input type="hidden" name="add" value="1">
</form>
<br><br>

'Move to next record
rsProducts.MoveNext( )
Wend
```

Adding More Product Information to Your Table

In order to provide more information on your product, you have to add at least one more field to your database table. You can have as many fields as you like, including a weight field for shipping purposes, or even an item color field. Open the tblProducts database table and add a new column named description. Set the data type of this field to long text, ntext, or memo, depending on your database platform. Save the change to the database, and then open the table and begin entering product descriptions for each of your products. Descriptions should educate the customer on specific information related to this particular product and contain any information they should know before making a purchase.

Product Details Page

The product details page makes a call to your `tblProducts` database table for one specific record, determined by the `id` QueryString parameter passed from the storefront page:

```
'Create and populate id variable for product
Dim Id
Id = Request.QueryString("id")
```

Next, ask the database for the specific record for that item, based on the product's Id field, with an SQL query like this:

```
"SELECT item_name, item_number, item_price, Id, description FROM tblProducts
WHERE Id = " & Id
```

> See the "Database Coding and Platform Choices" section of the Preface for the additional information needed to put this SQL statement to work with this and the other hacks in this book.

That query returns one record from your database table. Pull the returned record into a recordset named `rsProducts`. Keep the same recordset name you used on the storefront page, even though you are pulling in only one record. This provides consistency across your pages, so you can copy and paste code back and forth between pages. This means that since the record-sets share the same name, you can reuse the same code on both pages that reference recordset variables.

Giving your recordsets different names can be confusing and does not allow the two pages to share their code with one another. For instance, if you take the product name reference tag found in the storefront page (`<%=rsProduct("item_name")%>`) and paste it directly into the product detail page, it works properly without any editing.

You can now begin populating your page with the dynamic data used with the storefront page, as shown in Figure 5-9.

Take the code from your storefront and remove the `While` loop, because you have only one item to display. Then add the `description` field value for that item just below the button:

```
Product: <%=rsProduct("item_name")%><br>
Price: <%=rsProduct("item_price")%><br>
<a href="detail.asp?id=<%=rsProducts("Id")%>>Product details, click here</a>
<br>
Click the button below to Buy<br>
<form target="paypal" action="https://www.paypal.com/cgi-bin/webscr"
    method="post">
```

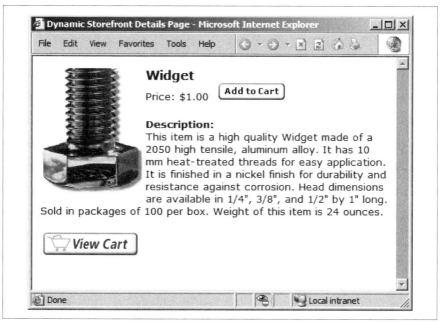

Figure 5-9. Adding details to a dynamic product page to present a more complete storefront

```
<input type="hidden" name="business" value="youremail@yourisp.com">
<input type="hidden" name="item_name" value="<%=rsProducts("item_name")%>">
<input type="hidden" name="item_number"
       value="<%=rsProducts("item_number")%>">
<input type="hidden" name="amount" value="<%=rsProducts("item_price")%>">
<input type="hidden" name="no_note" value="1">
<input type="hidden" name="currency_code" value="USD">
<input type="image" src="https://www.paypal.com/en_US/i/btn/x-click-but22.gif"
       order="0" name="submit">
<input type="hidden" name="add" value="1">
</form>
<br>
<%=rsProducts("description")%>
```

Hacking the Hack

This hack shows how to add a product description. However, the concept can be applied to any product-specific functionality you add to the page. For instance, you can add a function that allows the site visitor to send a link directly to the product details page to an email address. This is commonly referred to as a *Send to Friend* feature.

To implement this feature, you need to do two things. The first is to add a simple form that contains a text box in which to enter an email address of where to send the link to in the product details page. The second is to add a piece of code that actually performs the sending of the email and is located in a separate file named *sendtofriend.asp*. This example uses VBScript written for ASP pages. Here is the code to insert into the product details page:

```
<form action="sendtofriend.asp" method="post">
Send this page to a friend. Enter the recipient's email address below:
Recipient: <input type="text" name="email" value="">
<input type="hidden" name="Id" value = "<%=Request.QueryString("Id")%>">
<input name="" type="submit">
</form>
```

And here's the *sendtofriend.asp* page code:

```
<%
Set objCDO = Server.CreateObject("CDONTS.NewMail")
objCDO.From = "youremail@paypalhacks.com"
objCDO.To = Request.Form("email")
objCDO.Subject = "Link from web site"
objCDO.Body ="Click the link to visit the web page
    http://yoursite.com/details.asp?Id=" & Request.Form("Id")
objCDO.Send( )
%>
<html>
The link has been sent.
</html>
```

The first block of code allows the site visitor to enter the email address she wants to send the link to. It also places the product's unique identifier value into a hidden variable. The form posts itself to the second block of code found on another web page. This page simply sends a link to the specified recipient and includes a link to the product details page based on the product Id passed. The recipient can then click on the link in her email message to go directly to this product's details page.

Using this type of procedure, you add product-specific functionality to your product details page that can help you increase sales and provide customized information.

Insert Dynamic Images

#56   Include product images with your dynamic storefront and use it to activate the PayPal payment process.

Once you've added dynamic storefront details [Hack #55] to your site, you can include a product image that can be used as a PayPal button, as shown in Figure 5-10. The idea is that customers typically look for the most obvious object to click when they're interested in a product, and turning the product image into a PayPal button is an effective way to get more customers to complete purchases.

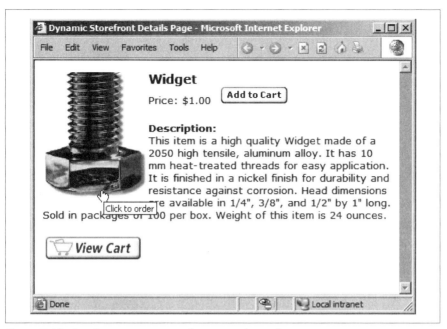

Figure 5-10. Displaying an image with your product information

Inserting the Image

Start by adding another database table column, image_file, to the tblProducts table created in "Create a Dynamic Storefront" **[Hack #54]** and populating it with the location (filename) of the image file to be displayed. So, for your widget, you might enter *widget.jpg*.

Next, take the code from "Add Dynamic Storefront Details" **[Hack #55]** and add the image_file column to your SQL query:

```
"SELECT item_name, item_number, item_price, Id, description, image_file
    FROM tblProducts WHERE Id = " & Id
```

> See the "Database Coding and Platform Choices" section of the Preface for the additional information needed to put this SQL statement to work with this and the other hacks in this book.

Then add your image file reference code to display the image on your product details page using the following line:

```
<img src="images/products/<%=rsProducts("image_field")%>">
```

In this example, the product images are stored in *images/products*. Insert this code in your page to include the dynamic image, just above the item name:

```
<img src="images/products/<%=rsProducts("image_field")%>">
Product: <%=rsProduct("item_name")%><br>
Price: <%=rsProduct("item_price")%><br>
<a href="detail.asp?id=<%=rsProducts("Id")%>>Product details, click here</a>
<br>
Click the button below to Buy<br>
<form target="paypal" action=
        "https://www.paypal.com/cgi-bin/webscr" method="post">
<input type="hidden" name="business" value="youremail@yourisp.com">
<input type="hidden" name="item_name" value="<%=rsProducts("item_name")%>">
<input type="hidden" name="item_number"
        value="<%=rsProducts("item_number")%>">
<input type="hidden" name="amount" value="<%=rsProducts("item_price")%>">
<input type="hidden" name="no_note" value="1">
<input type="hidden" name="currency_code" value="USD">
<input type="image" src="https://www.paypal.com/en_US/i/btn/x-click-but22.gif"
        border="0" name="submit">
<input type="hidden" name="add" value="1">
</form>
<br>
<%=rsProducts("description")%>
```

Link the Image to PayPal

To use the product image as a PayPal payment button, duplicate the purchase button code and replace the Buy Now image with the location of your product image [Hack #29]. The resulting code should look something like this:

```
<form target="paypal" action="https://www.paypal.com/cgi-bin/webscr"
        method="post">
<input type="hidden" name="business" value="youremail@yourisp.com">
<input type="hidden" name="item_name" value="<%=rsProducts("item_name")%>">
<input type="hidden" name="item_number"
        value="<%=rsProducts("item_number")%>">
<input type="hidden" name="amount" value="<%=rsProducts("item_price")%>">
<input type="hidden" name="no_note" value="1">
<input type="hidden" name="currency_code" value="USD">
<input type="image" src="images/products/<%=rsProducts("image_field")%>""
        border="0" name="submit">
<input type="hidden" name="add" value="1">
</form>

Product: <%=rsProduct("item_name"%><br>
Price: <%=rsProduct("item_price"%><br>
<a href="detail.asp?id=<%=rsProducts("Id")%>>Product details, click here</a>
<br>
Click the button below to Buy<br>
```

```
<form target="paypal" action="https://www.paypal.com/cgi-bin/webscr"
      method="post">
<input type="hidden" name="business" value="youremail@yourisp.com">
<input type="hidden" name="item_name" value="<%=rsProducts("item_name")%>">
<input type="hidden" name="item_number"
      value="<%=rsProducts("item_number")%>">
<input type="hidden" name="amount" value="<%=rsProducts("item_price")%>">
<input type="hidden" name="no_note" value="1">
<input type="hidden" name="currency_code" value="USD">
<input type="image" src="https://www.paypal.com/en_US/i/btn/x-click-but22.gif"
      border="0" name="submit">
<input type="hidden" name="add" value="1">
</form>
<br>
<%=rsProducts("description")%>
```

Of course, you might want to link the product image to a larger version of the image, a list of other products by the same manufacturer, or a page containing further details of the product. However, be careful not to discount the power of a big fat payment button on every product page: the easier it is for your customers to pay, the more likely they'll give you their business.

HACK #57 Build an Order-Tracking Page

Keep your customers informed of order status using an automated system.

The Internet sped up everything, including your customers' expectations. Once you have the code in place to display the merchant transaction ID on your return page [Hack #52] and insert payment details into a database [Hack #82], it's easy to create a page that enables customers to check on the status of an order. You need to place two new pages on your system: a query page that allows your customers to ask the question and a results page that gives them the answer. Figure 5-11 shows a completed results page.

An order-tracking page like this one is easy to implement and goes a long way in placating customers.

Asking the Question

The query page can be quite simple. All you need is a form that allows your customer to enter the transaction ID you previously provided. Once the customer clicks Submit, the results page takes over.

```
<html><body>
Enter the transaction ID corresponding to the order you wish to look up:
<form action="order_tracking.asp" method="post">
<input type="text" name="txn_id">
<input type="button" value="submit" name="submit">
```

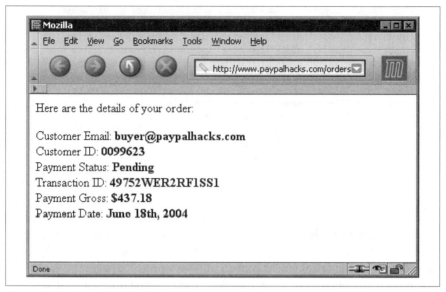

Figure 5-11. A completed order-tracking page

```
    </form>
    </body></html>
```

The form is only the beginning. Obviously, the preferred method is to display a list of all relevant transaction IDs, from which the customer can select one to view the transaction details. See "Quick-Link to Transaction Details" [Hack #22] for more information, as well as "Search for PayPal Transactions" [Hack #94] for a way to get this information using the PayPal API.

Getting the Answer

This example (especially the tblOrders table) assumes a database structure similar to the structure used in "Insert Payment Details into a Database with IPN" [Hack #82]. Any web scripting language will work for this task. This example uses ASP:

```
<%
'Read back customers input
Dim txn_id
Txn_id = Request ("txn_id")

'Connect to database and create recordset
connStore = "DRIVER={Microsoft Access Driver (*.mdb)};DBQ=
    "C:/InetPub/wwwroot/database/dbPayPal.mdb")
set rsOrder = Server.CreateObject("ADODB.Recordset")
rsOrder.ActiveConnection = connStore
```

```
rsOrder.Source = SELECT payer_email, payer_id, payment_status, txn_id,
    mc_gross, mc_fee, payment_date FROM tblOrders WHERE txn_id = '" &
    txn_id &"'"
rsOrder.Open( )
%>

<!--Check to see if the order information can be found; if so, display it.-->
<% If NOT rsOrder.EOF OR NOT rsOrder.BOF Then %>
Here are the details of your order:
<p>
Customer Email: <%=rsOrder("payer_email")%>
<br>Customer ID: <%=rsOrder("payer_id") %>
<br>Payment Status:  <%=rsOrder("payment_status") %>
<br>Transaction ID:   <%=rsOrder("txn_id") %>
<br>Payment Gross: <%=rsOrder("mc_gross") %>
<br>Payment Date: <%=rsOrder("payment_date") %>
<% Else %>
No matching Record Found. Please search again.
<% End If %>
```

Hacking the Hack

Here are a few ways you can extend this hack:

- Place another copy of the query form on the results page. This way, if your customers need to query for more than one transaction ID, they won't have to use their browser's Back button to enter another.

- Change the query page to accept a list of transaction IDs in a textarea box. Then modify the results page to display the results of searching for each.

- Use Instant Payment Notifications (IPN) to send an email with a tracking link [Hack #67].

Offer Discount Coupons

Reward good customers and entice new buyers with electronic coupons.

Everyone loves a sale. Customers like them because they get a bargain, and merchants like them because they increase sales. For instance, Amazon.com uses their Share the Love system to entice customers to advertise the products they've just purchased, in exchange for 10% off future purchases.

PayPal doesn't offer a built-in mechanism to process discounts, but you can set up electronic coupons for your customers with your own code. This hack provides two ways to pull it off: at the browser (a.k.a. client-side) with Java-Script, and at the server using Microsoft's Active Server Pages.

Accepting Coupons on the Client Side

While traditional coupons consist of slips of paper presented at the checkout counter of your local grocery store, electronic coupons are nothing more than distinct strings of numbers and letters.

This JavaScript-powered example allows a customer to specify a coupon code and then purchase an item at a discounted price:

```
<html>
<head>
<!-- -->
<script language = "JavaScript">
function on1Verify()
{
    var orderTotal=7.95;
    var on1Value=window.document.form1.on1.value;
    window.document.form1.on1.value="";
    if((on1Value < 990) && (on1Value > 988))
    {
      var newTotal=orderTotal-2;
      if(newTotal < 2)newTotal = 0;
      window.document.form1.on1.value="$2.00";
      window.document.form1.amount.value="$" + newTotal;
    }
    if((on1Value) < 989 || (on1Value > 989))
    {
      window.document.WEB_ORDER_FORM.on1.value=" -";
    }
}
</script>
</head>
<body>
<b>
<form name="form1" action="https://www.paypal.com/cgi-bin/webscr"
      method="post" target="paypal">
<input type="hidden" name="cmd" value="_cart">
<input type="hidden" name="add" value="1">
<input type="hidden" value="seller@example-domain.com" name="business">
<input type="hidden" name="item_name" value="Coupon Code 1">
<input type="hidden" name="item_number" value="001">
<input type="hidden" value="Selected" name="on0">Select<BR>
<select name="os0">
<option value="Option 1" selected>Option 1
<option value="Option 2">Option 2
<option value="Option 3">Option 3
</option>
</select><BR>
Enter Coupon number:<BR>
<input type="text" name="on1" size="10" onChange="on1Verify()">
<br><input type="hidden" value="DISCOUNT" name="os1">
Total amount due:<BR>
<input type="text" name="amount" value="7.95" size="10">
```

The circled numbers ❶ ❷ ❸ ❹ ❺ appear as annotations beside the corresponding code lines.

```
<input type="hidden" value="http://www.example-domain.com" name="return">
<input type="hidden" value="http://www.example-domain.com"
        name="cancel_return">
<BR>Shipping:<BR> <SELECT name="shipping">
<OPTION value="5.00" >Standard
<OPTION value="10.00" >Next Day
<OPTION value="15.00" >Over Night
</SELECT>
<input type="hidden" select_name="shipping" value="">
<input type="hidden" name="shipping2" value="5.00"> <BR>
Handling:<BR>
<input type="text" name="handling" value="2.00" size="10">
<p><input type="submit" value="Submit" name="B1">
</form></b>
</body>
</html>
```

Anyone who views the source of this page will be able to discover the code needed to obtain the discount. To avoid this problem, you might want to obfuscate your code **[Hack #36]** or use server-side coupon verification, as described later in this hack.

The normal price of the item is $7.95, as specified on lines ❶ and ❺. The customer enters a valid coupon code (here, the code 989 is tested on lines ❷ and ❹), the purchase price drops by $2.00 (line ❸). Figure 5-12 shows what the form looks like.

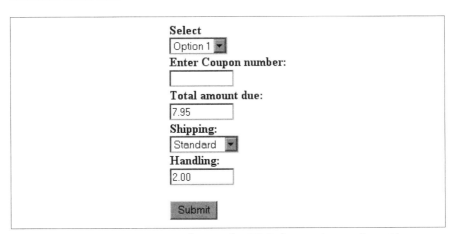

Figure 5-12. Processing coupons with a simple HTML form and some client-side JavaScript

Hacking the Hack

The code in the previous section is designed to accommodate a specific range of coupon codes. As shown, the range only allows 989, but you can increase this by changing line ❷ to:

```
if((on1Value > 5381)&&(on1Value < 5478))
```

and line 4 to:

```
if((on1Value < 5382) || (on1Value > 5477))
```

Doing so instructs the script to accept any coupon code between 5382 and 5473, inclusive.

Verifying Coupons on the Server Side

The previous solution shows how to use the browser for simple coupon processing, but for better security and more flexibility, you'll want to enable the discount at the server.

This example uses a special (presumably secret) URL to enable the discount. The URL itself serves as the coupon, and once your customer has visited this page, a discount of your choice will apply. From your customer's perspective, getting the discount price is simple:

1. The customer receives a promotional email from you that contains the coupon.

 Never send unsolicited email messages (also known as *spam*) to your customers. Let customers who want to hear about your specials *opt in* by adding their email addresses to your mailing list.

2. The customer clicks the coupon link, and the resulting page shows a "Thank You" or some other confirmation, followed by links to your shopping pages.

3. All applicable prices on your site subsequently reflect the discount for this customer.

Behind the scenes, the coupon page contains a script that sets a session variable for the customer's visit. Session variables are available with many scripting languages and are easy to implement with ASP, as in this example.

First, create the coupon page, the page shown to customers when they click your coupon links. This is also where the session variable is set:

```
<%
'Set the session variable
```

```
  Session("discount") = "true"
%>
<h1 align="center">Thanks for using your coupon</h1>
<p>Your discount has been enabled.</p>
<%
'Redirect to storefront
Response.Redirect("http://www.wwjcd.biz/shopping/")
%>
```

Give the script a particularly obscure URL to prevent customers from accidentally discovering it, such as:

```
http://www.wwjcd.biz/discount/farcvuznutz/discount.asp
```

Next, modify your PayPal buttons to check for the discount session variable:

```
<form action="https://www.paypal.com/cgi-bin/webscr" method="post">
<input type="hidden" name="cmd" value="_xclick">
<input type="hidden" name="business" value="sales@wwjcd.biz">
<input type="hidden" name="item_name" value="Jackie Chan Bobble Head">
<input type="hidden" name="item_number" value="BH-JC1">

<input type="hidden" name="no_note" value="1">
<input type="hidden" name="currency_code" value="USD">
<input type="image" src="https://www.paypal.com/en_US/i/btn/x-click-but23.gif"
       border="0" name="submit" alt="Make payments with PayPal - it's fast,
       free and secure!">
<% If Session("discount") = "true" Then %>
  <input type="hidden" name="amount" value=".90">
<% Else %>
  <input type="hidden" name="amount" value="1.00">
<% End If %>
</form>
```

Although you can see the code that checks for the discount setting (and the setting that is being checked), your buyers will never see it. Everything between the code markers (<% and %>) is processed and subsequently removed by your web server by the time your customers view the page.

HACK #59 Increase Search Engine Exposure

Modify the PayPal button code on your selling pages to make search engines spider them more effectively .

The most difficult part of selling your products on the Web is getting people to find them. If enough people visit your web page, sooner or later you will make a sale, regardless of what you are selling. It is just a matter of how many people need to see it before someone buys.

One of the most popular ways people find their ways to web sites is through search engines such as Yahoo!, Google, and MSN. These search engines create indexes that categorize and rank web pages based on their content. Most web page developers focus on the web page's text and metadata (such as its description and keywords).

However, there is one powerful, though often overlooked, tool that search engines weigh heavily: the web page's alt tags. Alt tags are used by non-graphical browsers and browsers for the visually impaired to help navigate through web pages easily. They can be used for a variety of HTML objects, but they are most commonly used in place of an image. This hack shows you how to use the alt tag in your PayPal buttons to increase search engine exposure.

Modifying the PayPal Button Factory Code

By default, the PayPal Button Factory creates the button code with the image's alt tag information populated with PayPal's own message: "Make payments with PayPal—it's fast, free and secure!" That could be useful in search engine ranking if a buyer is searching for sites that sell your item through PayPal. However, you can refine this text to increase the effectiveness of the tag. You can change many aspects of the PayPal form code [Hack #28] and still have the button function properly.

The item in this example is a widget that you are selling for one dollar. Combining that information with a few keywords increases the chances of having your web page spidered correctly. A better use for the alt content might be: "Buy a Thompson's widget here using PayPal for just $1." Here's an example in which the standard PayPal "Make payments..." message has been replaced with your own advertising:

```
<form action="https://www.paypal.com/cgi-bin/webscr" method="post">
<input type="hidden" name="cmd" value="_xclick">
<input type="hidden" name="business" value="sales@payloadz.com">
<input type="hidden" name="item_name" value="Widget">
<input type="hidden" name="item_number" value="Wid-001">
<input type="hidden" name="amount" value="1.00">
<input type="hidden" name="no_note" value="1">
<input type="hidden" name="currency_code" value="USD">
<input type="image" src="https://www.paypal.com/en_US/i/btn/x-click-but23.gif"
    border="0" name="submit" alt="Buy a Thompson's widget here using
    PayPal for just $1">
</form>
```

Applying the modified form code to your page increases the likelihood that when a person uses a search engine to look for a widget using a search engine, she is presented with your web page.

Hacking the Hack

You should also try to include keywords and description tags in your web page head that use the same keywords as you use in the alt attribute. This will give you a higher chance of being ranked for that text. You can also create duplicate form buttons, or even duplicate web pages, that use different sets of keywords in the document data and for the image alt tag values.

Sell Digital Goods with PayLoadz

#60   Deliver your digital goods automatically and securely without having to write your own application that relies on Instant Payment Notifications (IPN).

Using PayPal to sell goods from your web site allows your customers to make purchases without having to type all their financial information. Selling digital goods (documents, music, video, pictures, programs, etc.) affords the additional convenience of delivering your products over the Internet, rather than having to ship them, and comes as close to an ideal eCommerce scenario as you're going to get.

To sell digital goods online effectively with PayPal, you'll have to think about security and prompt fulfillment, both of which can be achieved with PayPal's Instant Payment Notification (IPN) system [Hack #73]. The problem is that IPN requires not only an ability to write code, but full access to a dedicated web server on which to run that code. This is where a third-party digital delivery provider such as PayLoadz (*http://www.payloadz.com*) comes in.

PayLoadz is a web-based service that allows you to sell digital goods securely, without user intervention, and—most importantly—without having to develop your own IPN system. Much like the way PayPal provides the back end for a pretty slick shopping cart system, PayLoadz provides the back end for IPN.

Before you get started with PayLoadz, you'll need a PayPal Business or Premiere account, as described in the introduction to Chapter 3.

Set up your free PayLoadz account by going to *http://payloadz.com* and clicking Sign Up. When the Edit Profile page appears, enter your business name and your PayPal email address (you won't need to provide your PayPal password). Specify URLs for your logo and for your cancel page, and customize the purchase email text.

With the Enable Price Checking feature, PayLoadz can check the amounts your customers pay to make sure they match the prices listed for your products. This works for mixed carts with your tangible goods [Hack #73] as well.

Turn on the IPN feature [Hack #65] in your PayPal account and insert the PayLoadz IPN script URL (provided for you when you sign up).

Then set up your digital goods on the PayLoadz web site so that it can handle fulfillment and track your sales, as shown in Figure 5-13.

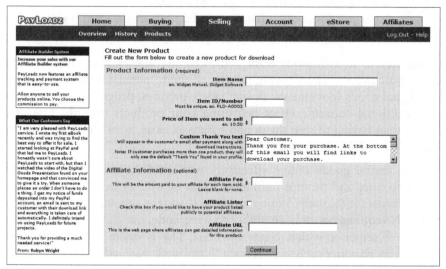

Figure 5-13. Setting up your digital goods at the PayLoadz web site

The PayLoadz system generates PayPal-compliant code that you add to your web pages, just like the code from the PayPal Button Factory [Hack #28].

While you can use your existing purchase buttons as generated by PayPal, the ones created by the PayLoadz system contain a customized return variable that allows your customers to download your products immediately after paying, which adds another level of redundancy to ensure proper delivery.

Finally, your customers click your special Pay Now buttons and are sent directly to PayPal to complete their transactions, as shown in Figure 5-14.

PayPal then contacts PayLoadz using IPN, and PayLoadz delivers your digital goods to your paying customers automatically, as shown in Figure 5-15).

Basic PayLoadz accounts are free, but for a monthly subscription fee (paid via PayPal, of course), you can store your files on the PayLoadz servers. This provides an enhanced level of security and means that you don't need to serve downloads from your own site. You can upgrade to the more robust paid version at any time.

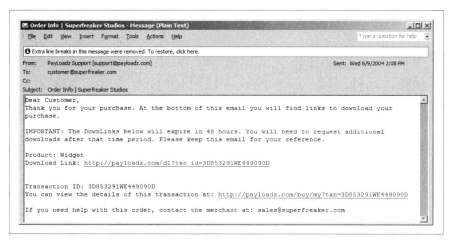

Figure 5-14. *An email directing the customer to the download*

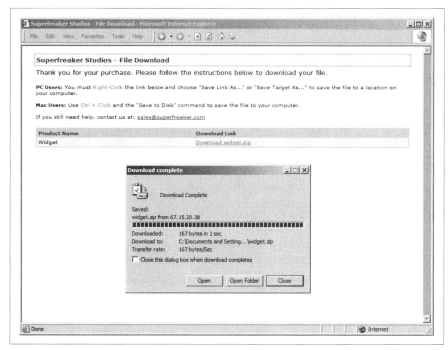

Figure 5-15. *Downloading files immediately after purchase*

See Also

To sell and deliver digital products on your own site, using your own code exclusively, see "Receive Instant Payment Notifications" [Hack #65].

## CHAPTER SIX

Managing Subscriptions
Hacks 61–64

Being paid once is a fine thing, but being paid repeatedly is fabulous. With a PayPal subscription button, you can offer your customers the chance to pay you again and again without any further human intervention. Subscription buttons allow you to collect automatically recurring payments easily for such things as club membership dues and monthly access to online content.

As mentioned in the introduction to Chapter 4, PayPal provides a tool to create subscription buttons for your site. Like ordinary Buy Now buttons, these are nothing more than HTML forms that can be placed on your pages. A customer clicks a Subscribe Now button to go to the PayPal site to confirm the new subscription, and the recurring payments begin.

For complete information about subscriptions and subscription buttons, see PayPal's Subscriptions and Recurring Payments Manual, available from within your PayPal account under the Merchant Tools tab. For now, keep a few facts in mind as you read this chapter:

- PayPal offers no facility for storing your content or for digital rights management (DRM) of your electronic resources. PayPal simply triggers regular payments from your buyers to you.

- Subscriptions can be canceled at any time by either you or your buyer. Use this as a selling point when asking customers to sign up. They will not require your cooperation if they decide to end the recurring payment.

 If you turn on Instant Payment Notification (IPN) [Hack #65], notice of any changes to your active subscriptions, such as cancellations, payments, or new subscriptions, will be sent to the IPN script you specify, and your server can take immediate action as necessary.

Sell Subscriptions to Your Online Content

Combine a database, PayPal subscriptions, and the IPN system to manage subscriber accounts.

If your web site offers something special that people are willing to pay for, such as access to a technical information database or specialized business-to-business commerce site, you might want to offer subscriptions. PayPal makes it easy. Using IPN, your web server, and your online database, you can easily create an entirely automated system.

> Many adult sites on the Internet are available on a subscription basis. Don't offer subscriptions to these sorts of sites with PayPal. Your site's content must be allowed under PayPal's Acceptable Use Policy; otherwise, you might find that your account has been limited [Hack #5].

For the purposes of this example, let's say you offer access to a Rhesus monkey marketing database for the low, low price of $30 per month. This opt-in database contains the monkey name, monkey age, caregiver name, and mailing address of over 10,000 monkeys across North America. You offer your subscribers, typically Rhesus monkey supply vendors, access to this information for marketing purposes.

You'll need four things to implement your subscription business model:

- A Subscribe button on your web site
- An online database that includes a subscribers table
- An IPN script to keep tabs on new, renewed, and expired subscriptions
- Dynamic pages that check a visitor's status before allowing access

Creating a Subscribe Button

The Subscribe button for your site can come straight from PayPal's button generator on the Merchant Tools page (log into PayPal and click the Merchant Tools tab). This example (created without encryption) should look familiar if you have created any unencrypted Buy Now or Donate Now buttons. The variables a3, p3, and t3 set the amount, period, and time unit of the subscription, respectively:

```
<html>
<head><title>Monkey Market Database</title></head>
<body>

<form action="https://www.paypal.com/cgi-bin/webscr" method="post">
```

```
<input type="image" src="https://www.paypal.com/en_US/i/btn/x-click-but20.gif"
    border="0" name="submit" alt="Make payments with PayPal - it's fast,
    free and secure!">
<input type="hidden" name="cmd" value="_xclick-subscriptions">
<input type="hidden" name="business" value="burchell@inebraska.com">
<input type="hidden" name="item_name" value="Monkey Market">
<input type="hidden" name="item_number" value="mm-1">
<input type="hidden" name="no_note" value="1">
<input type="hidden" name="currency_code" value="USD">
<input type="hidden" name="a3" value="30.00">
<input type="hidden" name="p3" value="1">
<input type="hidden" name="t3" value="M">
<input type="hidden" name="src" value="1">
</form>

</body>
</html>
```

Setting Up Your Database

Your access control database can be simple. A single table, shown in
Table 6-1, containing the email address and the password of your subscriber is all you need. For this example, the table subscribers contains two
alphanumeric fields: email and password. You could issue customer usernames to your subscribers, but you might be better served if you follow Pay-
Pal's example and use email addresses to identify users. Passwords can be
stored as plain text.

Table 6-1. A database to keep track of your subscribers

ID	email	password
4005	shannon@paypalhacks.com	sR3Du4#m77ca
4006	dave@paypalhacks.com	go3@c23-dad43
4007	david@paypalhacks.com	fae0v32c&ewf2

Processing Subscriber Notifications

You need to handle two kinds of notifications from PayPal: the addition of
new subscribers to your database when they sign up and removal of subscribers whose subscriptions lapse or are cancelled. Here's a snippet of ASP
that does this (see the "Database Coding and Platform Choices" section of
the Preface for database considerations):

```
<!-- Standard IPN processing here -->

<%

if Request.Form("txn_type") == "subscr_signup" then
```

```
' Add this subscriber to the database
' Use SQL like this:
set cInsSubscr = Server.CreateObject("ADODB.Command")
cInsSubscr.ActiveConnection = "DRIVER={Microsoft Access Driver
        (*.mdb)};DBQ="C:/InetPub/wwwroot/database/dbPayPal.mdb")
cInsSubscr.CommandText = "INSERT INTO subscriber (email, password) VALUES
    ( '" & Request.Form("payer_email") & "', 'drowssap')"
cInsSubscr.CommandType = 1
cInsSubscr.CommandTimeout = 0
cInsSubscr.Prepared = true
cInsSubscr.Execute( )

' Email the password to the new subscriber
elsif
Request.form("txn_type") == "subscr_cancel" then

' Remove a subscriber from the database
' Use SQL like this:
set cDelSubscr = Server.CreateObject("ADODB.Command")
cDelSubscr.ActiveConnection = "DRIVER={Microsoft Access Driver
        (*.mdb)};DBQ="C:/InetPub/wwwroot/database/dbPayPal.mdb")
cDelSubscr.CommandText = "DELETE * FROM subscriber WHERE email =
            '" & Request.Form("payer_email") & "'"
cDelSubscr.CommandType = 1
cDelSubscr.CommandTimeout = 0
cDelSubscr.Prepared = true
cDelSubscr.Execute( )

end

%>
```

 Don't really give every one of your subscribers the same password (drowssap in this example). Instead, use an algorithm for generating a password or let them choose a password for themselves in the subscription process.

Don't forget to turn on IPN in your PayPal account and point it at your IPN processing script [Hack #65].

Controlling Access to Your Valued Content

Now you have a list of valid subscribers that is automatically updated by PayPal and your IPN script. Next, you'll need to make use of this information by ensuring that visitors to your site are on the current subscriber list. In this example, all the members-only pages are dynamic ASP pages. The first thing the code does is check that the user is properly logged in. If not, the premium content is not displayed and the user is redirected to a Sign In page. You know the user is signed in if the *magic cookie* has been set.

```
<%
'content.asp
'Check for the magic cookie.
'If not found, redirect
if Response.Cookies("MagicMonkey) != "swordfish" then
 Response.Print("Please log in before accessing this page.")
 Response.Redirect("login.asp")
end
%>

<!-- Put your content here -->
```

The Sign In page simply asks for the user's email address and password. If this information shows the visitor is a valid subscriber, a cookie is set on the user's browser. The cookie contains the magic word that allows your subscribers access. Without this cookie, set to the proper magic word, no one can access subscriber-only content.

```
<%
'Sign in page: sign_in.asp
'Database connection code goes here
'Connect to database and create recordset
connStore = "DRIVER={Microsoft Access Driver (*.mdb)};
          DBQ="C:/InetPub/wwwroot/database/dbPayPal.mdb")
set rsCookies = Server.CreateObject("ADODB.Recordset")
rsCookies.ActiveConnection = connStore
rsCookies.Source = "SELECT * from subscribers WHERE email =
          '" & Request.Form("email") & "' AND password =
          '" & Request.Form("password") & "'"
rsCookies.Open( )

'IF the query turns up a match, execute this code:

'Set new cookie session in MagicMonkey
' "swordfish" happens to be today's magic cookie word
Response.Cookies("MagicMonkey") = "swordfish"

'Set cookie expiration
Response.Cookies("MagicMonkey").Expires = Now( ) + 1 'one day

Response.Print("Thank you for logging in. <a href="content.asp">Click
          here</a> to start selling stuff to a bunch of monkey lovers.")

'ELSE do this:

Response.Redirect("login.asp")
%>
```

Your page, *login.asp*, should contain an HTML form that asks for each customer's email address and password. Its data is posted to *sign_in.asp*.

Hacking the Hack

This example is purposefully simplistic. If the cookie is always the same, all a nonsubscriber needs to do to gain access is manually set the browser's cookies to include your magic word. In practice, you will want to change your magic cookie daily. Users will need to visit the Sign In screen each day and provide their email address and password to get that day's magic cookie. Better yet, use a one-way encryption algorithm to create a unique cookie each day for each subscriber.

Offer Tiered Subscriptions

Enhance simple subscription management to accommodate different levels of users.

Offering something of value for a small amount of money, and then selling your customer an upgrade to something of even greater value for a larger amount of money, is a great marketing plan. PayPal does this itself in a way; you can get some nice features for a low price (free) with a Personal account, and when you want more features you can upgrade to a Premier or Business account.

This hack shows you how to add *tiers* (or *service levels*) to your subscribers' accounts. You can create Subscribe buttons for each of your subscription levels, add a field to your database to indicate the subscriber's tier, check the tier of subscribers when users access pages, and give your customers an easy upgrade option.

Creating a Premium Subscription Button

Who knew the opportunities in marketing to lower primates? Thanks to a new partnership, you now own exclusive North American distribution rights to the customer data of Rhesus Research International, a leading monkey marketing firm in Europe and Asia (this example was introduced in "Sell Subscriptions to Your Online Content" [Hack #61]). You want to keep offering access to your North American data at the usual low price, but you want to add an option for buyers of your data who want to market to the rest of the world as well. Solve this problem by adding another subscription option at a higher price.

The following code includes the Subscribe button from "Sell Subscriptions to Your Online Content" [Hack #61] along with a new addition. Differences between the buttons are highlighted in bold:

```
<html>
<head><title>Monkey Market Database</title></head>
<body>

North American data only:
```

```
<form action="https://www.paypal.com/cgi-bin/webscr" method="post">
<input type="image" src="https://www.paypal.com/en_US/i/btn/x-click-but20.gif"
      border="0" name="submit" alt="Make payments with PayPal - it's fast,
      free and secure!">
<input type="hidden" name="cmd" value="_xclick-subscriptions">
<input type="hidden" name="business" value="burchell@inebraska.com">
<input type="hidden" name="item_name" value="Monkey Market">
<input type="hidden" name="item_number" value="mm-1">
<input type="hidden" name="no_note" value="1">
<input type="hidden" name="currency_code" value="USD">
<input type="hidden" name="a3" value="30.00">
<input type="hidden" name="p3" value="1">
<input type="hidden" name="t3" value="M">
<input type="hidden" name="src" value="1">
</form>
<br>

International option; includes Asia and Europe
<form action="https://www.paypal.com/cgi-bin/webscr" method="post">
<input type="image" src="https://www.paypal.com/en_US/i/btn/x-click-but20.gif"
      border="0" name="submit" alt="Make payments with PayPal - it's fast,
      free and secure!">
<input type="hidden" name="cmd" value="_xclick-subscriptions">
<input type="hidden" name="business" value="burchell@inebraska.com">
<input type="hidden" name="item_name" value="Monkey Market with
      International option">
<input type="hidden" name="item_number" value="mm-2">
<input type="hidden" name="no_note" value="1">
<input type="hidden" name="currency_code" value="USD">
<input type="hidden" name="a3" value="60.00">
<input type="hidden" name="p3" value="1">
<input type="hidden" name="t3" value="M">
<input type="hidden" name="src" value="1">
</form>

</body>
</html>
```

When subscriptions roll in, you (and your IPN script [Hack #65]) will be able to tell if they are standard or International by looking at the item_number.

Adding a Tier Field to Your Database

Modify your database (as shown in Table 6-2) to include a column called tier. This, along with the previously discussed [Hack #61] email and password, allows your system to keep track of the tier level for which your subscribers have paid.

Table 6-2. Adding a tier field to your database to keep track of subscriber levels

ID	email	password	tier
4005	shannon@paypalhacks.com	sR3Du4#m77ca	0
4006	dave@paypalhacks.com	go3@c23-dad43	1
4007	david@paypalhacks.com	faeOv32c&ewf2	2

Inserting Tier Information with Each New Subscription

Recall the approach to recording subscriptions **[Hack #61]** and modify the code to insert a value in the tier field based on the item_number reported:

```
<!-- Standard IPN processing here -->

<%

if Request.Form("txn_type") == "subscr_signup" then
 ' Add this subscriber to the database
 ' Is it an mm-1 or an mm-2 subscriber?
 If Request.Form("item_number") == "mm-1" then
 ' Use SQL like this:
  set cInsSubscr = Server.CreateObject("ADODB.Command")
  cInsSubscr.ActiveConnection = "DRIVER={Microsoft Access Driver (*.mdb)};
      DBQ="C:/InetPub/wwwroot/database/dbPayPal.mdb")
  cInsSubscr.CommandText = "INSERT INTO subscriber (email, password, tier)
      VALUES ( '" & Request.Form("payer_email") & "', 'drowssap', 1)"
  cInsSubscr.CommandType = 1
  cInsSubscr.CommandTimeout = 0
  cInsSubscr.Prepared = true
  cInsSubscr.Execute( )

 elsif Request.Form("item_number") == "mm-2" then

  set cInsSubscr = Server.CreateObject("ADODB.Command")
  cInsSubscr.ActiveConnection = "DRIVER={Microsoft Access Driver (*.mdb)};
      DBQ="C:/InetPub/wwwroot/database/dbPayPal.mdb")
  cInsSubscr.CommandText = "INSERT INTO subscriber (email, password, tier)
      VALUES ( '" & Request.Form("payer_email") & "', 'drowssap', 2)"
  cInsSubscr.CommandType = 1
  cInsSubscr.CommandTimeout = 0
  cInsSubscr.Prepared = true
  cInsSubscr.Execute( )

 end
 ' Email the password to the new subscriber
elsif
 Request.form("txn_type") == "subscr_cancel" then
 ' Remove a subscriber from the database
 ' Use SQL like this:

  set cInsPayment = Server.CreateObject("ADODB.Command")
```

```
    cInsPayment.ActiveConnection = "DRIVER={Microsoft Access Driver (*.mdb)};
        DBQ="C:/InetPub/wwwroot/database/dbPayPal.mdb")
    cInsPayment.CommandText = "DELETE * FROM subscriber WHERE email =
        '" & Request.Form("payer_email") & "'"
    cInsPayment.CommandType = 1
    cInsPayment.CommandTimeout = 0
    cInsPayment.Prepared = true
    cInsPayment.Execute( )

end

%>
```

Restricting Access Based on Tier

You will want to check for the magic cookie [Hack #61] before giving access to
pages. You will also want to set a cookie with its own secret word for the
tier. This page contains International content:

```
<%
'content_intl.asp
'Check for the magic cookie.
'If not found, redirect
if Response.Cookies("MagicMonkey") != "swordfish"
 or Response.Cookies("MagicMonkeyTier") != "lowtide" then
 Response.Print("Please log in before accessing this page.")
 Response.Redirect("login.asp")
end
%>

<!-- Put your content here -->
```

Don't forget to set the tier magic cookie word when subscribers log in:

```
<%
'Sign in page: sign_in.asp

'Connect to database and create recordset
connStore = "DRIVER={Microsoft Access Driver (*.mdb)};
        DBQ="C:/InetPub/wwwroot/database/dbPayPal.mdb")
set rsTier = Server.CreateObject("ADODB.Recordset")
rsTier.ActiveConnection = connStore
rsTier.Source = "SELECT tier FROM subscribers WHERE email =
        '" & Request.Form("email") & "' AND password =
        '" & Request.Form("password") & "'"
rsTier.Open( )

'Assign the result to tier
Dim tier
Tier = rsTier("tier")

'IF the query turns up a match, execute this code:
```

```
'Set new cookie session in MagicMonkey
'"swordfish" happens to be today's magic cookie word
Response.Cookies("MagicMonkey") = "swordfish"

'Set cookie expiration
Response.Cookies("MagicMonkey").Expires = Now() + 1 'one day

If tier > 1 then
 'Set International magic cookie
 Response.Cookies("MagicMonkeyTier") = "lowtide"

 'Set cookie expiration
 Response.Cookies("MagicMonkeyTier").Expires = Now() + 1 'one day
end

Response.Print("Thank you for logging in. <a href="content.asp">Click
    here</a> to start selling stuff to an International bunch of monkey
    lovers.")

'ELSE do this:

Response.Redirect("login.asp")
%>
```

Encouraging Subscribers to Upgrade

You can allow your current subscribers to upgrade to a better subscription by giving them a Modify Subscription button. Take the HTML code for your top-tier subscription and add a modify line. For example, the following code lets your original subscribers get on board with the new International offering:

```
Upgrade now to the new International option; includes Asia and Europe
<form action="https://www.paypal.com/cgi-bin/webscr" method="post">
<input type="image" src="https://www.paypal.com/en_US/i/btn/x-click-but20.gif"
    border="0" name="submit" alt="Make payments with PayPal - it's fast,
    free and secure!">
<input type="hidden" name="cmd" value="_xclick-subscriptions">
<input type="hidden" name="business" value="burchell@inebraska.com">
<input type="hidden" name="item_name" value="Monkey Market with
    International option">
<input type="hidden" name="item_number" value="mm-2">
<input type="hidden" name="no_note" value="1">
<input type="hidden" name="currency_code" value="USD">
<input type="hidden" name="a3" value="60.00">
<input type="hidden" name="p3" value="1">
<input type="hidden" name="t3" value="M">
<input type="hidden" name="src" value="1">
<input type="hidden" name="modify" value="2">
</form>
```

This can be a better solution than asking your customers to cancel one subscription and add another. Your records will also be simpler as a result, because PayPal will continue to use the same subscription ID in your records.

In your IPN script, add checking for a txn_type of subscr_modify. If you see that value, you need to change your database to reflect the new service tier. For example, your SQL might look like this:

```
"UPDATE subscriber SET tier =
        2 WHERE email = '" & Resquest.Form("email") & "'"
```

Time Your Subscriptions to End on Specific
#63 Dates

Use some simple JavaScript and PayPal's trial period to calculate the lengths
of new subscriptions, assuring they all expire at the same time.

Imagine you own a diaper service for Rhesus monkeys. Your customers subscribe by the month, and every month some customers allow their subscriptions to lapse. You need to get these customers back on board so you get some help from your brother-in-law Leon, a guy with a knack for bringing monkey owners around. Market research suggests lapsed subscribers are best contacted seven to nine days after dropping the service, just when the smell has started to get the attention of local law enforcement. But Leon doesn't want to call two or three people a day. He'd rather make 60 or 90 calls all at once.

PayPal doesn't offer a feature to set the date a subscription will expire; the subscription expires at a time that corresponds to the date the customer signed up. For example, a monthly subscription started on the 12th will run until the 12th of the next month. But you can use this hack to ensure that every new subscription will be billed on the first of the month, keeping Leon as happy as a Rhesus monkey in a fresh nappy.[*]

Hacking the Trial Period

One handy feature of PayPal's subscriptions is the trial period. It allows you to set an introductory price for new subscribers that changes to the standard rate when the trial period expires. For example, you might offer access to your online information service for $1 during a three-day trial period, after which the price jumps to $100 a month.

To time your subscriptions to expire on the same day, bend the terms of the trial period so that each customer is charged a prorated amount for the bal-

---

[*] No simians were harmed in the writing of this hack, with the possible exception of the author.

ance of the month, after which the standard monthly rate kicks in. The Java-Script code makes this easy by completing these tasks:

1. Calculate how many days are left in the current month.
2. Find the prorated price by dividing the monthly subscription fee by the number of days in a month (31 days in this example) and multiplying by the number of days left.
3. Stuff the calculated values into the subscription button when the buyer clicks Subscribe.

Just use this for your subscription sign-up page:

```
<html>
<head>
<title>Prorated Subscription</title>
</head>
<body>
<script language="JavaScript">
function CalcDate( ) {

var subend

//Set the start day to today
today=new Date( )

//Set the end date
//If it is December now, then the ending date needs to be January 1 of
    next year
if (today.getMonth == 12) {
  subend=new Date(today.getFullYear( )+1, 1, 1)
} else {
  subend=new Date(today.getFullYear( ), today.getMonth( )+1, 1)
}

//Set 1 day in milliseconds
var one_day=1000*60*60*24

//Calculate the difference between the two dates, convert to days, and put
    it in the day_count variable
var day_count = (Math.ceil((subend.getTime( )-today.getTime( ))/(one_day)))

//Set the subscription fee, then calculate the prorated value
var sub_fee = 10
var prorated_fee = Math.floor(((sub_fee/31)*day_count)*100)/100

//Write the values to the form on click
document.fmSubscribe.p1.value = day_count
document.fmSubscribe.a1.value = prorated_fee
}
</script>
```

```
<form action="https://www.paypal.com/cgi-bin/webscr"
      method="post" name="fmSubscribe">
<input type="image" src="https://www.paypal.com/en_US/i/btn/x-click-but20.gif"
      onClick="CalcDate()" border="0" name="submit">
<input type="hidden" name="cmd" value="_xclick-subscriptions">
<input type="hidden" name="business" value="burchell@inebraska.com">
<input type="hidden" name="item_name" value="Monkey Nappy Service">
<input type="hidden" name="item_number" value="Sub-001">
<input type="hidden" name="no_note" value="1">
<input type="hidden" name="currency_code" value="USD">
<input type="hidden" name="a3" value="10.00">
<input type="hidden" name="p3" value="1">
<input type="hidden" name="t3" value="M">
<input type="hidden" name="src" value="1">
<input type="hidden" name="sra" value="1">

<!-- Values for the "trial period" -->
<input type="hidden" name="a1" value="">
<input type="hidden" name="p1" value="">
<input type="hidden" name="t1" value="D">
</form>

</body>
</html>
```

Hacking the Hack

PayPal allows you to have two subscription trial periods. If you'd like to offer new subscribers a special rate and also have them all expire on the same schedule, use the first trial period for the discount (or even free) trial and the second trial period to prorate the balance of the month. Set the second trial period to the number of days left in the month after accounting for the days in the first trial.

For a three-day free trial, for instance, the trial period section of the button might look like this:

```
<!-- Values for the "trial period" -->
<input type="hidden" name="a1" value="0">
<input type="hidden" name="p1" value="3">
<input type="hidden" name="t1" value="D">
<input type="hidden" name="a2" value="">
<input type="hidden" name="p2" value="">
<input type="hidden" name="t2" value="D">
```

Don't forget to modify the JavaScript code to figure the end date of the second (prorated) trial period, which may fall at the end of *next* month.

HACK #64 Manage Subscription Passwords the Easy Way

Use PayPal's Password Management feature and a PayPal-provided Perl script to get a subscription service up and running quickly.

PayPal offers a subscription service [Hack #61] that enables you to set up your customers to pay you on a recurring basis. But if you offer access to an online resource, it can be a pain to manage all the subscribers manually. You'll have to monitor your PayPal account or email notifications, activate service each time you get a new subscriber, email customers their usernames and passwords, and deactivate the accounts of canceled subscribers precisely at each subscription's end of term. It goes on and on. That ain't any kind of fun.

If you are an experienced programmer, you can take advantage of Instant Payment Notifications (IPN) [Hack #65] to update subscriber lists and send out passwords automatically, but that requires a fair amount of knowledge, expertise, and patience. To help online merchants, PayPal offers a Password Management feature, including a complementary Perl script, that makes things much easier.

The Password Management feature takes PayPal's standard subscriptions service one step further by automatically generating usernames and passwords for your subscribers. PayPal displays the newly created username and password to each new subscriber upon signup. Subscribers should probably write them down, because they aren't memorable. For example, a username might be pp-cookankle with the password saga!glint. Occasionally, you'll get even stranger combinations!

Shortcut to the Subscription Page

Subscribers can always find their usernames and passwords in the subscription details page at the PayPal web site. You can provide your customers with a shortcut to this page with this link (where *merchant_email* is the email address of the merchant—in this case, you):

> *https://www.paypal.com/cgi-bin/webscr?cmd=_subscr-find*
> *&alias=merchant_email*

The link takes each subscriber to his own History page at PayPal and shows a list of any and all subscriptions purchased from you. Merchants can also pull down a list of subscribers, including usernames and passwords, in a downloadable log.

.htpasswd and .htaccess

To use Password Management, you must run your own Apache web server on Unix or Linux (or use a hosting provider that offers it; the vast majority of hosts do). Password Management works with the *.htpasswd* and *.htaccess* files used by Linux/Unix and Apache, as described at *http://httpd.apache.org/docs/ howto/auth.html*. Apache consults these password files before it allows (or denies) access to your premium content directories.

The Perl script in this hack works in conjunction with the Password Management option on the PayPal system, IPN, and your web server to automatically add and remove users from your *.htpasswd* and *.htaccess* files and thus provide immediate password-protected access to new subscribers.

> PerlDiver is a useful tool when deploying Perl scripts. It tells you the path to your home directory, the path to your sendmail program, and which Perl modules are installed on your server. All three are pertinent to Password Management installation. PerlDiver is available for free at *http:// www.scriptsolutions.com/programs/free/perldiver/*.

Getting the Code

Even though Perl is a programming language, you don't need to know how to program in order to install this script successfully. Familiarity with Perl is, of course, helpful, as is some experience in creating and editing files and directories on Unix or Linux systems.

It's usually possible to perform a complete installation using File Transfer Protocol (FTP)—a method of transferring files between computers—to upload the file to your server. If not, you might need to connect to your server with Telnet or SSH (or with some other server access program provided by your hosting provider). In any event, use the method with which you are most comfortable.

First, obtain the PayPal Perl script from the PayPal web site:

1. Log into PayPal and click the Merchant Tools tab.
2. Click Subscriptions and Recurring Payments.

> While you're here, make note of the Subscriptions Password Management checkbox. To use Password Management for a subscription, you'll need to enable this feature.

3. Click the "IPN and server modifications" link.
4. Click the "Download Perl script" link and save the Manual and Script to your hard drive.

The script is packed into a gzipped TAR file. Windows users can use WinZip (*http://www.winzip.com*) to decompress this file. Unix and Mac OS X users should go to the command line and type gunzip paypal.tar.gz and then tar xvf paypal.tar to extract the script and *README* file.

The complete installation instructions are too lengthy to discuss here, but the manual provided by PayPal does a decent job. Among other things, the manual covers the setup of basic authentication with Apache, installation and configuration of the script, and updates you'll need to make your Pay-Pal account configure IPN.

The PayPal manual sometimes refers to the password file as *.htpassword* (as opposed to the more standard *.htpasswd*). This is okay; the file can be named anything you choose, so long as it is referenced properly in your Perl script and Apache configuration files.

For your reference, Figure 6-1 shows a typical directory structure for a web site. Unfortunately, every hosting provider seems to have a different naming convention and organizational structure, so this hierarchy will probably be slightly different from what you find on your web server.

Figure 6-1. A typical hierarchy of directories and files that make up a web server

If you encounter any problems, make sure your files are installed to the correct locations, that you've set the file privileges with chmod, and that the file location of your *.htaccess* file is specified in your *paypal.pl* Perl script.

Once you have everything set up, you should give it a thorough testing and then roll it out to your customers. The script will handle incoming Instant Payment Notifications and make updates to your password files automatically.

Adding Users Manually

In order to manage users on your web site manually, open your *.htpasswd* file for editing (any plain-text editor will do). You'll notice that it is made up of a long list of text strings that look like this: pp-oaktunnel:8fusre9fhs. The first part is the PayPal-generated username, the second part is a scrambled version of the password, and the two are separated by a colon (:). The Pay-Pal Perl script automatically inserts and deletes lines in this file.

To remove a user, simply delete the corresponding line from the file. Or, to temporarily disable a subscriber's access without deleting the line altogether, just add the word OFF in front of the user's password. You can reinstate access by removing the OFF prefix at any time.

> When you are just getting started with a Password Management installation, you'll probably want to set up some temporary user accounts for testing purposes. Adding a few test accounts here means that you don't have to set up secondary PayPal accounts and purchase subscriptions from yourself just to test the system.

Adding users is a little more complicated, because the passwords are scrambled with the Unix crypt( ) function. The easiest way to generate an encrypted password is to use a web-based tool such as the one at *http://www.earthlink.net/cgi-bin/pwgenerator.pl*. Next, insert the username:password combo just as you would edit any other file on your web server. If you add a username:password combination to the end of the list, make sure to press Return or Enter so that your cursor moves to the next line before you save the file.

If you want to add a user from the Unix command line (and without having to edit the *.htpasswd* file manually), use the htpasswd utility that comes with Apache, like this:

```
htpasswd -b -d /usr/web/mysite.com/.htpasswd newuser newpass
```

In this command, */usr/web/mysite.com* is the full path of your *.htpasswd* file, and *newuser* and *newpass* are the username and password of the new user, respectively.

Hacking the Hack

There are some commonly requested enhancements to the *paypal.pl* Perl script that are reasonably easy and safe to perform:

Multiple currencies
   The *paypal.pl* Perl script supports subscriptions funded by U.S. dollars (USD) only, but you can modify it to support the other currencies that PayPal uses (GBP, CAD, JPY, and EUR).

Multiple subscription terms

PayPal's Perl script handles only one set of subscription terms. However, you can add support for a more complicated pricing structure, such as discounts for longer-term commitments.

Consider the following hypothetical subscription. You'd like to charge your customers 10 euros per month, or 100 euros annually for subscribers who sign on for a full year (the annual rate provides a savings of 20 euros).

The PayPal signup button for 10 euros per month would then look like this:

```
<form method="post" action="https://www.paypal.com/cgi-bin/webscr">
<input type="hidden" name="cmd" value="_xclik-subscriptions">
<input type="hidden" name="business" value="pay@paypalhacks.com">
<input type="hidden" name="a3" value="10.00">
<input type="hidden" name="p3" value="M">
<input type="hidden" name="t3" value="1">
<input type="hidden" name="currency_code" value="EUR">
<input type="hidden" name="src" value="1">
<input type="submit" value="10.00 Euros per Month">
</form>
```

And the button for 100 euros per year would look like this:

```
<form method="post" action="https://www.paypal.com/cgi-bin/webscr">
<input type="hidden" name="cmd" value="_xclik-subscriptions">
<input type="hidden" name="business" value="pay@paypalhacks.com">
<input type="hidden" name="a3" value="100.00">
<input type="hidden" name="p3" value="Y">
<input type="hidden" name="t3" value="1">
<input type="hidden" name="currency_code" value="EUR">
<input type="hidden" name="src" value="1">
<input type="submit" value="100.00 Euros per Year">
</form>
```

To enable both of these scenarios, make the following edits to the *paypal.pl* script. First, replace these lines from the *paypal.pl* script:

```
# If you have an initial trial period set it here. For example one
# month would be '1 M'
my $PERIOD1 = '';

# If you have a second trial period set it here. For example one
# month would be '1 M'
my $PERIOD2 = '';

# Set this to your recurring or normal period. For example one
# month would be '1 M'
my $PERIOD3 = '1 M';

# Set this to the dollar amount for your initial trial period. For
# example a free trial would be '0.00'
my $AMOUNT1 = '';
```

```
# Set this to the dollar amount for your second trial period. For
# example a $1.00 trial would be '1.00'
my $AMOUNT2 = '';

# Set this to the dollar amount for your recurring or normal period.
# For example $1.00 would be '1.00'
my $AMOUNT3 = '10.00';
```

with this code:

```
# Join button a
my $PERIOD1a = '';
my $AMOUNT1a = '';
my $PERIOD3a = '1 M';
my $AMOUNT3a = '10.00';

# Join button b
my $PERIOD1b = '';
my $AMOUNT1b = '';
my $PERIOD3b = '1 Y';
my $AMOUNT3b = '100.00';

# Join button c
my $PERIOD1c = '';
my $AMOUNT1c = '';
my $PERIOD3c = '';
my $AMOUNT3c = '';

my $CURRENCY = 'EUR';
```

This example allows you to configure up to three subscription tiers; just fill in the details of your subscriptions here.

 This modification doesn't support the middle subscription period, PERIOD2, which is seldom used.

Next, replace these lines:

```
sub validate_signup {
  # validate the terms and amounts
  if ((param("period1") ne $PERIOD1)
     || (param("period2") ne $PERIOD2)
     || (param("period3") ne $PERIOD3)
     || (param("amount1") ne $AMOUNT1)
     || (param("amount2") ne $AMOUNT2)
     || (param("amount3") ne $AMOUNT3)) {
    error_notify("This customer did not sign-up according to your payment
       terms. Although payment was accepted the account was not activated.",
       "validate subscription terms", 0, 1);
    return undef;
```

with this code:

```perl
sub match_terms {
  # validate the terms and amounts
  my $p1 = shift;
  my $a1 = shift;
  my $p3 = shift;
  my $a3 = shift;

  if (($p1 eq param("period1") && $a1 eq param("mc_amount1")) &&
    ($PERIOD2 eq param("period2") && $AMOUNT2 eq param("mc_amount2"))&&
    ($p3 eq param("period3") && $a3 eq param("mc_amount3")) &&
      ($CURRENCY eq param("$mc_currency"))) {
      return 1;
  } else {
      return undef;
  }
}

sub validate_signup {
  # validate the terms and amounts
  if (match_terms($PERIOD1a, $AMOUNT1a, $PERIOD3a, $AMOUNT3a) ||
    match_terms($PERIOD1b, $AMOUNT1b, $PERIOD3b, $AMOUNT3b) ||
    match_terms($PERIOD1c, $AMOUNT1c, $PERIOD3c, $AMOUNT3c)) {
  } else {
      error_notify("Although payment was accepted the account was not
activated.",
                "validate subscription terms", 0, 1);
      return undef;
  }
}
```

See Also

For information on Apache's password protection for directories and tools
to modify the *.htpasswd* file, see *Apache: The Definitive Guide* by Ben Laurie
and Peter Laurie (O'Reilly).

— *Patrick Breitenbach and Dave Burchell*

## CHAPTER SEVEN

IPN and PDT
Hacks 65–86

One of the questions asked most often by merchants considering PayPal as a payment processor is, "How will I know when the customer pays?" If a merchant is employing any sort of automation or digital fulfillment, the question becomes, "How will my site know when the customer pays?" Obviously, since customers must leave your site to complete payment at the PayPal web site, your site (or its database) won't know when your customer has paid until it has been notified by PayPal.

To that end, PayPal has developed two technologies for developers: Instant Payment Notification (IPN) and Payment Data Transfer (PDT). These technologies notify the merchant's web server when payment has been attempted, whether or not it was successful, and details about the sale.

What IPN and PDT Are

Instant Payment Notification (IPN) is a means by which PayPal contacts your server directly every time a transaction completes; in other words, IPN is a call-back routine and part of an asynchronous process (in that the notification can happen any time after the transaction). This design has its benefits, such as accommodating eChecks that can take three to four days to process.

Payment Data Transfer (PDT), on the other hand, is fueled directly by your customer's actions. First, you enable PayPal's Auto Return feature, such that when a payment is completed, the customer is immediately returned to your site, along with some transaction information. Restricting the navigation options in this way drives the payment process in a linear (and thus synchronous) fashion, making the PayPal transaction virtually seamless to your customer. The site is notified of the payment immediately, and your more impatient customers might not head for the complaint box so quickly.

The big advantage of IPN over PDT is that the PayPal server keeps trying until it successfully notifies your server of a transaction (if the customer closes the browser window or clicks the browser's Stop button, a PDT will be interrupted). The big advantage of PDT, on the other hand, is that the customer doesn't have to wait for the asynchronous IPN transaction to take place (IPN usually happens within a few seconds, but it can take up to four days in extreme cases).

IPN and PDT aren't necessarily mutually exclusive; in fact, there are times when you'd want to use both technologies. For instance, say you're selling downloadable software (known in the trade as *digital fulfillment*). You might choose to employ PDT so that a customer could pay and be immediately sent to a download page, without having to wait for a confirmation email. But you might also employ IPN so that you could be certain that any and all transactions were recorded automatically by your server and that your customer could return to your site days later and still retrieve your product.

How IPN Works

Simply put, IPN is the means by which PayPal can inform your server of a payment, a change in payment status, or other, possibly more urgent information. IPN differs from nearly every other way merchants use PayPal, because the IPN transaction is initiated by PayPal. Except for IPN (and PDT), all parts of the PayPal system are *user initiated*: nothing happens unless you, as the account holder, take action. IPN, on the other hand, can be triggered at any time (even when you are not at your computer), hours or even days after the last payment was made to your account.

IPN carries out this communication using HTTP, the same protocol used when you access the PayPal system with your web browser. In the case of IPN, however, roles are reversed: PayPal acts as an automated browser, making a request of your web site, which acts as the web server. This swapping of traditional positions can be confusing, but once you know that IPN posts originate at PayPal and request the IPN script on your site just like any other web browser on the Internet might, IPN becomes much easier to *grok*.*

---

* To make full use of IPN, it's helpful to profoundly understand the process. To *grok* the concepts involved (as opposed to merely grasping them), helps elevate you to the status of Geek. (The term *grok* was coined by Robert A. Heinlein in his novel *Stranger in a Strange Land*.)

To get started with IPN, see "Receive Instant Payment Notifications" [Hack #65].

Advantages of PDT

The advantage of using PDT over IPN is that it enables you to track orders more efficiently. The best way to think about PDT is to consider where it fits in the three steps of a customer purchase:

1. Your customer selects what he wants to buy on your web site, and during the checkout process, all the order items are handed to PayPal.

2. PayPal processes the payment and confirms the sale to the user on the PayPal web site and via email.

3. Your site receives the order information via PDT, records the sale in your site's database (if you so choose), and shows the user a nice receipt, tailored to the order.

This is a much cleaner transaction experience for your customers than the process afforded by IPN, because they can see their order results immediately on your site. It also allows you to track only those orders that have been completed.

To get started with PDT, see "Process Payments like a Credit Card with PDT" [Hack #85].

—Rob Conery and Dave Burchell

HACK #65 Receive Instant Payment Notifications

Set up the IPN system to have PayPal automatically send transaction details to your server to process immediately after receiving a payment.

PayPal makes it easy for merchants to accept payments by placing payment buttons on their web sites. While this system can be sufficient to initiate transactions, it does nothing to help process payments once they're made. IPN fills this gap.

PayPal's IPN feature sends a behind-the-scenes server-to-server post to a page of your choice, almost instantly after a customer clicks the Pay button and completes the transaction at the PayPal web site.

To begin using IPN, log into PayPal, click Profile, and then click Instant Payment Notification Preferences to see the screen shown in Figure 7-1. Turn on the feature by checking the box, and then specify the URL of the script on your server that you would like to receive the transaction details.

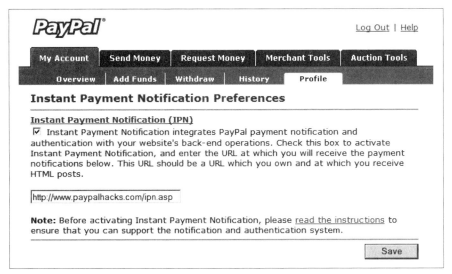

Figure 7-1. Using the Instant Payment Notification Preferences page to enable IPN and specify the location of your transaction-processing script

The address you specify will never be seen by your customers and should contain only Common Gateway Interface (CGI) code or dynamic server technology, such as PHP, JSP, Perl, or ASP (explained later in this hack).

The Code

Here is the sample IPN code, which is available from the PayPal web site. It's written in VBScript for Active Server Pages (ASP), which means you need a server capable of handling Microsoft Active Server Pages. If you'd rather develop your IPN script in Perl, PHP, or JSP, you can get the corresponding sample code at *http://www.paypal.com*, but the concepts discussed here will be the same, regardless of the platform you're using (see the "Database Coding and Platform Choices" section of the Preface for further information).

```
<%@LANGUAGE="VBScript"%>
<%
Dim Item_name, Item_number, Payment_status, Payment_amount
Dim Txn_id, Receiver_email, Payer_email
Dim objHttp, str

' read post from PayPal system and add 'cmd'
str = Request.Form & "&cmd=_notify-validate"
```

```
' post back to PayPal system to validate
set objHttp = Server.CreateObject("Msxml2.ServerXMLHTTP")
objHttp.open "POST", "https://www.paypal.com/cgi-bin/webscr", false
objHttp.setRequestHeader "Content-type", "application/x-www-form-urlencoded"
objHttp.Send str

' assign posted variables to local variables
Item_name = Request.Form("item_name")
Item_number = Request.Form("item_number")
Payment_status = Request.Form("payment_status")
Payment_amount = Request.Form("mc_gross")
Payment_currency = Request.Form("mc_currency")
Txn_id = Request.Form("txn_id")
Receiver_email = Request.Form("receiver_email")
Payer_email = Request.Form("payer_email")

' Check notification validation
if (objHttp.status <> 200 ) then
 ' HTTP error handling
elseif (objHttp.responseText = "VERIFIED") then
 if Payment_status = "Completed" Then
  ' check that Txn_id has not been previously processed
  ' check that Receiver_email is your Primary PayPal email
  if Receiver_email = "youremail@yourisp.com" Then 'Email is correct
  ' check that Payment_amount/Payment_currency are correct
  ' process payment
  end If
 end If
elseif (objHttp.responseText = "INVALID") then
 ' log for manual investigation
else
 ' error
end if
set objHttp = nothing
%>
```

(Bullet markers along left margin: ❶ at Item_name line, ❷ at Payer_email line, ❸ at `if Payment_status = "Completed" Then`, ❹ at `' check that Txn_id`, ❺ at `if Receiver_email =`, ❻ at `' process payment`, ❼ at `end If`)

Running the Code

The first section of code with which to be concerned, from line ❶ to line ❷, retrieves the values passed to you by PayPal and assigns them to variables. Field formats and descriptions for the 50 supported variables can be found in the Integration Guide, available at *https://www.paypal.com/ipn*.

The next section, from line ❸ to ❼, contains code to check the transaction and process the order. Simply replace the commented lines of pseudocode with your own code.

Now, you'll need to complete several steps to process a transaction. The first If/Then statement (line ❸) checks to see if the Payment_status variable has a value of Completed.

Next, you'll need to check that the transaction ID has not been previously processed (line ❹). One way to accomplish this is to record the txn_id value into a database [Hack #54]. Then, query the table, pull the results into a recordset named rsCheck, and then check to see whether the record exists:

```
' check that Txn_id has not been previously processed:
connStore = "DRIVER={Microsoft Access Driver (*.mdb)};
    DBQ="C:/InetPub/wwwroot/database/dbPayPal.mdb")
set rsCheck = Server.CreateObject("ADODB.Recordset")
rsCheck.ActiveConnection = connStore
rsCheck.Source = "SELECT txn_id FROM tblOrders WHERE txn_id =
    '" & txn_id & "'"
rsCheck.Open( )

If rsCheck.EOF And rsCheck.BOF Then 'Not a duplicate, continue processing
 ' check that Receiver_email is your Primary PayPal email
 ' check that Payment_amount/Payment_currency are correct
 ' process payment
End If
```

> See the "Database Coding and Platform Choices" section of the Preface for the additional information needed to put this SQL statement to work with this and the other hacks in this book.

You might want to process pending payments (typically from eChecks) so that you can automatically notify customers that there will be a delay in fulfilling the order. If the payment_status value is Pending, you can record the pending payment into your database table, but you will also need to adjust your duplicate transaction query to ignore the pending transactions you would otherwise be recording. Pending payments ultimately post two notifications to your IPN script: one when the purchase is made (with a status of Pending) and a second when the payment has cleared (with a status of Completed).

Finally, the check on line ❺ compares the recipient's email address with your address to ensure that the IPN was not spoofed. You also want to make sure that the price has not been tampered with [Hack #73]. When all is said and done, replace line ❻ with your own server logic to process the order.

HACK #66 Troubleshoot Instant Payment Notifications

Effectively diagnose processing problems and overcome some of IPN's stumbling blocks.

The IPN system is one of the most powerful features of the PayPal system. Deploying it requires a certain level of programming skill, but even with perfect programming, there can be issues that arise in deploying any new system for the first time. In the case of implementing IPN, there are several things you can do to help diagnose any issues that arise.

The first step in testing your IPN system is to make a live purchase on the system so that the script gets called by PayPal [Hack #65].

Adding Email to IPN

A good way to help diagnose problems is to have your IPN processing page send you all the variables and their values as they were posted to the PayPal site. You can do this by inserting a server mail component function that emails you the complete form post from PayPal when your IPN page is called. You can add the code to send an email and also to include a switch to turn this function on and off with the following code, written in VBScript for Active Server Pages:

```
Dim vTesting
vTesting = 1 'Uncomment for test mode on
'vTesting = 0 'Uncomment for test mode off
If vTesting = 1 Then 'Send test email
 Dim TestCDO
 Set TestCDO = Server.CreateObject("CDONTS.NewMail")
 TestCDO.From = "youremail@yourisp.com"
 TestCDO.To = "youremail@yourisp.com"
 TestCDO.Subject = "IPN Variables"
 TestCDO.Body = Request.Form( )
 TestCDO.Send( )
 Set TestCDO = Nothing
End If
```

With this code added to the basic IPN processing code [Hack #65], the IPN page sends you an email with all the transaction data as posted by PayPal. This can help you determine whether the problems are with the data being passed back.

Using a Return URL

The next way to test your IPN script is to check to see if your IPN page is throwing any errors. You can do this easily by redirecting to your IPN page after payment (using the return variable) and having the IPN information sent when you hit the page. This provides the same functionality that normally occurs behind the scenes, except you are able to see it firsthand. You need to add the following code to your test purchase button to accomplish this:

```
<input type="hidden" name="rm" value="2">
<input type="hidden" name="return" value="http://yoursite.com/ipn.asp">
```

When this code is added to your purchase button, PayPal redirects you back to your IPN script after payment and a form post is sent that allows you to see if the page has an error on it.

 If you're using Internet Explorer, you should also configure your browser to show descriptive server errors by disabling the "Show friendly HTTP error messages" option, found in Tools → Internet Options → Advanced. Now, when a page with an error is loaded, you'll get a descriptive message regarding the error and the line on which it occurred.

Capturing Errors

One way to find out if your IPN script is causing an error is to insert error-capturing code within your IPN page. When a page error occurs, you can get an email letting you know that an error has occurred and what the error was. This example uses ASP written in VBScript. First, you have to add the following piece of code to the top of your IPN page:

```
<% On Error Resume Next %>
```

That line makes sure that the page continues to process if an error is detected. Then, at the bottom of your IPN page, insert the following:

```
<%
ErrorCheck( )
Function ErrorCheck( )
  If Err.Number <> 0 then   'if there is an error then the html table will be
      written out
  Dim ErrorCDO
  Set ErrorCDO = Server.CreateObject("CDONTS.NewMail")
  ErrorCDO.From = "youremail@yourisp.com"
  ErrorCDO.To = "youremail@yourisp.com"
  ErrorCDO.Subject = "IPN Error"
  ErrorCDO.Body = "Error: " & Err.Number & " " & VbCrLf & "Description: " &
      Err.Description & ""
  ErrorCDO.Send( )
  Set ErrorCDO = Nothing
  End If
End Function
%>
```

Once you add this code to your IPN script, you'll be notified via email when an error has occurred.

Since the page uses an On Error Resume Next statement, it assumes that the post worked properly and does not send an error back to the PayPal system or try again. Without this statement, PayPal would continue to repost the information back to your IPN script until it was successful. Therefore, you should use this technique only during testing phases and not in a live implementation.

Using a Third-Party Testing Script

Another easy way to test your IPN page is to use a third-party testing script that simulates a PayPal purchase to your IPN script without having to make an actual purchase. The best third-party testing script is located at *http://www.eliteweaver.co.uk/testing/ipntest.php*. Test your script by simply entering your IPN page's web address. You also have to change the following line in your IPN page (the postback line) so your script does not try to send the posted data back to PayPal as it causes an Invalid response from their system:

```
objHttp.open "POST", "https://www.paypal.com/cgi-bin/webscr", false
```

Change it like so:

```
objHttp.open "POST", "http://www.eliteweaver.co.uk/cgi-bin/webscr", false
```

Then, you can fill in the script form with any information you like and submit it to simulate the post to your IPN script. You can find a list of all available testing scripts at *http://www.paypal.com/cgi-bin/webscr?cmd=p/pdn/3p-solutions-ipntools-outside*.

HACK #67 Send a Purchase Confirmation Email with IPN

Automate communication with customers by sending simple order-confirmation emails.

In this hack, your web server uses IPN to learn about purchases a customer makes and sends the customer an email confirming her purchase. To use this hack, you need to have an environment that allows you to execute server-side scripts that can send email. This example uses Microsoft's Active Server Pages (ASP), but the concepts apply to any scripting language you choose.

Before using this example, set up and test the basic IPN script described in "Receive Instant Payment Notifications" [Hack #65]. You'll add the code presented here to that basic script, giving your system the ability to send email messages to customers after each purchase.

All popular web scripting environments provide a tool for sending electronic mail. Microsoft Windows server environments, for example, have a Common Data Objects (CDO) mail component preinstalled. Regardless of the platform, the email messages require a subject, a message body, the recipient's address, and the sender's address. You can find the recipient's address and other information about the sale in the IPN posting, such as the payer_email variable:

```
Payer_email = Request.Form("payer_email")
```

The Code

Place this code in your IPN script after the IPN information has been verified. In PayPal's sample scripts, the following code should appear at the 'process payment comment:

```
'Get the customer's email address
Dim payer_email
Payer_email = Request.Form("payer_email")

'Get information about the purchase the customer made
Dim item_name, item_number
Item_name = Request.Form("item_name")
Item_number = Request.Form("item_number")

'Create the body of the email
Dim mail_body
Mail_body = "Thank you for your order. Below are the details." & VbCrLf
        & "Item Name: " & item_name & VbCrLf & "Item Number: "
        & item_number & ""

'Create an email object and send the message
Dim MailCDO
Set MailCDO = Server.CreateObject("CDONTS.NewMail")
MailCDO.From = "sales@yoursite.com"
MailCDO.To = payer_email
MailCDO.Subject = "Order Information"
MailCDO.Body = mail_body
MailCDO.Send( )
Set MailCDO = Nothing
```

When your site makes a sale, the code is executed and an email is sent to the customer verifying her order information. Keeping your customer informed in this way is a good practice, because it assures the customer that she made the purchase she intended to, and builds your reputation as a responsive merchant.

Process Shopping Carts with IPN

#68   Modify your IPN code to handle multiple products purchased through PayPal's Shopping Cart system.

When a payment is made for a good on the PayPal system through Single Item Purchase or Web Accept buttons, the product information is passed back to your IPN page in the same format as that in which it was submitted. This means your IPN processing page has to handle only one set of values in order to process the order. In the case of Shopping Cart purchases, your IPN page can expect to receive product information for one or more items. It needs to be able to handle this scenario effectively in order to process orders without errors.

In order for your page to be able to work with both Web Accept and Shopping Cart orders, you need to check which type of payment is being made, to see how many items are being ordered (if the order is a Shopping Cart), and finally, to populate the variable values accordingly for each item in the cart.

The Code

Here is a block of ASP VBScript code written in two sections. The first handles orders from Shopping Carts and the second handles orders for Single Item Purchases. They are used together in a single IPN page:

```
If txn_type = "cart" Then 'Shopping cart purchase

Dim num_cart_items, i
num_cart_items = Request.Form("num_cart_items")

For i=1 to num_cart_items
Request.Form("item_name" & i)
Request.Form("item_number" & i)
Request.Form("option_name1_" & i)
Request.Form("option_selection1_" & i)
Next

Else 'Not a shopping cart purchase

Request.Form("item_name")
Request.Form("item_number")
Request.Form("option_name1")
Request.Form("option_selection1")

End If
```

The Results

When the block of code is executed on your IPN page (place it after the code from "Receive Instant Payment Notifications" [Hack #65]) after a payment has been made, it uses the txn_type variable to determine whether the payment is being made for a Shopping Cart purchase. If txn_type is set to cart, the payment is for a Shopping Cart and the first block of code in the If/Then statement will be executed.

Within the If/Then statement, you initially pull into the num_cart_items the number of items that have been purchased. Using that value, you then perform a For/Next loop that takes the number of items in the cart and executes a block of code that number of times. In this case, the block of code simply requests the values of the variables as they have been passed back. Your code can perform other functions, but in order to use the values for the items in the cart, they must be called using this format.

If the purchase is not for a Shopping Cart, but for a Single Item Purchase or Web Accept, the second block of code runs and creates only one set of product variables. In this case, you can call the variable values using the same form element names that were posted to the PayPal system initially.

HACK #69 Use IPN with eBay Listings

Include additional variables with auction payments to help fortify the connection between eBay and your PayPal transaction history.

When the IPN system is activated for auction payments, your IPN script receives a form post with the transaction information. If you have your IPN profile preferences set to On, your processing script always gets hit when a payment is made, even for auction payments.

In order to process posts for auctions, your IPN script needs to be able to recognize that the payment is being made for an auction and adjust accordingly. In some cases, you might want to process only certain sections of code for auctions, or you might want to omit certain sections of your IPN page in the case of auction payments. There are five additional variables you need to watch for while dealing with IPN pages that can potentially receive posts for auction payments: item_number, auction_buyer_id, auction_closing_date, and auction_multi_item, and for_auction.

The item_number variable, which is normally populated with your user-defined unique ID-tracking value, is sent populated with the auction number. If these new variables are not accounted for, or you do not have a way of dealing with the item_number value as passed back by auctions, you might have a problem with your entire system.

The Code

This hack shows you how to set up your IPN script to look for an auction payment, process one block of code for an auction payment, and process another section of code for nonauction payments. This example illustrates how to insert the auction buyer ID, the auction number, the auction closing date, and the multi-item counter variable for the auction into the separate database table tblAuctions.

```
'Process payment
If Request.Form(for_auction) = "true" then 'Auction payment received
 'Insert into tblAuctions table
 'Create and populate auction variables
 Dim auction_id, auction_buyer_id, auction_closing_date, auction_multi_item
 auction_id = Request.Form("item_number")
 auction_buyer_id = Request.Form("auction_buyer_id")
 auction_closing_date = Request.Form("auction_closing_date")
 auction_multi_item = Request.Form("auction_multi_item")

 'Database connection info here
 set cInsAuction = Server.CreateObject("ADODB.Command")
 cInsAuction.ActiveConnection = "DRIVER={Microsoft Access Driver (*.mdb)};
     DBQ="C:/InetPub/wwwroot/database/dbPayPal.mdb")
 cInsAuction.CommandText = "INSERT INTO tblAuctions (auction_id,
     auction_buyer_id, auction_closing_date, auction_multi_item) VALUES
     ('" & auction_id & "', '" & auction_buyer_id & "', '" &
     auction_closing_date & "', '" & auction_multi_item & "')"
 cInsAuction.CommandType = 1
 cInsAuction.CommandTimeout = 0
 cInsAuction.Prepared = true
 cInsAuction.Execute( )

End If
If for_auction <> "true" Then 'Normal payment
 'Create and populate normal variables
 Dim item_number
 Item_number = Request.Form("item_number")
 'Normal payment code here
End If
```

The Results

When you place the code in your IPN processing page, it enables your script to handle payment calls for both auctions and normal Web Accept payments. If you did not build this type of functionality into your script, your system might not function properly, because the item_number variable is populated with different information in the case of an auction.

The first section uses an If/Then statement to determine whether the post is being made for an auction. The for_auction variable lets your page determine whether this is the case. If the variable has a value of 1, the payment is for an auction, and the code uses the aforementioned additional variables (including the modified item_number variable) to make a database insertion into a table created to track auction payments. If the payment is not for an auction, the for_auction variable has a value of 0 and the section of code is not activated.

The second block of code does the exact opposite of the first section. It checks to see if the for_auction variable has a value other than 1 (true). If it has a value other than 1, the code block that handles the processing of your normal payments is activated. You should place all of your normal transaction processing code in this section.

Track Your eBay Products with IPN

Easily process eBay sales easily by automatically storing completed transactions in a database.

The eBay and PayPal combination is hard to beat. It gives anyone who wants to sell unique items the ability to market goods and accept payment for that item without any programming expertise or an expensive merchant account. Since eBay purchased PayPal, their efforts to integrate the two have made the process of doing business on eBay with PayPal almost seamless. This improvement includes PayPal's IPN system. When an auction is completed and it has been paid for through PayPal, an IPN call is made to your IPN script (listed in your PayPal account's Profile settings, if you have enabled IPN). This POST contains a lot of the same information as the IPN generated by a normal web purchases. However, because of the nature of an auction, the notification lacks some values we normally rely upon. Fortunately, this hack provides a workaround.

The main issue is that the item_number value supplied by IPN after payment for an auction item is actually the auction number generated by eBay, not the unique identifier you assigned to the product for internal use. This means that when an item is purchased through eBay, you have no way of determining (with your IPN script) which item that is. The workaround is to tack your internal identifier for the item to the end of the auction title, allowing our database and IPN script to process the order normally.

Preparing Your Database

This example pulls up product details from your database after receiving an IPN that tells you your item sold and has been paid for with PayPal. This could be useful if you like to send an automated confirmation email to your buyers with complete details about the product. To store this information, your database requires the item_number, item_name, and description fields, as shown in Table 7-1.

> You might also want a count_inventory field for keeping track of how many of an item have been sold.

Table 7-1. *A database table to track the stuff you sell on eBay*

item_number	item_name	description
6001	Vitamins	Some children may develop a rapid...
6002	Sulfuric Acid	As seen on boxcar advertisements...
6004	Calculator	Now with a 7 and an 8!
7001	Imitation Gruel	Favored by camp counselors

Listing the Item Number on eBay

Have the item's unique internal identifier on hand as you list it on eBay. The length of the item numbers you use must be consistent for all the items you are selling on eBay. For instance, suppose the item we are selling is a *Widget* with an item number of WID-01 stored in our database. The item number is six characters long. If you list another item called *Gidget* on eBay, you can choose GID-02 (which is also six characters long) as its item number.

The eBay auction title field accepts 55 characters. However, since you will be using your item number in the auction title (with a space), you have only 48 characters left for your auction title. Type up to 48 characters for the auction's title, and then enter a space and the item number. For example, when you list your Widget for sale on eBay, the auction title will look like this: Widget WID-01. It might look a bit strange at first, but it should not throw your customers off too much. When a payment for this item is made through PayPal at the auction's end, the IPN page will have the item's unique internal identifier passed back to it in the auction title.

> When listing items, be sure not to add any trailing spaces after the item number as you type the auction title. You rely on the last six characters of the auction title to identify the item properly, so a trailing space will throw off your processing.

The Code

In your IPN script, pull out the appended item number from the auction title. The auction title is passed back in the item_name field as with normal web payment IPNs. So, for the example auction in the previous section, you would receive a value of Widget WID-01 in the item_name field. Copy that value to a variable and then assign its last six characters to a variable for the item number:

```
Dim Auction_title
Dim Item_number
Auction_title = Request.Form("auction_title")
Item_number = Right(auction_title, 6)
```

Your IPN script can now query your database using that item number. For instance, here's a SQL query to get this product's information:

```
SELECT * FROM tblProducts WHERE Item_number = '" & item_number & "'"
```

> See the "Database Coding and Platform Choices" section of the Preface for the additional information needed to put this SQL statement to work with this and the other hacks in this book.

That query pulls from the database the description of the item you just sold. You could modify it to update the inventory count or perform other functions usually associated with web site payments, such as automatically delivering digital goods. As it stands, the query gives you all the information you need to email your customers your full description of the item they just purchased.

Deliver Digital Goods with IPN

HACK #71

Use IPN to have your server automatically send digital goods to customers as soon as they purchase them from your web site.

The Internet revolution allows instant gratification when purchasing an item. You can purchase digital goods—eBooks, digital music, video files, software, and anything else that can be delivered via the Internet—from the comfort of your customer's home and use them almost instantly.

This hack shows you how to leverage PayPal's ease of use, security, and brand name to sell digital goods with large margins and low overhead. PayPal's IPN system [Hack #65] lets you deliver those goods without any interaction as a seller.

The Code

The code in this hack uses Microsoft VBScript, but the same process can be implemented with any web scripting language.

> Since this solution employs IPN to deliver a product without any action on your part, you should take steps to ensure that the payment is legitimate (e.g., no price tampering has taken place) [Hack #73].

This script, when used in conjunction with the IPN script from "Implement Price Checking with IPN" [Hack #73], sends your customer an email with your digital product as an attachment:

```
'Declare and populate email address for delivery
Dim payer_email
Payer_email = Request.Form("payer_email")

'Create file variable and set path to file
Dim file_location
file_location = "C:\InetPub\wwwroot\yoursite\filestore\file.zip"

'Send an email to customer and attach file
Dim objCDO
Set objCDO = Server.CreateObject("CDOSYS.NewMail")
objCDO.From = "sales@paypalhacks.com"
'Add customer email address
objCDO.To = payer_email
'Add file attachement
objCDO.AttachFile(file_location)
objCDO.Subject = "PayPal Hacks Software Exo"
objCDO.Body = "Thank you for your order. Your file is attached to this
email."
objCDO.Send( )
Set objCDO = Nothing
```

❶ `file_location = "C:\InetPub\wwwroot\yoursite\filestore\file.zip"`

❷ `objCDO.From = "sales@paypalhacks.com"`

❸ `objCDO.Subject = "PayPal Hacks Software Exo"`

❹ `objCDO.Body = "Thank you for your order. Your file is attached to this email."`

Place your digital product in a file (presumably zipped up) on your server, and specify the full path and filename in the file_location variable (line ❶). Include your email address as the return address (line ❷); in most cases, this should be the same as the email address used for your PayPal account. Finally, you'll want to customize the subject and message body text (lines ❸ and ❹, respectively) to suit your needs.

> When delivering files via email, be sure to keep the file size relatively small (less than 500 KB). Otherwise, you run the risk of overfilling your customer's email inbox or having the message rejected by the customer's ISP.

See Also

This hack shows the most simplistic way to implement digital goods sales for your site. For an improved method, see "Deliver Digital Goods with a Return Page" [Hack #72].

Deliver Digital Goods with a Return Page

Instead of forcing customers to wait for an email, present an instant download link to customers as soon as they complete the checkout process.

Although you can deliver digital goods with IPN [Hack #71], there might be times you want to allow customers instant access to their purchases with a *return page* (via PDT). Email messages can be lost, might bounce, or might not be desired at the same address used in the buyer's PayPal account. PayPal provides a way to redirect your customers back to your web page after they have completed a purchase with PayPal. This return page can be used as another means to provide a data file to your customers and can be quicker than waiting for the email to arrive.

However, if you simply have the digital goods waiting for the customers once they reach the return page, they could avoid the payment step altogether. For example, a quick inspection of the Buy Now button code shows exactly where the return URL is. Someone who wants the product but doesn't want to pay for it could just type that URL into a browser.

You can prevent this by recording verified transactions with IPN, then checking against the list with a dynamic return page. To implement this hack, add form variables to your purchase buttons, create a database table, add a database update to the IPN page, and create a return page that checks the database for an appropriate transaction status before providing the file for download.

Augmenting the PayPal Button Code

You need to add two new variables, return and rm, to your button code. The first variable, return, defines the page to which your customers should be returned when they click Continue after making a payment. The second variable, rm, tells the PayPal system to send transaction data to that page using the POST method. Your return page uses that information to consult your database and determine whether to make the download available.

Add the return and rm variables between the button's opening and closing <form> tags. The new button should look like this:

```
<form target="paypal" action=
      "https://www.paypal.com/cgi-bin/webscr" method="post">
<input type="hidden" name="business" value="youremail@yourisp.com">
<input type="hidden" name="item_name" value="Widget">
<input type="hidden" name="item_number" value="Wid-001">
<input type="hidden" name="amount" value="1.00">
<input type="hidden" name="no_note" value="1">
<input type="hidden" name="currency_code" value="USD">
<input type="image" src="https://www.paypal.com/en_US/i/btn/x-click-but22.gif"
      border="0" name="submit">
```

```
<input type="hidden" name="add" value="1">
<input type="hidden" name="return" value="http://yoursite.com/return.asp">
<input type="hidden" name="rm" value ="2">
</form>
```

PayPal prompts the customer to return to your *return.asp* page after making the payment.

Creating an IPN Page

Use the IPN page created in "Deliver Digital Goods with IPN" **[Hack #71]**, which introduced the concept of selling digital goods and delivering the file via email. Modify it to insert information about the purchase into the database when a purchase transaction has been completed. Insert the new code just below the code that sends the email to the customer.

We first need a way to uniquely identify the order. PayPal gives us a unique transaction ID with each order.

> The merchant and customer each get a different unique transaction ID. Neither party can see the other's transaction ID. See "Display the Merchant Transaction ID on Your Return Page" **[Hack #52]** for details.

In this simple system, the transaction ID is the only identifying piece of information that is required. A simple SQL call to the database stores the transaction ID in a list of completed orders. Create a new variable and populate it with this value:

```
'Create and populate transaction id variable
Dim txn_id
txn_id = Request.Form("txn_id")
```

Insert the transaction ID into the database with a SQL statement, like this:

```
INSERT INTO tblOrders (txn_id) VALUES ('" & txn_id &'")
```

Finally, create a table in your database called tblOrders with just one field, txn_id, of a text type.

Building the Return Page

The final component in this system is the return page, the page the customers will see after they finish making payment and click Continue. Because the rm variable in the Buy Now button is set to 2, this page will receive a POST from PayPal that contains all of the transaction details. The return page looks up the transaction ID (txn_id) received in the tblOrders table of the database. If the transaction is there, you know the customer has paid and you can give access to the data file.

The IPN script is called when the buyer clicks the Pay button at PayPal, so a matching transaction ID should be present in the system by this time. However, the transaction ID might not be in your system yet, because the IPN script might not have finished processing the order. If you don't have the transaction ID yet, the return page displays a message that lets the buyer know he will get the file via email.

> Some customers will not click on the Continue link that returns them to your page, but will instead either close their browser or remain on the PayPal web site. In such a case, the return system will not be activated and we must rely on the file delivery via email.

Here's the code for the return page:

```
<%@LANGUAGE="VBSCRIPT"%>
<%
'Process information

'Create and populate transaction id variable
Dim txn_id
txn_id = Request.Form("txn_id")

'Query the database for the txn_id
'Connect to database and create recordset
connStore = "DRIVER={Microsoft Access Driver (*.mdb)};
     DBQ="C:/InetPub/wwwroot/database/dbPayPal.mdb")
set rsOrderCheck = Server.CreateObject("ADODB.Recordset")
rsOrderCheck.ActiveConnection = connStore
rsOrderCheck.Source = "SELECT txn_id FROM tblOrders WHERE
     txn_id = '" & txn_id & "'"
rsOrderCheck.Open( )
%>
<html>
<body>
<%
If Not rsOrderCheck.EOF Or Not rsOrderCheck.BOF Then
'Order is valid, display download link
%>
<a href="/filestore/file.zip">Click here to downlaod your file</a>
<%
Else
'Order is invalid or not yet complete; display message
%>
Your order is being processed. Please check your email for the
     file delivery.
<%
End If
%>
</body>
</html>
```

See the "Database Coding and Platform Choices" section of the Preface for the additional information needed to put this SQL statement to work with this and the other hacks in this book.

When this page is loaded after payment is made, it will provide the download for the customer. It will also guard against people who might fraudulently try to get a free download by going directly to your return page without paying.

Providing a direct link to the file can be dangerous because the customer can copy the link location (`/filestore/file.zip` in this example) and pass it along to others.

H A C K Implement Price Checking with IPN
#73
Prevent fraudulent transactions by comparing the value of the goods purchased with the amount received.

PayPal has taken many steps to ensure that their system is secured against fraudulent transactions. However, just like any online eCommerce system, there are always ways for an unscrupulous person to attempt to cheat you. The PayPal Buy Now and Shopping Cart buttons, for example, are normally displayed as plain text in your web page's source code, which means that anyone can view your HTML code or—more importantly—copy and modify the code, and then submit a spoof payment (presumably with a lower price) to PayPal. And since PayPal doesn't maintain an active database of all the current prices of your products, it's up to you to engage in some proactive price checking.

See "Hack-Proof Your Payment" [Hack #36] for ways to hide your payment button code from customers and reduce the possibility of spoofed payments.

Obviously, the primary concern is the price, given how easily it can be changed from, say, $18.00 to $.18. While a merchant who is able to view each and every transaction will likely notice when a $100 item was purchased for $.01, but it can, of course, be easy to miss this kind of thing, especially for high-volume merchants. And if you have a fully automated fulfillment system, such as for digital goods [Hack #71], you'll need to employ some sort of price checking.

The following solution employs the trusty IPN system to check whether a customer has paid the correct amount.

Simple Price Checking with Single Item Purchases

The PayPal IPN system posts the variables as they were originally submitted to PayPal, so a spoofed price will be reflected in our IPN postback from PayPal. Because PayPal does not store any of your product information on their servers, you have to query your product information to ensure it matches the price the customer paid.

To use a price-checking system on your site, you need to be able to run a dynamic server page technology (e.g., ASP, as is used in this example) and a simple database (e.g., Microsoft Access). The table in this example, tblProducts, has only two columns: item_number, containing a list of all of the unique product numbers, and item_price, in which the corresponding prices are stored. Naturally, your product database will be more sophisticated, but it will likely have analogous fields.

Here is some skeleton code, written in ASP, that does rudimentary price checking for items purchased with Buy Now buttons:

```
'Declare and populate our price checking variables
Dim item_number, item_amount
item_number = Request.Form("item_number")
item_amount = "Request.Form("mc_gross")

'Connect to database and create recordset
connStore = "DRIVER={Microsoft Access Driver (*.mdb)};DBQ=
    "C:/InetPub/wwwroot/database/dbPayPal.mdb")
set rsPriceCheck = Server.CreateObject("ADODB.Recordset")
rsPriceCheck.ActiveConnection = connStore
rsPriceCheck.Source = "SELECT item_price FROM tblProducts
    WHERE item_number = 'item_number'"
rsPriceCheck.Open( )

'Compare the values to see if amount paid is equal to or
    greater than required

If rsPriceCheck("item_amount") >= item_amount Then
 'Price paid is at least as much as required, process order
 'Order processing code here
Else
 'Price paid is less than required, stop order processing
 'Send alert to purchaser and merchant
End If
```

See the "Database Coding and Platform Choices" section of the Preface for the additional information needed to put this SQL statement to work with this and the other hacks in this book.

This code relies on the `mc_gross` variable, which is equal to the purchase price plus any shipping, handling, or tax charges applied to the order (note that `mc_gross` does not include the deduction of any applicable PayPal fees).

> This code merely checks to see if the price paid is equal to or higher than the price in your database. You'll want to account for shipping and sales tax, because these values can also be spoofed by customers.

Price Checking for Shopping Cart Purchases

PayPal does not pass back individual item prices in Shopping Cart transactions. If a customer buys three items worth $1.00, $2.00, and $5.00, respectively (and agrees to pay $3.50 for shipping), you don't get any of those individual values in the IPN data. Rather, the `mc_gross` variable will have a value of the total amount paid (in this case, $11.50). Thankfully, PayPal does pass back the individual `item_number` fields, which means that you can still look up the individual prices in your database.

> In the long run, however, it might be easier to keep a running total on file for each customer's Shopping Cart so that you can easily cross-check this value with the amount paid.

As described in "Hack Shopping Cart Buttons" **[Hack #45]** and "Integrate a Third-Party Shopping Cart with PayPal" **[Hack #50]**, the PayPal Shopping Cart system returns an item number for each item in the cart. The variables are in the form `item_number`*n*, where *n* is the cart number for that item, starting with 1. PayPal also provides the `num_cart_items` variable to indicate the number of items in the cart. To verify the order, add the values of each item as listed in your database and compare the total to the gross amount paid:

```
Dim item_number, mc_gross, I, num_cart_items, price_check
mc_gross = Request.Form("mc_gross")
num_cart_items = Request.Form("num_cart_items")
price_check = 0

For i=1 to num_cart_items

 'Populate variable with value
 item_number = Request.Form("item_number" & i)

 'Execute SQL query on database with item_number value
 'Connect to database and create recordset
 connStore = "DRIVER={Microsoft Access Driver (*.mdb)};
     DBQ="C:/InetPub/wwwroot/database/dbPayPal.mdb")
 set rsPriceCheck = Server.CreateObject("ADODB.Recordset")
 rsPriceCheck.ActiveConnection = connStore
```

```
    rsPriceCheck.Source = "SELECT item_price FROM tblProducts
        WHERE item_number = 'item_number'"
    rsPriceCheck.Open( )

    'Add value from database to our running count
    price_check = price_check + rsPriceCheck("item_price")

Next

If price_check = mc_gross OR price_check > mc_gross Then
  'Price paid is at least as much as required, process order
  'Order processing code here
Else
  'Price paid is less than required, stop order processing
  'Send alert to purchaser and merchant
End If
```

This ASP code assumes a quantity of 1 for each cart item. If you offer multiple quantities of items, you will need to take the item_quantity value into account by multiplying the database price value by the price of the item.

Sending a Price Check Alert

Once you see a problem with an order, it's up to you to send an alert. Use any simple mail component available to you and your server technology. In ASP, you can use the Common Data Objects (CDO) mail component with the following code:

```
Dim PriceErrorCDO
Set PriceErrorCDO = Server.CreateObject("CDOSYS.NewMail")
PriceErrorCDO.From = Request.Form("receiver_email")
PriceErrorCDO.To = Request.Form("receiver_email")
PriceErrorCDO.CC = Request.Form("payer_email")
PriceErrorCDO.Subject = "IPN Price Checking Error"
PriceErrorCDO.Body = "There has been a price-checking error
        on the following transaction: " & Request.Form("txn_id") & ""
PriceErrorCDO.Send( )
Set PriceErrorCDO = Nothing
```

This email alert code sends an email to the recipient of the payment (you), but you might also want to send an automatic email to the customer to indicate that there will be a delay in processing the order.

If you want a truly automated system, you can simply refund any irregular payments using the PayPal API "Refund Payments with the API" [Hack #91].

Provide an Order Summary with IPN

#74   Present order-specific information on the return page after the customer makes payment.

The return URL and the IPN processing script are two pages on your site that can receive posts containing details of a purchase. Used separately, these two pages can enable you to create a more robust eCommerce system by providing order-specific customization.

Using the return page, for instance, you can display the order number [Hack #52] to the customer for later use. Using the IPN system, on the other hand, you can send a customized email to the customer [Hack #71], giving her that same order number for tracking purposes. When these two features are used together, they can be even more powerful in terms of their ability to present your customer with valuable information.

This hack uses the return page to show the buyer whether the order has been processed successfully by the IPN system. By itself, this feature might not be worth much, but the functionality is called on for more advanced functions, such as delivering digital goods [Hack #72].

When a customer reviews the payment information at PayPal and clicks the Pay button, PayPal sends a POST to your IPN page with the purchase information. The customer is directed to a PayPal page that shows them the payment confirmation message. There, the buyer sees a Continue button that, when pressed, returns the user back to the return page at your site. Order-specific information is also sent to this page.

In almost all cases, the IPN page will already have been hit and have processed the information, so you have the transaction information in your local system. With that information, you can customize the return page to give your customer order-specific information.

> Exactly when your IPN page is hit by the PayPal system—and, therefore, the exact time the customer's order information is made available to your system—is not defined by PayPal. While it usually occurs quite quickly (the *I* in IPN stands for *Instant*), the possibility exists for IPN postings to be queued up at PayPal and delayed for minutes or longer. For best results, build your software to be tolerant of this possibility.

In this example, you simply display a message that notifies the customer of whether the order has been completed in your system. While this hack only displays a message, you can include other things as well. You might also want to display any error information, such as a price-checking error [Hack #73].

This hack relies on an IPN page that inserts payment details into your database [Hack #82] which checks the database table to determine whether the order has been processed.

The Code

The return page receives purchase details from PayPal through a form POST (if enabled; see "Using a Return URL" in [Hack #66] for more information). Included in the purchase details is the order transaction ID, passed as txn_id. Compare this unique variable to your database to see if the order has been inserted into the table, which indicates whether it has been processed by your system.

 See the "Database Coding and Platform Choices" section of the Preface for the additional information needed to put this SQL statement to work with this and the other hacks in this book.

First, you need to pass the value as presented by PayPal into a local variable using the following code:

```
<%
'Create local transaction id variable and populate
Dim txn_id
Txn_id = Request.Form("txn_id")
%>

'Query the database table and find the record (if it is there yet).
connStore = "DRIVER={Microsoft Access Driver (*.mdb)};
     DBQ="C:/InetPub/wwwroot/database/dbPayPal.mdb")
set rsOrder = Server.CreateObject("ADODB.Recordset")
rsOrder.ActiveConnection = connStore
rsOrder.Source = "SELECT payment_status FROM tblOrders
     WHERE txn_id = '" & txn_id & "'"
rsOrder.Open( )
%>
<% If Not rsOrder.EOF Or Not rsOrder.BOF Then 'order exists %>
Your order has been processed successfully. The payment status for
     this order is: <%=rsOrder("payment_status")%>
<% End If %>

<!-- Tell the customer if the order information has not yet been processed -->
<% If rsOrder.EOF Or rsOrder.BOF Then 'order does not exist %>
Your order is still being processed.
<% End If %>
```

As this hack illustrates, the return page and the IPN page are more powerful when used in conjunction with one another.

> Ideally, you don't want to use your return page to process any of the payment information. You want to use the return page only to read the values from PayPal or read the information created by your IPN page. The return page is not completely reliable, because customers might close their browsers when they see the payment confirmation screen at PayPal, rather than follow the Continue link.

H A C K   Upsell Your Customers
#75
Use the return variable to provide a list of items in which a customer might also be interested.

Although you can use IPN to provide an order summary [Hack #74], you're missing a sales opportunity if you don't use this page to advertise your other products, a technique known as *upselling*. For instance, say you're selling bicycle parts and someone comes along and buys a bottom bracket from your web site. Using this technique, your web site would then present this customer with a small ad listing some of the cranksets, pedals, and derailleurs you sell. It's easy to do, and it works better than you might expect.

The Return Page's Job

The return page is the page you show your customers once they are done paying for an item. To help you upsell your customers, this page has several jobs to do:

Retrieve information about the products purchased. In order to use this hack, you also need to insert cart details into a database [Hack #83] (or something like it) to keep a running record of purchases your customers have made.

Consult your sales database to find out what other buyers of this item have purchased. The heavy lifting in this hack comes from a single database query that is used to search the contents of the database table [Hack #74] to find a list of products that have been purchased by other customers.

Display a link and brief description for each. "Add Dynamic Storefront Details" [Hack #55] shows how to link directly to the other product's details page so that customers can continue shopping if they choose.

The Code

Here's the ASP code that does it all:

```
<% 'Find the number of the item just purchased
Dim item_number
Item_number = Request.Form("item_number") %>

'Find products purchased by other buyers
connStore = "DRIVER={Microsoft Access Driver (*.mdb)};DBQ=
        "C:/InetPub/wwwroot/database/dbPayPal.mdb")
set rsProducts = Server.CreateObject("ADODB.Recordset")
rsProducts.ActiveConnection = connStore
rsProducts.Source = "SELECT DISTINCT item_number FROM tblOrderDetails
        WHERE (payer_email IN (SELECT payer_email FROM tblOrderDetails WHERE
(txtItemNumber = 'item_number')))"
rsProducts.Open( )
%>

<% If Not rsProducts.EOF Or Not rsProducts.BOF Then 'it exists %>
<%
'While recordset still has products, loop code
While NOT rsProducts.EOF
%>
<a href="http://yoursite.com/product_detail.asp?item_
number=<%=rsProducts("item_number)%">Link Text Here</a><br>
<%
'Move to next record
rsProducts.MoveNext( )
Wend
%>
<% End If %>
```

> See the "Database Coding and Platform Choices" section of the Preface for the additional information needed to put this SQL statement to work with this and the other hacks in this book.

Running the Code

Simply save this file in a public folder on your web server, and then set your return page to the URL of the page [Hack #85]. When a customer pays, this code looks up the product that was just purchased and uses a SQL statement to look up past purchases of this product to see what other products those customers purchased along with it.

Enable Multiple IPN Pages

HACK #76

Use a multiplexer script inspired by PayPal's code samples to duplicate the IPN posting to multiple scripts.

PayPal's IPN facility enables you to process your orders in real time. By specifying a script on your site, you can automatically update your database, add a name to your subscriber list, or email a custom order confirmation. PayPal's system is capable of making a call to only one IPN page per transaction, but with some code and tweaking, we can call more than one script.

The IPN Multiplexer

Any IPN script [Hack #65] accepts data from PayPal, verifies it, then goes about its business. The following multiplexer script is no different, but its mission is simply to pass the information on to your secondary scripts.

```
' read post from PayPal system and add 'cmd'
str = Request.Form & "&cmd=_notify-validate"

' post back to PayPal system to validate
set objHttp = Server.CreateObject("Msxml2.ServerXMLHTTP")

objHttp.open "POST", "https://www.paypal.com/cgi-bin/webscr", false
objHttp.setRequestHeader "Content-type", "application/x-www-form-urlencoded"
objHttp.Send str

' assign posted variables to local variables

' Check notification validation
if (objHttp.status <> 200 ) then

' HTTP error handling
elseif (objHttp.responseText = "VERIFIED") then
' PayPal says the posting is good; post the data to the secondary scripts.

objHttp.open "POST", "http://othersite1.com/ipnpage.asp", false
objHttp.setRequestHeader "Content-type", "application/x-www-form-urlencoded"
objHttp.Send str

objHttp.open "POST", "http://othersite2.com/ipnpage.asp", false
objHttp.setRequestHeader "Content-type", "application/x-www-form-urlencoded"
objHttp.Send str

objHttp.open "POST", "http://othersite3.com/ipnpage.asp", false
objHttp.setRequestHeader "Content-type", "application/x-www-form-urlencoded"
objHttp.Send str
```

When this IPN script is called, it performs the PayPal verification process to ensure the transaction is a real one. It then posts the information to your secondary IPN scripts. Each script you use should follow the form of a typical IPN processor script "Receive Instant Payment Notifications" [Hack #65].

Turning off Secondary Verification to Eliminate Extra Postings

The multiplexer in the previous section does the job of assuring the posting data is genuinely from PayPal [Hack #65] Once its authenticity is verified, the data is passed along to the secondary scripts.

If your secondary IPN scripts do what they're supposed to do, they will each reverify this information for themselves. There is nothing wrong with this, but if you would like to cut down on the bandwidth your site uses, you might want to remove any redundant verification by eliminating the lines in the subordinate scripts that post data back to PayPal.

 If you decide to turn off IPN validation in the secondary scripts and their location is known to spoofers, you potentially open up your system to falsified data. Ensure that security is adequate before taking this step.

Hacking the Hack

Here are a couple tips for working with this hack:

Embrace code multiculturalism. Because the scripts communicate with each other—and with the PayPal system—using the standard, documented HTTP protocol, you need not stay with one programming language for the multiplexer and the secondary scripts it serves. You can use the multiplexer in ASP/VBScript, while deploying a secondary one in Perl, and another in Python.

Test off-site. Who says your IPN script's data needs to originate with Pay-Pal? Build a system tester that simply posts data to your IPN script. You can see exactly what will happen when your customer tries to buy an odd item from your site or how your system will handle a payment from a hacked button. Be sure to comment out the verification step before testing and reenable it before putting your system back into production. See "Test IPN and PDT in the Sandbox" [Hack #99] for other testing methods.

Use Mass Pay to Create an Affiliate System
HACK #77
Automate payout incentives to affiliates and resellers with PayPal's Mass Pay feature.

A great way to increase your sales is to provide incentives for other people to promote your products and services. This is typically done with an *affiliate* program, in which you reward those who send traffic to your site by paying them a small fee, usually either a fixed amount per sale or a percentage of the items sold as a result of the affiliate's efforts.

Managing an affiliate system involves tracking all the successful sales from referrals by your affiliates and then paying the affiliates their due on a regular basis. This hack uses IPN [Hack #65] to track affiliate referrals and PayPal's Mass Pay feature to pay all your affiliates at once.

> When you use Mass Pay, you (the sender) pay the PayPal fees [Hack #14].

Creating Your Business Model

The following code employs a simple business model, in which each affiliate gets one dollar for each sale you receive as a result of their referral, regardless of the amount of the sale.

Here's how it works:

1. Create a sign-up system on your web site, in which prospective affiliates enter their email addresses. Instruct each affiliate to open a PayPal account with that email address.

2. Generate a custom button [Hack #28] for each affiliate, as described in the next section.

3. Instruct the affiliate to place the button on his site. If you want to be creative, supply some custom payment button images [Hack #29] to spruce up the button appearance and help attract attention.

4. Visitors to your affiliate's site see your product advertisement, crave it instantly, and click the Buy Now button. The payment is sent to you and you deliver the product.

5. Use IPN to record the affiliate's email address (and any other relevant information) into a database.

6. Use Mass Pay to send a buck per sale to the affiliate responsible.

Building a Button for Your Affiliate

Each affiliate's button should be like any other Buy Now button [Hack #28], with two important exceptions.

First, include the email address of your affiliate in the custom variable of the button (make sure the payment still goes to you, however). Second, specify the location of your IPN script for handling affiliate program payments in the notify_URL variable:

```
<form action="https://www.paypal.com/cgi-bin/webscr" method="post">
<input type="hidden" name="cmd" value="_xclick">
<input type="hidden" name="business" value="sales@superfreaker.com">
```

```
<input type="hidden" name="item_name" value="Widget">
<input type="hidden" name="item_number" value="Item-123">
<input type="hidden" name="amount" value="10">
<input type="image" name="Submit" value="Submit" src="buynow.gif">
<input type="hidden" name="notify_url"
       value="http://yoursite/affiliate_ipn.asp">
<input type="hidden" name="custom"
       value="affiliate@theirisp.com">
</form>
```

Save this button code into a text file and email it to each affiliate. Better yet, create a script on your server that does this automatically, and take yourself out of the loop entirely.

Recording Referred Purchases

The IPN script specified in the notify_url variable receives a post of the transaction details from PayPal when a sale is made from the affiliate's site. The script writes the affiliate tracking information to a tab-delimited text file, along with the amount of the reseller incentive. This example is written in Microsoft VBScript and uses a Windows File System Object to manipulate the file.

Use the following VBScript code in conjunction with a standard IPN validation script, such as the one in "Receive Instant Payment Notifications" [Hack #65]:

```
Const fsoForWriting = 2
Dim objFSO
Dim objTextStream

Set objFSO = Server.CreateObject("Scripting.FileSystemObject")

'Open the text file
vFilePath = "C:\InetPub\yoursite\affiliates\output\MassPay.txt"
Set objTextStream = objFSO.OpenTextFile(vFilePath, fsoForWriting, True)

'Write the new line to the file
objTextStream.WriteLine custom & "       " &
         (rsAffiliateFees.Fields.Item("AffiliateFee").Value)

'Close the file and clean up
objTextStream.Close
Set objTextStream = Nothing
Set objFSO = Nothing
```

Replace the example filename on line ❶ with the full path of the file in which to save your affiliate data. Make sure you have the proper permissions to write to the file on your server. When using IIS on Windows, for example, you'll probably need to set IUSER (Internet guest) write permissions.

The long space in quotation marks on line ❷, used to separate the custom variable (here, the affiliate's email address) from the dollar amount paid to the affiliate, is really a tab (ASCII code 9). See *http://www.paypal.com/cgi-bin/webscr?cmd=p/ema/batch_format-outside* for the latest updates to the specification.

Notifying Your Affiliates

You might want to let your affiliates know whenever you've received a payment as a result of an affiliate referral. They'll be more likely to stay enthusiastic about your affiliate program if they can see it working. Add the following code to your IPN script, after the main IPN processing code [Hack #65]:

```
Dim InvCDO
Set InvCDO = Server.CreateObject("CDONTS.NewMail")
InvCDO.From = receiver_email
InvCDO.To = custom
InvCDO.Subject = "Affiliate Sale"
InvCDO.Body = "You have an affiliate sale. Your affiliate account has
        been credited and will be paid according to the schedule
        in the affiliate program aggreement."
InvCDO.Send( )
Set InvCDO = Nothing
```

Paying Your Affiliates en Mass

Making a Mass Payment is easy, especially since the file in which you've recorded your affiliate sales, *MassPay.txt*, already contains the information in the proper format.

Because sales sometimes fall through (due to customer returns, problems with payments, etc.), you might prefer to wait a good period of time (e.g., 30 days) after the sale before paying your affiliates. And for bookkeeping purposes, you might want to schedule affiliate payments to occur quarterly.

To make the affiliate payments, upload your data file, and PayPal does the rest:

1. Download the *MassPay.txt* file from your server and save it on your local hard disk.

2. Log into your PayPal account, and click the Mass Pay link near the bottom of the page.

3. On the Mass Payment Overview page, click Make a Mass Payment.

4. Click Browse to locate the *MassPay.txt* file, or type the full path of the file in the box, and then click Continue when you're done.

5. Review the details of the transaction and the first few lines of the *MassPay.txt* file you just uploaded, and then send your payment. You and your affiliates will be notified by PayPal that the payments have been made.

Hacking the Hack

You can further enhance this system with the following:

- Create a statistics page on the fly so that affiliates can see their sales figures and possibly fine-tune their earnings (and thus boost your sales).

- Use a task scheduler (or a Unix cron job) on your server to mail the *MassPay.txt* file to yourself each week.

- This hack is only the beginning; you can use Mass Pay for customer rebates, pay-to-surf rewards, employee benefits, survey incentives, and more.

Manage Your Inventory with IPN

Indicate whether the products on your web site are in stock using up-to-date inventory data maintained by some add-ons to your IPN processing script.

Merchants who sell tangible goods typically don't have an unlimited supply of any item. When you sell out of something, you might no longer want it to appear on your web site: you can't sell what you don't have. Managing inventory counts for each order and updating your web pages accordingly can be a time-consuming and tedious process, but it can be mostly automated with PayPal's IPN system.

This hack consists of a database table, tblProducts, that holds our inventory count, an IPN processing page that manages the count, a web page that displays an out-of-stock message when appropriate, and an email notification to alert you when the inventory count for a particular item is running low (or has been depleted).

Updating the Inventory Count

Create a database table, tblProducts, that contains fields for the product's unique item number, item_number, and the initial inventory count, count_inventory, as shown in Table 7-2.

Table 7-2. A database table to manage your store inventory

item_number	item_name	count_inventory
6001	Vitamins	6
6002	Sulfuric Acid	5612
6004	Calculator	0
7001	Imitation Gruel	77

When a payment is made, PayPal will post the transaction details to your IPN processing page. Included in these details is the unique item number, for which you'll need to query your database for the in-stock inventory. Finally, decrement the value by the number of products purchased:

```
Dim item_number
Dim count_inventory_new

item_number = Request.Form("item_number")
quantity = Request.Form("quantity")

'Retrieve the current inventory count from the database
'Connect to database and create recordset
connStore = "DRIVER={Microsoft Access Driver (*.mdb)};
    DBQ="C:/InetPub/wwwroot/database/dbPayPal.mdb")
set rsInventoryCount = Server.CreateObject("ADODB.Recordset")
rsInventoryCount.ActiveConnection = connStore
rsInventoryCount.Source = "SELECT count_inventory FROM tblProducts
    WHERE item_number = " & item_number
rsInventoryCount.Open( )

count_inventory_new = rsInventoryCount("count_inventory") - quantity

'Store the reduced inventory count in the database
set cInsPayment = Server.CreateObject("ADODB.Command")
cInsPayment.ActiveConnection = "DRIVER={Microsoft Access Driver
    (*.mdb)};DBQ="C:/InetPub/wwwroot/database/dbPayPal.mdb")
cInsPayment.CommandText = "UPDATE tblProducts SET count_inventory =
    " & count_inventory_new & " WHERE item_number = " & item_number & ""
cInsPayment.CommandType = 1
cInsPayment.CommandTimeout = 0
cInsPayment.Prepared = true
cInsPayment.Execute( )
```

This code only handles the inventory count; see "Receive Instant Payment Notifications" [Hack #65] for the complete code necessary to implement IPN.

Creating the Selling Page

An inventory count will not do much good if the web store allows people to purchase items that are no longer available. You can remove the Buy Now button for an out-of-stock item with a simple conditional statement on a dynamic page.

Start by placing the current inventory count into the rsInventoryCount variable, using a SQL statement something like this:

```
SELECT count_inventory FROM tblProducts WHERE item_number = 'Wid-001'
```

> See the "Database Coding and Platform Choices" section of the Preface for the additional information needed to put this SQL statement to work with this and the other hacks in this book.

Next, compare that value to zero, and display the button only if the item is available:

```
<%
If rsInventoryCount("count_inventory") > 0 Then
 'We have it in stock, display PayPal purchase button
%>
<form action="https://www.paypal.com/cgi-bin/webscr" method="post">

<input type="hidden" name="cmd" value="_xclick">
<input type="hidden" name="business" value="business@paypalhacks.com">
<input type="hidden" name="item_name" value="<%=rsProduct("item_name")%>">
<input type="hidden" name="item_number" value="<%=rsProduct("item_number")%>">
<input type="hidden" name="amount" value="<%=rsProduct("item_price")%>">
<input type="hidden" name="no_note" value="1">
<input type="hidden" name="currency_code" value="USD">
<input type="image" src="https://www.paypal.com/en_US/i/btn/x-click-but23.gif"
        border="0" name="submit">

</form>
<% Else
 'We do not have any left, show OoS message %>
%>

We're sorry, this item is out of stock.

<% End If %>
```

> You might not want to use a value of zero as your threshold, especially if it is a high-volume item. Real-world values might be different than the electronic inventory count, due to defective merchandise from your supplier or offline transactions. Try setting the number to, say, three instead. Or, display a message to your customers that inventories are low and they should contact you directly to assure quick fulfillment.

Alerting Yourself if Inventory Is Low

Finally, set up a script to email yourself or let your staff know when inventory is low or has become depleted. Insert this code into your IPN processing script:

```
If count_inventory_new < 5 Then
  'Low count, send email
  Dim InvCDO
  Set InvCDO = Server.CreateObject("CDONTS.NewMail")
  InvCDO.From = "sales@paypalhacks.com"
  InvCDO.To ="sales@paypalhacks.com"
  InvCDO.Subject = "Order More Inventory"
  InvCDO.Body = "We need to order more of item # " & item_number
  InvCDO.Send( )
  Set InvCDO = Nothing
End If
```

If, immediately after a purchase, you have fewer than five of the item left in your inventory, you'll get an email that contains a warning, along with the product's item_number.

> There will be some lag time between the instant your customer hits the Buy Now or Checkout button and the time that that transaction is complete. Since this means it might be possible for two customers to be in the process of purchasing a single remaining item, you'll want to keep the threshold sufficiently high (five, in this case) sufficiently high so that this doesn't happen.

HACK #79 Display Donation Goals on Your Web Site

Use donation buttons and IPN to display actively updated donation goals.

As a web site owner, you might want to provide information or entertainment to your visitors without charging for the service or cluttering up your site with advertising. However, you might also need funds to pay site expenses or to support a worthy cause. The PayPal Donate Now button enables webmasters to collect payments from willing donors.

Donation buttons on web sites do not give visitors much information apart from the cause to which they are donating. Contributors have no idea how many other people have donated or how much has been raised already. Visitors might be more inclined to donate once they know others have, or if they believe their donation will make a difference in achieving a goal for a fund drive. Providing donation goals and a tally of the amount collected to date can induce potential donors to contribute—and contribute in larger amounts.

Another way to entice donors is to offer several suggested donation levels [Hack #40].

This hack illustrates how to use your donation button to display a donation goal and the current amount collected. To implement this hack, you need to set up your site to receive Instant Payment Notifications [Hack #65] and connect the notifications to a local database using dynamic server page technology. This example uses VBScript for ASP, but it could as easily be done with PHP, Perl, Python, or Java.

Recording Donations

To keep a record of donations as they are made, first install a script to process PayPal's IPN feature and add a record to your database for each transaction [Hack #82].

Next, use a SQL query such as this one to get the sum of all donations in your database:

```
SELECT SUM(mc_gross) AS TotalDonated FROM tblOrders
```

See the "Database Coding and Platform Choices" section of the Preface for the additional information needed to put this SQL statement to work with this and the other hacks in this book.

For instance, if you have a table that looks like Table 7-3, the SUM(mc_gross) function returns the sum of the mc_gross column ($323.10 in this case).

Table 7-3. A database table to track the donations

ShowName	mc_gross	date
Monty	$0.05	12/7/1943
Barney	$300.00	5/6/2004
Seymour	$23.05	7/10/2004

Put the result into the rsDonationGoal("TotalDonated") variable. If you've received three donations for $3, $5, and $7, respectively, the value for rsDonationGoal("TotalDonated") will be $15.

Naturally, if you're accepting donations for more than one cause, you'll need to narrow the SQL query so that it returns only donations that relate to the donation goal at hand.

Building the Donation Page

The donation page consists of three items: your donation goal (in dollars) as static text, the total amount collected thus far (drawn from your database), and the PayPal donation button (displayed somewhere prominently, of course):

```
<p>Please help us achieve our donation goal of $10,000.</p>
Total Amount collected so far: <%=rsDonationGoal("TotalDonated")%>
<br>
<form action="https://www.paypal.com/cgi-bin/webscr" method="post">
<input type="hidden" name="cmd" value="_xclick">
<input type="hidden" name="business" value="sales@paypalhacks.com">
<input type="hidden" name="item_name" value="Donation">
<input type="hidden" name="item_number" value="Donation-001">
<input type="hidden" name="no_note" value="1">
<input type="hidden" name="currency_code" value="USD">
<input type="hidden" name="tax" value="0">
<input type="image" src=
        "https://www.paypal.com/en_US/i/btn/x-click-but21.gif"
        border="0" name="submit">
</form>
```

Hacking the Hack

You might also want to display the number of donations you have already received. Start by adding another SQL query to calculate the count of donations table:

```
SELECT COUNT(Id) AS CountDonated FROM tblOrders
```

Then, use this new CountDonated variable in your ASP page:

```
Total number of donations collected so far:
<%=rsDonationGoal("CountDonated")%>
```

Or, calculate the average donation with this bit of SQL:

```
SELECT AVG(mc_gross) AS AverageDonated FROM tblOrders
```

and display it on your ASP page:

```
Average Donation Amount: <%=rsDonationGoal("AverageDonated")%>
```

All this extra information makes your cause appear more credible and helps donors pony up the dough. If you really want to make it fancy, you can display a recent donor list [Hack #80] on the same page.

Display a Recent Donor List

Extend your donation system by allowing users to be recognized for their contributions.

"Display Donation Goals on Your Web Site" [Hack #79] shows how to display donation goals for your web site with the intention of encouraging more and larger contributions. This hack shows how to recognize your donors for their contributions by displaying a list of the five most recent donors, the amount they donated, and a small note if the donor chooses.

The Donation Button

The donation button needs to be modified to present donors with two fields. The first asks whether the donor would like to have her name displayed on the web page. The second allows her to enter a short note if she wishes. As with a Buy Now button, the optional button variables on0, os0, on1, and os1 are used to pass the donor's answers along to PayPal.

> As explained in PayPal's Integration Guide (*https://www.paypal.com/en_US/pdf/integration_guide.pdf*), the optional fields on0, os0, on1, and os1 work for donations in the same way they do for the Buy Now button. (You also won't see these options in the donation button generator under PayPal's Merchant Tools tab.)

This donation button collects the information we need. (Note the similarity to the button code in "Display Donation Goals on Your Web Site" [Hack #79].)

```
<form action="https://www.paypal.com/cgi-bin/webscr" method="post">
<input type="hidden" name="cmd" value="_xclick">
<input type="hidden" name="business" value="sales@payloadz.com">
<input type="hidden" name="item_name" value="Donation">
<input type="hidden" name="item_number" value="Donation-001">
<input type="hidden" name="no_note" value="1">
<input type="hidden" name="currency_code" value="USD">
<input type="hidden" name="tax" value="0">
<input type="hidden" name="on0" value="Display name on donors page">
Do you want your name displayed on the "recent donors" page?
<select name="os0">
 <option value="Yes" selected>Yes</option>
 <option value="No">No</option>
</select>
<br>
<input type="hidden" name="on1" value="Public note for donors' page">
Note for "recent donors" page (optional):
<input type="text" name="os1" maxlength="255">
```

```
<input type="image" src=
    "https://www.paypal.com/en_US/i/btn/x-click-but21.gif"
    border="0" name="submit">
</form>
```

When this form is submitted to PayPal by your donor, it passes the values for the optional fields along to PayPal, where the choices are displayed on the Confirm Your Payment page. This gives your donors a chance to reread the choices and use the Cancel button if they made a mistake.

The Database Table

The database schema for this hack is based on "Insert Payment Details into a Database with IPN" [Hack #82] and "Insert Cart Details into a Database" [Hack #83]. Those hacks cover recording the payment information and the payment detail information.

To store the donors' recognition choices, you need to add two fields to your database. You could create a new table for this information, but for simplicity, this example assumes you have added two fields—named ShowName and DonorNote, of types integer and text, respectively—to the tblPayments table, as shown in Table 7-4.

Table 7-4. A database table to track the donations you receive

ShowName	mc_gross	DonorNote
1	$0.05	Give 'til it hurts
0	$300.00	Why not?
1	$23.05	This is our entire annual budget

 To make the Confirm Your Payment page look friendly and readable to your donors, set os0 to either Yes or No. When reading option_selection1 (the value sent by the donor's browser as os0), remember to look for a Yes or a No and populate your database table with a value of 1 or 0, respectively. (By the way, why does PayPal accept a variable called os0 and send you back its value in a variable called option_selection1? Why indeed....)

The IPN Page

Your IPN page functions much like the IPN page described in "Insert Payment Details into a Database with IPN" [Hack #82]. However, you need to insert two new field values, one that indicates the donor's choice whether to display her name and one to hold the donor's note:

```
'Create new variables and populate them
Dim ShowName
Dim DonorNote
If Request.Form("os0") = "Yes" Then
 ShowName = 1
Else
 ShowName = 0
End
DonorNote = Request.Form("os1")
```

Include these values in the SQL statement to insert the values into the database.

```
INSERT INTO tblPayments (payer_email, payer_id, payment_status, txn_id,
    mc_gross, mc_fee, payment_date, first_name, last_name) VALUES ('"
    & payer_email & "', "' & payer_id & "', '" & payment_status & "', '"
    & txn_id & "', " & mc_gross & ", " & mc_fee & ", '" & payment_date
    & "', '" & first_name & "', '" & last_name & "', " & ShowName
    & ", '" & DonorNote & "')
```

The Donation Page

Now that you have the donation data flowing into your database, you can use it on your Donations page. Query the database table for the five most recent entries:

```
SELECT TOP 5 first_name, last_name, mc_gross, ShowName, DonorNote
    FROM tblPaymnets ORDER BY Id DESC
```

See the "Database Coding and Platform Choices" section of the Preface for the additional information needed to put this SQL statement to work with this and the other hacks in this book.

Once the query has been made, iterate over the five records and display each one, substituting Anonymous for any donors who choose not to be acknowledged publicly:

```
<%
While NOT rsDonation.EOF
%>
<br>
Donor:
<% If rsDonation("ShowName") = 1 Then 'Show the name %>
<%=rsDonation("first_name")%> <%=rsDOnation("last_name")%>
<% Else 'Do not show the name %>
Anonymous
<% End If %>
Amount: <%=rsDonation("mc_gross")%>
<% If rsDonation("DonorNote") <> "" Then 'Note is not empty, show note %>
Note: <% rsDonation("DonorNoate")%>
```

```
<% End If %>
<br>
<%
 rsDonation.MoveNext()
End
%>
```

Hacking the Hack

You can encourage more donations—and donations of higher values—by displaying lists of the most generous and the most recent donors.

Query the database for the top five donations by amount, sorted with the largest donation first:

```
SELECT TOP 5 first_name, last_name, mc_gross, ShowName, DonorNote
      FROM tblPaymnets ORDER BY mc_gross DESC
```

The code to display this information is identical to the code used in the previous section of this hack.

HACK #81 Capture Customer Information with IPN

Use the data passed back from PayPal to keep a record of your customers and their information.

One of the key benefits of using PayPal is that customers do not have to enter information repeatedly whenever they buy something. As a merchant, you sometimes need to obtain the information on file at PayPal so that you can fulfill orders without having to contact your customers directly. You can capture the customer's information as it is stored at PayPal by using the IPN system whenever he makes a purchase from you; that way, you have it on hand in your local system for later use.

One such set of values that PayPal manages is the customer's shipping information. You can take the information passed back to you by PayPal and populate your local database so that you'll have that customer's information on file for later use. For instance, you might want to send a promotional mailing to all your customers' shipping addresses. You can also use the information to fulfill orders by printing shipping labels from your database or integrating with a shipping service such as UPS.

There are many other reasons why you would want to have a local copy of the customer's information, such as for site personalization, customer profile maintenance, and sales performance evaluations. This hack allows you to insert into a local database all the available information for a customer that PayPal passes back to you.

The following script is highly valuable when you are building an online eCommerce system. It helps with customer support issues, shipping information, and marketing and sales evaluation. It also serves as the procedural basis on which to insert other sets of data passed back to you by PayPal [Hack #83].

The Database Table

Create a new database table named tblCustomers to store your customers' information. This table contains all of the available fields: first_name, last_name, payer_business_name, address_name, address_street, address_city, address_state, address_zip, address_country, address_status, payer_id, and payer_email. Each of the fields should be entered into your database defined as text values.

Next, add a field named Id and set it as the table's primary key with an auto increment of one and no duplicates allowed. This additional field enables you to work with unique records in your advanced store functionality [Hack #54]. Once the table is ready, simply save it, and you can begin creating your script that populates the table with data.

The IPN Page

Your IPN page is passed your customer's information as soon as the transaction completes. This hack uses VBScript for Microsoft Active Server Pages (ASP) and SQL queries to interact with the database. First, retrieve the values that are posted from PayPal and place them in temporary variables so you can work with them inside your VBScript code:

```
Dim first_name, last_name, payer_business_name, address_name,
        address_street,
address_city, address_state, address_zip, address_country,
        address_status, payer_id, payer_email

first_name = Request.Form("first_name")
last_name = Request.Form("last_name")
payer_business_name = Request.Form("payer_business_name")
address_name = Request.Form("address_name")
address_street = Request.Form("address_street")
address_city = Request.Form("address_city")
address_state = Request.Form("address_state")
address_zip = Request.Form("address_zip")
address_country = Request.Form("address_country")
address_status = Request.Form("address_status")
payer_id = Request.Form("payer_id")
payer_email = Request.Form("payer_email")
```

Once you have the variables populated with values, you are ready to insert them into your database table. The following SQL query adds the items to the database:

```
INSERT INTO tblCustomers (first_name, last_name, payer_business_name,
    address_name, address_street, &_address_city, address_state,
    address_zip, address_country, address_status, &_ payer_id,
    payer_email) VALUES ('" & first_name & "', "' & last_name & "', '" &
    payer_business_name & "', '" & address_name & "', '" & address_street
    & "', '" & address_city & "', '" & address_state & "', '" & & "', '"
    & address_zip & "', '" & address_country & "', '" & address_status
    & "', '" & payer_id & "', '" & payer_email & "')
```

See the "Database Coding and Platform Choices" section of the Preface for the additional information needed to put this SQL statement to work with this and the other hacks in this book.

Each time a new record is added to the table, a unique ID number is automatically generated for that record in the Id column. Uploading this page to your server and setting your IPN preferences to use this page as your IPN script causes the code to execute whenever a transaction is made in your account. When the page is called in the server-side post by PayPal, the transaction details are passed to this page, including the variable values. They are then recorded into your local database, creating a record on your own system.

HACK #82 Insert Payment Details into a Database with IPN

Record the data from IPN into a database to facilitate simple bookkeeping.

Capturing transaction-specific information is a vital part of expanding an online store, because it provides a platform of information on which to build value-added services and upselling techniques. For example, "Upsell Your Customers" [Hack #75] provides a list of similar products purchased by other customers.

This functionality is required for complete security against spoofing in some vending applications. It allows you to check whether a transaction has already been processed.

The Database Table

Create a new database table, tblOrders, in which to store your order information. This table contains information about your customers' orders, but not any information related to the products your customers actually ordered.

Your database table should consist of the fields and data types shown in Table 7-5.

Table 7-5. A table to store order information retrieved with IPN

Variable	Data type
Id	An autonumber type, set as the primary key
Payer_email	Text field
Payer_id	Text field
Payment_status	Text field
Txn_id	Text field
Mc_gross	Money, or a floating point type with 2 places of precision
Mc_fee	Money

The IPN Page

Once the table has been created, install your IPN script to populate it with information posted by PayPal's IPN facility. Start by creating new local variables and capturing the posted values into your IPN page:

```
Dim payer_email, payer_id, payment_status, txn_id, mc_gross, mc_fee,
    payment_date

payer_email = Request.Form("payer_email")
payer_id = Request.Form("payer_id")
payment_status = Request.Form("payment_status")
txn_id = Request.Form("txn_id")
mc_gross = Request.Form("mc_gross")
mc_fee = Request.Form("mc_fee")
payment_date = Request.Form("payment_date")
```

Now that you have the values temporarily placed in your page, you can perform the database insert using the following SQL query:

```
INSERT INTO tblOrders (payer_email, payer_id, payment_status, txn_id,
    mc_gross, mc_fee, payment_date) VALUES ('" & payer_email & "', "' &
    payer_id & "', '" & payment_status & "', '" & txn_id & "', " &
    mc_gross & ", " & mc_fee & ", '" & payment_date & "')
```

When the values are inserted into the tblOrders database table, a unique ID number will be generated by the database for the Id field. Note that the mc_gross and mc_fee variables are not surrounded by single quotes; they are inserted into your database as numeric values.

Insert Cart Details into a Database

#83   Record the contents of customers' Shopping Carts into a database to build a
complete order-tracking subsystem.

This hack records a list of products a customer has purchased, in addition to the corresponding payment and customer information. There are two situations in which you'll record purchase information: purchases of a single item (with the Buy Now button) and Shopping Cart transactions.

The first is fairly straightforward and serves as a primer for the more complex Shopping Cart insertion into your database. This hack is necessary for many merchants, because the PayPal history does not keep track of the individual items purchased in Shopping Cart transactions. For Shopping Cart purchases, the history provides only transaction information without any product detail. However, the PayPal IPN system does POST the individual cart values back to us in real time, so we can use that information to create our own payment history with full details.

The Database Table

Create a new database table to hold only the product detail information, as shown in Table 7-6.

Table 7-6. A database table that stores a customer's purchases

item_number	item_name	txn_id
6001	Vitamins	3498573409587349958
6002	Sulfuric Acid	4593845793487543432
6004	Calculator	3453120231232468962
7001	Imitation Gruel	2349821342013093232

This table will be used later with the transaction table to give a complete view of any specific transaction.

You will not record any of the payment information in this table, because you have already captured it in "Insert Payment Details into a Database with IPN" [Hack #82].

You can join the tables using the transaction ID as the key; it will be the same in both tables for any one transaction. The minimal information you'll capture for each product purchased will be the product's name and item number, so create two fields named item_name and item_number with text data types.

The PayPal system does not provide individual product price information via IPN. To overcome this limitation, you must query an item's price from another table [Hack #73] and calculate the price for the item based on the item_number passed by the IPN system.

Name the new table tblOrderDetails and save the database. It is now ready to have information inserted into it by your IPN script.

Single-Item Purchases IPN Page

Because you're looking for the item_name and item_number variables, you need to create two new temporary variables to hold these values. Also, you need to capture the transaction ID so that you can query your database later for the information regarding a specific transaction. Create and populate the variables with the following code:

```
Dim item_name, item_number, txn_id
Item_name = Request.Form("item_name")
Item_Number = Request.Form("item_number")
Txn_id = Request.Form("txn_id")
```

Next, execute this SQL statement to insert these values into the database:

```
INSERT INTO tblOrderDetails (item_name, item_number, txn_id) VALUES
        ('" & item_name & "', '" & item_number & "', '" & txn_id & "')
```

Once the script is activated, the values passed back for any transaction are inserted into your tblOrderDetails database table.

A Shopping Cart IPN

Since Shopping Carts pass one or more products for any single transaction, you need to check the IPN data for the item name and number of each product. First, use the num_cart_items variable to find out how many items the customer purchased. Create a local variable to hold the number of cart items and populate it with the following code:

```
'Get number of cart items purchased
Dim num_cart_items
Num_car_items = Request.Form("num_cart_items")
```

For Shopping Cart transactions, the item_name and item_number variables are appended with their corresponding cart item count. To get the value of the first item in the cart, examine item_name1; the name of the third item in the cart (if it exists) is stored in item_name3. Using the item_name$i$ or item_number$i$ format, where the i is the cart item count, you can get the values for all the items in the cart.

Use a For loop in your IPN script to iterate through all the products your customer purchased, inserting the information about each into your database as you go.

```
'Get number of cart items purchased
Dim num_cart_items
Num_car_items = Request.Form("num_cart_items")

'Create new count variable
Dim i

For i=1 to num_cart_items

   set cInsDetails = Server.CreateObject("ADODB.Command")
   cInsDetails.ActiveConnection = "DRIVER={Microsoft Access Driver
       (*.mdb)};DBQ="C:/InetPub/wwwroot/database/dbPayPal.mdb")
   cInsDetails.CommandText = "INSERT INTO tblOrderDetails (item_name,
       item_number, txn_id) VALUES ('" & Request.Form(item_name & i) &
       "', '" & Request.Form(item_number & i) & "', '" & txn_id & "')"
   cInsDetails.CommandType = 1
   cInsDetails.CommandTimeout = 0
   cInsDetails.Prepared = true
   cInsDetails.Execute( )

Next
```

Note that the transaction ID variable remains the same, regardless of what cart item you are on, because all the items were purchased as part of the same transaction.

HACK #84 Track Google Referrals

Use Google's AdWord Conversion Tracking system and PayPal's IPN system to track sales made from Google advertising.

Google has emerged from the search engine wars as the clear winner to date. Its fast, accurate search results are presented in a way that enables users to get search results quickly without the tool getting in the way, unlike many other search engine portals. It is the most widely used search engine on the Internet, and its builders continue to innovate.

Among those innovations is a self-service advertising system that enables small merchants to get wide exposure in a cost-effective, pay-per-click arrangement. When a web surfer looking for an item—a widget, say—goes to Google and types the name of the product into the search box, not only are the search results from the Google Page Ranking system displayed, but so are small, text-based ads related to widgets. As a widget vendor, you can target your AdWords ads to be displayed when a surfer enters certain widget-centric combinations of keywords. However, Google charges you only when a person actually clicks on your ad.

In the field of marketing, the effectiveness of an advertising effort is measured by its *conversion rate*. The conversion rate can be measured in a variety of ways, but generally it is the sales generated by advertising, divided by the number of *impressions* (times a consumer sees the ad). For AdWords, Google defines a conversion as "when a click on your ad leads directly to user behavior you deem valuable, such as a purchase, signup, page view, or lead." This corresponds to the marketing industry's *response to purchase* conversion rate: the number of purchases divided by the number of clicks-through. Understanding the conversion rate of a given ad can help you refine your AdWords ad copy and decide if the campaign is bringing the return on investment you expect.

Google provides a mechanism to help you tally purchases that come from customers clicking AdWords ads. This mechanism is triggered by a small piece of code you place in your transaction processing system. This hack shows how to enable a Google AdWords ad in your PayPal eCommerce system and track sales from that ad's referrals. The system consists of three parts:

- A tracking-enabled Google AdWords placement
- A PayPal-enabled selling page
- An IPN page with the Conversion Tracking Code

Modifying Your Google AdWord Placement

You need to have one or more Google AdWord placements that refer people to your PayPal selling page. You can have as many ad placements as you like.

Log into the Google AdWord system (*http://adwords.google.com*), go to your campaign summary, and click the Conversion Tracking tab to display the screen in Figure 7-2.

You will see an option to select Basic Tracking or Customized Tracking; select the Customized Tracking option. Select the Purchase/Sale option from the tracking options, which brings you to a page that has a generated a snippet of tracking code. Copy and paste the code into a text editor. It should look something like this:

```
<!-- Google Conversion Code -->
<script language="JavaScript">
<!--
google_conversion_id = 1234567890;
google_conversion_language = "en_US";
if (1) {
  google_conversion_value = 1;
```

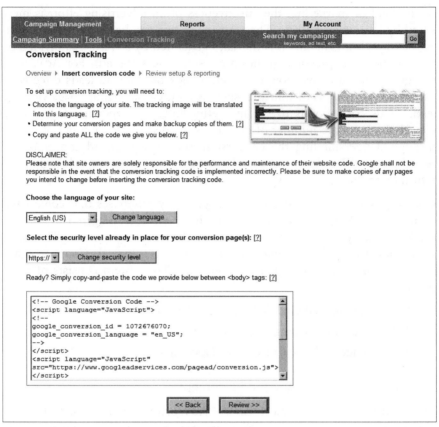

Figure 7-2. Obtaining the AdWord code from Google's Conversion Tracking page

```
}
google_conversion_label = "Purchase";
-->
</script>
<script language="JavaScript" src=
    "https://www.googleadservices.com/pagead/conversion.js">
</script>
<noscript>
<a href="https://services.google.com/sitestats/en_US.html" target=_blank>
<img height=27 width=135 src=
    "https://www.googleadservices.com/pagead/conversion/1234567890/
?value=1&label=Purchase&hl=en">
</a>
</noscript>
```

You'll place this code in your IPN processing page. But first, copy the Google conversion ID from this code (on the fourth line, in this example) for use in your AdWord placement. Use the Edit function from the Ad Group detail page to change the Destination URL. This URL is not displayed to the visitor, but when the ad is clicked, this is the URL to which visitors are sent. Visitors are directed to the PayPal-enabled sales page named *widget.asp*, and the URL includes a parameter, convid, set to the value of your Google conversion ID:

```
http://www.yoursite.com/widget.asp?convid=1234567890
```

Setting up Your Selling Page

To enable the selling page *widget.asp* to track ad referrals, it needs to include a PayPal button that passes the conversion ID provided by Google to the PayPal system. Do this by putting a standard Buy Now button on the *widget.asp* page, then adding the PayPal-defined custom variable to the button code. This tag should be added between the opening and closing <form> tags. The custom variable will be hidden from the site visitor and will be populated with the convid variable that was passed as a querystring. Populating the custom variable with this value can be done in a variety of ways, including with JavaScript, but since this example uses ASP for the IPN processing anyway, put it to use here as well:

```
<input type="hidden" name="custom" value="<%=Request.QueryString("convid")%>">
```

Now, the PayPal button is able to pass on the Google conversion ID to PayPal. When the transaction is processed, PayPal sends the conversion ID on to your IPN processing page.

Creating Your IPN Processing Page

The IPN page finishes the job of tracking conversions. Take the code you copied from Google in the preceding section and paste it into your IPN page after the standard IPN processing chores (the section that begins with process payment in PayPal's example scripts). Since the code is meant for client-side interpretation, you need to temporarily interrupt the server-side code processing by escaping the processor and adding your script. In ASP, stop the server-side processing with a %> tag and start it again with a <% tag:

```
'process payment
'stop server-side processing scripts and add conv code
%>
<!-- Google Conversion Code -->
<script language="JavaScript">
<!--
google_conversion_id = <%=Request.Form("custom")%>;
google_conversion_language = "en_US";
if (1) {
 google_conversion_value = 1;
}
google_conversion_label = "Purchase";
```

```
-->
</script>
<script language="JavaScript" src=
    "https://www.googleadservices.com/pagead/conversion.js">
</script>
<noscript>
<a href="https://services.google.com/sitestats/en_US.html" target=_blank>
<img height=27 width=135 src=
    "https://www.googleadservices.com/pagead/conversion/<%=
    Request.Form("custom")%>/?value=1&label=Purchase&hl=en">
</a>
</noscript>
<%
'continue processing server-side processing scripts
```

When an order is placed at your web site from a Google AdWord referral, the Google Conversion tracking system is activated. You can log into your Google AdWords account and evaluate your campaign's effectiveness in Google's conversion tracking system, as shown in Figure 7-3.

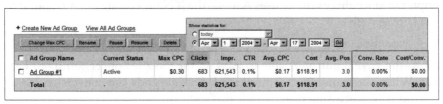

Ad Group Name	Current Status	Max CPC	Clicks	Impr.	CTR	Avg. CPC	Cost	Avg. Pos	Conv. Rate	Cost/Conv.
Ad Group #1	Active	$0.30	683	621,543	0.1%	$0.17	$118.91	3.0	0.00%	$0.00
Total			683	621,543	0.1%	$0.17	$118.91	3.0	0.00%	$0.00

Figure 7-3. Measuring your campaign's effectiveness with Google's conversion tracking system

See Also

- For practical ways to calculate and use conversion rates in your marketing campaigns, see *Strategic Database Marketing : The Master Plan for Starting and Managing a Profitable, Customer-Based Marketing Program* by Arthur M. Hughes (McGraw-Hill).
- For the nitty-gritty details on AdWords and conversion tracking, see Chapter 9, "Making Money with Google," of *Google: The Missing Manual* by Sarah Milstein and Rael Dornfest (O'Reilly).

HACK #85   Process Payments like a Credit Card with PDT

Use PDT to transact payments synchronously and deliver your product or confirmation screen immediately—and without waiting for the IPN postback.

As explained in the introduction to this chapter, PDT is one of two technologies (along with IPN) that are used to send transaction information back to your server. PDT has the distinct advantage of allowing you to provide a seamless transition from payment to delivery of goods.

To use PDT with your web site, you must first configure some options in your PayPal Profile:

1. Log into PayPal and click the My Account tab.
2. Click Profile and then click the Website Payment Preferences link.
3. Change the Auto Return option to On.

> It's vital that you turn on the Auto Return option. Without it, PDT won't work at all.

4. Enter a return URL: the address of a page (or more specifically, a script) on your site that can process the information sent back to it from Pay-Pal and display an order summary to each customer. Details of this page follow.
5. Change the Payment Data Transfer option to On.

Your site is now configured for use with PDT.

> When you save your PDT preferences, an identity token is generated and appears with a message at the top of the Website Payment Preferences page. In future visits, your identity token appears in the Payment Data Transfer section, below the On and Off options. Eventually, you will need to pass this identity token, along with the transaction token, to Pay-Pal in order to confirm that a payment is complete.

When a transaction has completed, PayPal redirects the customer to the URL you specify, with the following transaction parameters (among others) appended to the URL:

Transaction number (tx)
    The most important of the parameters sent back by PayPal. Use this in the next section to get the full set of transaction information.

Status (st)
    The status of the transaction, normally set to Completed.

Amount of sale (amt)
    The dollar (or whatever currency used) amount of the sale.

Currency (cc)
    The three-digit currency code indicating the currency used for the sale.

Once PayPal has sent this information to your site (e.g., the URL supplied in the return URL parameter), the rest is up to you and your web site in terms of how to record the transaction and fulfill the order. In the next section, you'll see how this is done.

PDT in Action

At this point, all that's left is to make sure you have a PDT handling page for the return trip. This example is written in C# for Microsoft ASP.NET.

The first order of business for the handling page (*PDTHandler.aspx*) is to grab the transaction number from the URL:

```
String strTransactionID=Request.QueryString["tx"].ToString();
```

This is where the identity token comes into play. You'll need to POST a form request and send the identity token and the transaction ID back to PayPal, as well as set a command parameter (cmd) to notify-synch. The result of this exchange will be the full PDT suite of information. To do this programmatically using C#, open a request against PayPal's server, and then place the response into a string variable:

```
string sOut = "";
string MyIDToken = "MyIdentityToken";
string transactionID = Request.QueryString["tx"].ToString();
string sCmd = "_notify-synch";

string serverURL = "https://www.paypal.com/cgi-bin/webscr";

try{
  string strFormValues = Request.Form.ToString();
  string strPassValue;
  string strResponse;

  // Create the request back
  HttpWebRequest req = (HttpWebRequest) WebRequest.Create(serverURL);

  // Set values for the request back
  req.Method = "POST";
  req.ContentType = "application/x-www-form-urlencoded";

  //Append the transaction ID, ID Token, and command
  //to the form
  strPassValue = strFormValues +
          "&cmd = _notify-synch&at = "+MyIDToken+"&tx = "+transactionID;

  req.ContentLength = strPassValue.Length;

  // Write the request back IPN strings
  StreamWriter stOut = new StreamWriter (req.GetRequestStream(),
                  System.Text.Encoding.ASCII);
```

```
stOut.Write(strPassValue);
stOut.Close( );

// Do the request to PayPal and get the response
StreamReader stIn = new StreamReader(req.GetResponse( ).GetResponseStream( ));

strResponse = stIn.ReadToEnd( );

stIn.Close( );
sOut= Server.UrlDecode(strResponse);

} catch(Exception x){
//if there is an error with the PDT response,
//you will need to handle it here, making sure you trap
//the raw PDT (if received) as well as the transactionID
//etc so you can query PayPal again should anything go
//wrong
}
```

 You can only query PayPal for the PDT response a limited number of times per transaction. After five unsuccessful responses from PayPal, you will no longer be able to query for the transaction details. This limit has been imposed for PayPal performance and security reasons. For more mission-critical applications, or if your server's connection to the Internet is flaky, you might want to employ IPN as well.

The data you receive in the PDT response is a grouping of name=value pairs, with the first parameter set to either SUCCESS or FAILURE.

 To see the full output of the PDT, refer to the Payment Data Transfer Manual, available at *https://www.paypal.com/pdt*.

Once the PDT response is placed into a string variable, loop through the string and pull out the data you need to record the order:

```
string GetPDTValue(string key){
```

❶ ```
   String [] PDTbits=PDT.Split('\n');
```

```
   string theField="";
   string theValue="";
   string thisLine="";
   string sOut="";
```

❷ ```
   for(int i=0;i< PDTbits.Length;i++){
     thisLine=PDTbits[i].ToString( );
```

③
```
      if(thisLine.IndexOf("=")>-1){
        theField=thisLine.Substring(0,thisLine.IndexOf("="));
        theValue=thisLine.Remove(0,thisLine.IndexOf("=")+1);
```

④
```
      if(theField==key){
        sOut = theValue;
        }
      }
    }
    return sOut;
  }
```

The PDT data is sent back in a single string using a linefeed as the record delimiter. On line 1, the split routine is used to assemble an array from these records. Then, the script loops (line 2) through the array, looking for the key=value pairs (line 3). When the specified key is found (line 4), the return variable, sOut, is set with the key name.

Using this GetPDTValue function, you can pull out any individual values you need to record the order into your database and prepare a nice receipt page for the customer (one of the tasks you must perform when you use PDT). For the full list of PDT parameters, refer to the Payment Data Transfer Manual.

Tracking Your Users: Before and After

If you decide to personalize the shopping experience for each customer, it is important to know who is buying what from your site. If you have any kind of customer login, you need to pass this information to PayPal so that you'll know who your customers are when they return to your site.

A great way to track your user before and after the PayPal transaction is to send along the user's identifier in the custom parameter [Hack #28]. To do so, use the following code, where *user_ID* is some identifying number or string assigned to the particular customer (usually an integer key from a database):

```
<input type=hidden name="custom" value="user_ID">
```

When this value is returned to you in the PDT response, you can retrieve it using the GetPDTValue from the previous section:

```
string strCustomerID=GetPDTValue("custom");
```

You could also use HTTP cookies to do this, but the custom field is more reliable, because it won't break if the customer has configured her browser to reject cookies.

Retrieving the Order

PayPal sends the items purchased in a simple numbered sequence. For a single-item purchase, PayPal returns a simple parameter called item_number:

```
item_number=HTHTKEPO
```

When a customer purchases more than one item, PayPal adds an integer value to the end of each parameter to identify the item number, like this:

```
item_number1=HTHTKEPO
item_number2=DREGFEF
item_number3=ERTRTDFD
```

The values to the right of the equals signs correspond to the product IDs you send PayPal, presumably taken from your database (these could be SKU codes, product names, or whatever). See "Hack Shopping Cart Buttons" [Hack #45] to use PDT with PayPal's Shopping Cart, or check out "Integrate a Third-Party Shopping Cart with PayPal" [Hack #50] if you're using your own shopping cart system.

The following code retrieves the details of an order:

```
string productNumber=GetPDTValue("item_number");
```

❶ if(productNumber!=""){
      //only one item purchased

❷   //process order here

    }else{
      string itemTag="item_number";
      string thisItem="";

❸   for(int i =0; i < 1000; i++){
       thisItem = itemTag + i.ToString();
       productNumber = GetPDTValue(thisItem);

       if(productNumber!=""){

❹   //process shopping cart item here

       }else{

        //no more items found; exit the loop
        break;

       }
      }
    }

Since the item_number field is present if only a single item was ordered, the first check (line ❶) redirects the code if the field exists. Otherwise, the code proceeds to the next section, which begins a loop (line ❸) to look for multiple items in the Shopping Cart. Either way, you must add code (on lines ❷and ❹) to retrieve the quantity and other details from the PDT data string using the same GetPDTValue function.

—*Rob Conery*

Synchronizing PDT and IPN

#86

Ensure that your product is delivered, even when PDT fails and the return page never shows, by introducing redundancy with IPN.

PayPal's PDT system [Hack #85] automatically redirects your customers back to your web page after they pay and sends the transaction information along with them. While this is an effective way to deliver products and services to your customers without forcing them to wait for IPN to contact your server, it's certainly not infallible. If you care about record keeping, you'll want to use IPN to record payment details into a database [Hack #82] so that you don't miss any payments.

This hack shows how to coordinate PDT with IPN to ensure that every transaction is processed by your server. The potential problem here is that when using PDT, or even the return variable feature, your customer can be redirected back to your web site before the IPN system has finished processing. You can address this issue by checking your local database to see whether or not the transaction details have been inserted yet; this refreshes the return page until the order has been processed and the IPN data has been received.

The reason you still need to use the IPN system is that the PDT is intended to be used only for a one-time query when the transaction takes place. If that query fails, the data for that transaction is lost forever. The IPN system has a high level of redundancy; it continues to call your IPN processing script for up to four days until it processes successfully.

The Code

The following ASP code simply reads the transaction data passed from PDT and then checks your local database to see if the IPN has finished processing the transaction. If not, it repeatedly refreshes the page (every five seconds) until it finds the corresponding transaction in the database. Use this as your PDT return page:

```
<%
❶  Response.AddHeader "Pragma","no-cache"
```

```
      Response.Expires = 0
      Response.buffer = true
      Response.clear

❷    'Create transaction id variable
      Dim txn_id
      txn_id = Request("txn_id")

❸    'Check if IPN has been processed with database query and recordset
      Dim rsOrderCheck
      Set rsOrderCheck = Server.CreateObject("ADODB.Recordset")
      rsOrderCheck.ActiveConnection = MM_connPayloadz_STRING
      rsOrderCheck.Source = "SELECT tblOrderDetails.* FROM tblOrderDetails
           WHERE tblOrderDetails.txn_id = '" & txn_id & "'"
      rsOrderCheck.Open( )

❹    'Count how many times you refresh the browser
      Dim vRCount
      If Request("rcount") = "" Then
        vRCount = 1
      Else
        vRCount = cInt(Request("rcount")) + 1
      End If
      %>
      <html>
      <head>
      <% If rsOrderCheck.EOF And rsOrderCheck.BOF Then 'ipn not processed yet %>
❺    <meta http-equiv="refresh" content="5;URL=
           http://paypalhacks.com/pdtpage.asp?txn_id=<%=Request("txn_id")%
           &rcount=<%=vRCount%>">
      <% End If %>
      </head>
      <body>
      <% If rsOrderCheck.EOF And rsOrderCheck.BOF Then 'ipn not processed yet %>
❻    Please wait while we locate your order.
      This may take up to 30 seconds.
      <% Else 'ipn has been processed %>
❼    IPN has been processed, insert content here.
      <% End If %>
      </body>
      </html>
```

Line ❶ tells the browser and server not to cache the page content, but rather
to expire it immediately; this makes sure that new content appears when it is
available. Then, line ❷ initializes the transaction ID, and line ❸ checks it
against the database. Line ❺ contains the meta refresh tag, which refreshes
the page automatically if the recordset is empty (e.g., if IPN has not processed the order yet).

Place your own messages on lines ❻ and ❼ to inform the customer that the
order is still being processed and that the order is ready, respectively.

This example illustrates synchronizing the PDT and IPN system, but you can also use the same technique presented here for your return page if you are not using the PDT system. For information on using the return page for order processing, see "Process Payments like a Credit Card with PDT" [Hack #85].

Hacking the Hack

Normally, the IPN system contacts your server and completes the process in a matter of seconds after the customer pays. However, there are times when the IPN system can take longer (up to several minutes or even hours). This can be caused by load on the PayPal system, on your site, or any number of other possibilities. In the event of such a delay, the repeated refreshing of the page is likely to induce seizure in your customer or, at the very least, try his patience.

To address this issue, you might want to limit the number of times the browser is refreshed and display a message to the customer if that limit is reached (something to the effect that his order is still being processed and he should contact you or get a cup of coffee or something). Simply add the following snippet of code before the opening <html> tag:

```
<%
'Redirect customer to order search timeout page
If vRCount => 5 Then
  Response.Redirect("ordertimeout.asp")
End If
%>
```

This code simply checks the number of times the browser has been refreshed (vRCount, set on line ❹ in the original code) and interrupts the process after five unsuccessful tries (this means that at least 30 seconds have passed since the customer was first sent to your PDT page).

The PayPal Web Services API
Hacks 87–100

PayPal's Web Services application programming interface (API) is the means by which you can interface directly with the PayPal platform to build applications and web sites that leverage features on the PayPal web site. Essentially, this means that you can integrate your order-processing and customer-service systems with the payment information stored on the PayPal web site.

No longer are you bound by the patchwork services afforded by services like Instant Payment Notification (IPN) [Hack #65] and Payment Data Transfer (PDT) [Hack #85]. Instead, the API provides a more seamless link between your application and the PayPal engine, allowing you to write slick, robust order-processing applications to help grow your business.

 Currently, you cannot use PayPal's API to process credit card payments directly from your site. Your customers must still visit the PayPal web site to send payments to you, but you can subsequently use the API to retrieve the details about such payments, including those funded by credit cards.

The geek-impaired might not immediately see the benefit of writing more code to essentially duplicate the functionality that exists on the PayPal web site, but here are some specific benefits to consider:

- Individual merchants can automate administrative tasks they do repeatedly.
- Large merchants who conduct thousands of transactions a day no longer have to log into PayPal to review their transactions, view specific transaction details, or perform refunds [Hack #91]. This allows customer care representatives to work more efficiently.

- Third parties can provide solutions to small or large businesses. Some solutions require customers to pay via the PayPal web site, but you can provide some services in which PayPal is never seen by the user. Therefore, you can make it appear as if you are providing the payment service (e.g., Mass Pay [Hack #96]. In addition, most of the administrative PayPal functionality can remain on your site.

> You might be wondering at this point exactly how API, IPN, and PDT differ. In simplest terms, IPN and PDT are notifications initiated by PayPal (in the form of web requests) that let your server know when a transaction has completed. The API, on the other hand, is initiated by you and allows you to execute core PayPal functions from your application, whenever and however you like. These technologies can be used together for further automation.

Due to security concerns, the API is limited to a subset of the things you can do on the PayPal site. Specifically, you can do the following things:

- Search for a transaction with the date, name, email, and other parameters [Hack #94].
- Retrieve the details of a single transaction [Hack #93], given the PayPal transaction ID.
- Refund a payment [Hack #91] (in full, or partially).
- Make payments from your account to other accounts using PayPal's Mass Pay service [Hack #96].

> A little programming experience will be extremely helpful in making use of the hacks in this chapter, most of which were written for Visual Studio .NET. See the "Database Coding and Platform Choices" section of the Preface for more details.

Most of the API functionality is usable by merchants as is, but there are ways to extend the basic functionality to do wonderful things that will make people mumble your name as you walk valiantly by—which is the point of this book anyway, isn't it?

Create a Developer Account

The first thing you need to do to access the PayPal API is set up a developer account at PayPal Developer Central. It's simple, and best of all, it's free. There is a wealth of information on the Developer Central site, including:

- Sample code provided by PayPal that demonstrates most of the API
- A moderated forum where you can ask (and receive answers to) common or obscure API-related questions
- The PayPal Sandbox [Hack #87], a test area in which you can run merchant transactions without using actual funds

PayPal Developer Central is located at *https://developer.paypal.com*. To create a developer account, click the registration link and enter basic information about yourself, such as your name, company, email address, as well as some optional profile questions.

After completing the sign-up form, an email will be sent only once to the email account you specify. Click the email link to activate your account. Make sure you don't lose this email, because if you do, you will not be able to register again with the same email address.

When you're finished, you will be registered as a developer, at which point you'll be able to log into PayPal Developer Central, as shown in Figure 8-1.

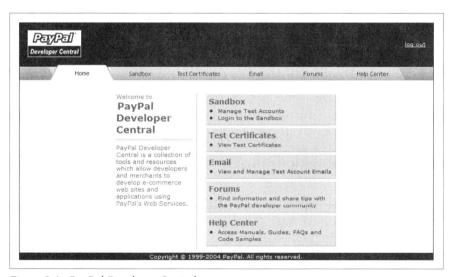

Figure 8-1. PayPal Developer Central

Developer Central is divided into five areas:

The Sandbox
   Create test user accounts and test your code [Hack #87].

Test Certificates
   Create and keep track of your SSL certificates [Hack #87].

Email

Manage pseudo-email messages sent from the Sandbox.

Forums

Ask questions and discuss the API with other developers in a user-to-user forum moderated by PayPal developers.

Help Center

How-tos, sample code, and links to other forums (e.g., eBay and PayPal general forums).

Now that your developer account is set up, it's time to have some fun in the Sandbox.

—*Rob Conery and Dave Nielsen*

HACK #87   Set up the Sandbox

Create phony accounts and use phony money to test your API code, all without spending a dime.

Go to http://paypalhacks.com for downloadable code and API updates.

PayPal Developer Central includes an environment called the PayPal Sandbox, in which you can test your PayPal Web Services applications, as well as IPN and PDT features (discussed in Chapter 7). The Sandbox looks and behaves like the PayPal web site, with one important exception: no real money is transacted. You can create and access multiple test accounts in the Sandbox, which means that you can create both a business and a buyer account without the hassle of setting up real email, credit card, and bank accounts.

Before PayPal created its Sandbox, you would have had to create two real PayPal accounts and use real money to test your code. There was no way to get around this, but you could send test payments in pennies—$0.01 for a widget or $0.02 for a gumball—and then refund the transactions immediately thereafter. As you can imagine, this process quickly became burdensome. Although some companies (such as Eliteweaver) offered good IPN-testing solutions, ultimately nothing was able to replace the comfort of knowing that your code worked against the real thing.

Creating a Sandbox Account

Creating a Sandbox PayPal account is similar to creating a live PayPal account. The web pages look and behave almost identically. Here's how to do it:

1. Log into Developer Central with your new developer account and click the Sandbox tab.

2. Click the Create Account link, at which point a familiar page appears: the PayPal sign-up page.

> It might be a little jarring to see the PayPal account sign-up page, but if you look to the top-left corner, you'll see a PayPal Sandbox logo, verifying that you did swallow the blue pill and are indeed working within a simulated PayPal environment.

3. To create a business account, select the Business Account option. Select your country and click the Continue button.

4. On the next page, enter any existing address and phone number. This information never leaves the Sandbox, so the information you enter here makes little difference. Click the Continue button when you're done.

5. On the Enter Your Information page, type an email address and password. To make it easy on yourself, use a simple email address such as business@mysite.com and an easy-to-remember password such as qwertyui. You don't have to use a real email account, because the Sandbox emails never leave the Sandbox.

> Real currency is not involved when using the Sandbox, so there isn't much of a security issue. You might choose to use the same password for every Sandbox account you create. Having to manage multiple passwords is pointless and can slow down your development team.

6. You also need to provide answers to two security questions. Again, this information never leaves the Sandbox. Enter something obvious, such as your own last name, for Mother's Maiden Name and the city you work in for City of Birth. Finally, enter the Security Measure characters and click the Sign-up button.

7. Next, you will be asked to confirm your email address. But before you do, repeat steps 1 through 6 to create a second Sandbox account, from which you can send test payments. To create a buyer account, select Personal Account (instead of Business Account) in step 3. You'll be asked fewer questions this time.

You might want to create both types of personal accounts (Standard and Premier) to mimic the different types of Pay-Pal users who will be buying things from your site. To create a Premier account, answer Yes when asked "Would you like this to be a Premier Account?"

8. Once both your Business and Personal accounts are set up, they will appear under the Sandbox tab, as shown in Figure 8-2. For each account you create, you will see the email address, the account type, the country in which the account is registered, the account balance and currency, and whether the account is confirmed and verified.

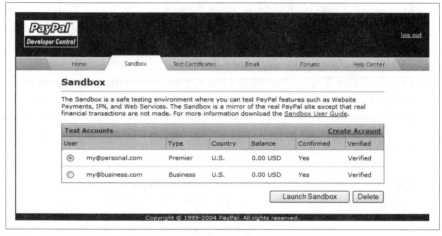

Figure 8-2. Buyer and Seller accounts in the Sandbox

Confirming Your Sandbox Email Addresses

Just as you would on the live PayPal site, you must confirm your newly cre-ated PayPal Sandbox accounts before you use them. Normally, PayPal would send a real email to a newly added email address for confirmation, but email sent on behalf of pseudo-accounts would be confusing, to the say the least. So, for security and other reasons, PayPal's Developer Central web site includes a self-contained pseudo-email–messaging system to catch and display emails generated by the PayPal Sandbox.

To view these emails, log into the Developer Central web site and click the Email tab. A list of emails from PayPal to your various accounts will be dis-played here. Click the subject link of any email to open the email message, as shown in Figure 8-3.

To confirm your Sandbox account:

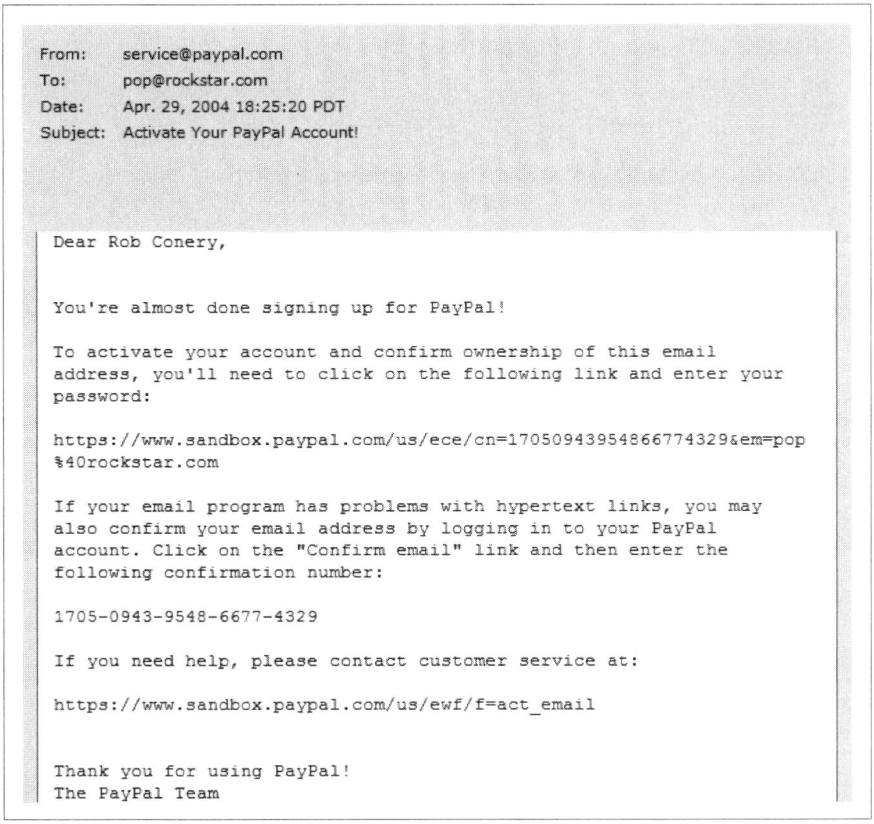

```
From:     service@paypal.com
To:       pop@rockstar.com
Date:     Apr. 29, 2004 18:25:20 PDT
Subject:  Activate Your PayPal Account!


Dear Rob Conery,


You're almost done signing up for PayPal!

To activate your account and confirm ownership of this email
address, you'll need to click on the following link and enter your
password:

https://www.sandbox.paypal.com/us/ece/cn=17050943954866774329&em=pop
%40rockstar.com

If your email program has problems with hypertext links, you may
also confirm your email address by logging in to your PayPal
account. Click on the "Confirm email" link and then enter the
following confirmation number:

1705-0943-9548-6677-4329

If you need help, please contact customer service at:

https://www.sandbox.paypal.com/us/ewf/f=act_email


Thank you for using PayPal!
The PayPal Team
```

Figure 8-3. The PayPal Sandbox account verification process

1. Copy the URL from the Activate Your PayPal Account email.
2. Open a new browser window, paste the URL into your browser's address bar, and press Enter.
3. Enter the password for your account and click Submit.

You will need to follow this process for every new Sandbox account you've created.

Verifying Bank Accounts in the Sandbox

PayPal uses bank accounts to verify [Hack #2] that their members are who they say they are.

 Bank accounts are also used to add and withdraw funds [Hack #20].

Adding a bank account to a Sandbox account is relatively straightforward and has the added bonus of instantly making you rich—at least in the world of the PayPal Sandbox.

To add a bank account to your PayPal Sandbox account:

1. Log into the Sandbox with your business account and click Add Bank Account on the My Account/Overview page.

2. The Add Bank Account page will be conveniently pre-populated with a fake bank account number. Add a name for the account and click Add Account. Be sure to make note of the account numbers used for the bank account, because you will need them in the future to add multiple users or enable other features.

 At the time of this writing, the Sandbox displays this account number only once: at the moment of its creation. So, write it down somewhere, because you won't see it again. One way to remind yourself of this bank account information is to use the routing number and bank account as part of the account name (e.g., BofA-325272157_10448249836185934481). If you do forget the account numbers, you might want to abandon this Sandbox account and open another.

3. At this point, PayPal would normally make two small deposits into your pseudo-account and then ask you to confirm the amounts that were deposited. However, since the account numbers and the corresponding accounts are fake, you won't be able to visit your bank's web site to get the information [Hack #2]. Instead, PayPal provides an easy way to accomplish this step right on the site. Click the Get Verified link on the My Account/Overview page to view the Get Verified page.

4. On the Get Verified page, click "Add and confirm a checking account" to be taken to the Confirm Bank Account page. Select the bank account you would like to confirm and click Submit. Click Continue when you see "Your U.S. Bank Account Has Been Confirmed."

Repeat this process for your buyer account.

Adding Funds (and Getting Rich Quick)

When you've verified all your accounts, the last step is to put some money in your Personal (buyer) account.

 You do not have to add funds to your account before making a payment, because PayPal will let you fund payments from your fake bank account or fake credit card, just as in real life.

To add funds, log into the Sandbox with your Sandbox buyer account, and from the My Account tab, click Add Funds. Click the Transfer Funds from a Bank Account link and follow the instructions. You need to put some money into your Personal account only, since that's the account from which you'll be making your pseudopayments.

> The transaction will be held as Pending until you actually view the details of the transaction and click Clear Transaction or Fail Transaction. For the purposes of this hack, select Clear Transaction here.

This might be the most fun of all the things mentioned in this book, because you can, on a whim, transfer any amount of money into your account and become a pseudomillionaire in seconds! (And you thought this was going to be about the coding!)

—*Rob Conery and Dave Nielsen*

Make Your First API Call
Make your first API call by issuing a refund from the command line.

As a programmer, you know that web services are the "next big thing." They're supposed to make it easy for two computers to exchange information. PayPal Web Services, however, handle money and therefore require an extra level of security. The extra layers are quite easy to implement, but you'll need to take the following configuration steps prior to executing your first call:

1. Set up an SSL certificate issued by PayPal.
2. Install Simple Object Access Protocol (SOAP) libraries or set up a web reference to SOAP-enable your application

Setting Up the SSL Certificate

Your web site might already have an SSL certificate that it uses for secure communication, but at the time of this writing, PayPal does not support using certificates from other certificate authorities (CAs). This means that you'll need to generate an SSL certificate from the PayPal Sandbox [Hack #87], and then later, the PayPal live site when your application goes live [Hack #100]. Here's how to request an API certificate:

1. Log into your PayPal Sandbox Business account and click the Profile tab.
2. Click the API Access link and then click the API Certificate Request link.

3. In the Certificate Profile section, enter your merchant information (First Name, Last Name, Company, Volume, and Expected Use are required fields). While the Volume and Expected Use fields are required, they are mainly for PayPal informational purposes only.

4. In the Account Name and Password section, enter a password.

> Make sure to write down your account name and password, because there will be no way to get a reminder later on. This account name and password, along with a certificate file, will be required when you connect to the PayPal API. If you do forget your password, you will need to create a new SSL certificate request.

5. In the Terms of Use section, check Yes and click Continue. Review your Certificate Profile and click Generate Certificate. Your API Certificate file will be created and made available for you to download.

6. Once the API certificate file is generated, click Download and save the text file (*cert_key_pem.txt*) to your local hard drive.

This API certificate file is a text file, but it is not yet in the format required to connect to the PayPal API. You'll need to convert it into a PKCS12 (*.cer*) file using a cryptographic tool such as OpenSSL (*http://www.openssl.org*). To avoid having to compile the OpenSSL source code yourself, you can download a precompiled Windows version, as described in the "Installing OpenSSL for Windows" sidebar.

SOAP-Enabling Your Application

In order for your application to access PayPal's Web Services, you'll need to install a module or code library that can call a SOAP-based web service. Some development tools, such as Visual Studio .NET, are set up to support web services out of the box.

> For the sake of simplicity and consistency, the rest of this chapter uses code written in C# using Visual Studio .NET. If you are using another language, such as Java, VB, C++, PHP, or Perl, review the PayPal Web Services page (*http://www.paypalhacks.com/resources/*).

To access a web service from within a development environment such as Visual Studio .NET, you need the URL of the Web Service Description Language (WSDL) file that describes the web service and, possibly, a valid security certificate. Typically, you would set up a web reference to abstract the SOAP-specific details of the web service, allowing you to access the web ser-

Installing OpenSSL for Windows

Download and install Shining Light Productions' Win32 OpenSSL from *http://www.slproweb.com* (at the time of this writing, v0.9.7d is the recommended version).

To convert the text certificate file into SSL (PKCS12) format using OpenSSL, open the Windows command prompt (cmd.exe in Windows XP/2000, or command.com in Windows 9x/Me). Start OpenSSL by typing c:\openssl\bin\ openssl at the prompt (the pathname may be different on your system). At the OpenSSL prompt, type the following command, where c:\cert_key_pem.txt is the location of your text certificate file and c:\mycert.p12 is the location of your new SSL (PKCS12) file to create:

```
pkcs12 -export -in c:\cert_key_pem.txt -out c:\mycert.p12
```

The next step involves installing the certification and is dependent upon the type of application you're creating (e.g., a desktop application or a web application) and the development tool you're using to create it. This hack connects to the PayPal API from a desktop application created from within the Microsoft Visual Studio .NET development environment. If, however, you are using another development environment such as Java, or if you are developing a web application under Apache, you'll need to see the developer tool documentation at *http://www.paypalhacks.com/resources*.

vice as you would any other class or function call. Once you validated a web service using its WSDL file in the Visual Studio .NET Web Reference Wizard, a web reference would be added to your project and you'd be able to access its methods just like any other class in your project.

Currently, PayPal does things differently. For security reasons, PayPal requires that you not only install a security certificate, but also provide your digital certificate account name and password to access the PayPal API.

To set up a proxy web reference in Visual Studio .NET, open your Visual C# Windows Application. In your project's Solution Explorer, right-click the References folder and select Add Web Reference. In the Add Web Reference box, type the URL of the appropriate PayPal Sandbox WSDL file:

Sandbox: *http://api.sandbox.paypal.com/wsdl/PayPalSvc.wsdl*
Sandbox (alternate): *http://www.paypalhacks.com/wsdl/PayPalSvc.wsdl*
Live PayPal site: *http://api.paypal.com/wsdl/PayPalSvc.wsdl*

Then click Go. (The wizard does not work well with https, so use http.) If successful, the Web Reference wizard displays the description of the PayPalAPIInterface and the methods it contains. As of this writing, the methods are BillAgreementUpdate(), BillUser(), GetTransactionDetails(),

Installing Certificates into IE

To access PayPal's API using Visual Studio .NET, you need to import the .*p12* certificate file you created into Internet Explorer to register the certificate in the computer's registry.

Before you access the secure PayPal API with Microsoft development tools, Microsoft requires that you create a valid security certificate. To do this, import the .*p12* certificate file into Internet Explorer and then export the certificate as a .*cer* file, all from within Windows.

To import the .*p12* certificate, double-click the .*p12* file (e.g., *mycert.p12*) to open the Windows Import Certificate Wizard. Follow the prompts and accept the defaults. You will be required to enter the password you provided when you created the PayPal API certificate file earlier in this hack. When finished, you will see a confirmation message that the import was successful. Click OK.

To export the certificate as a .*cer* file, open the Tools menu in Internet Explorer and select Internet Options. Choose the Content tab and then click the Certificates button to display the Certificates screen. The Certificates screen lists the certificates currently installed on your computer; select the certificate you just imported (it's under the Personal tab) and click Export. Accept the default options. When prompted to select a File Format, select "DER encoded binary X.509 (.CER)" and click Next. Enter the filename and location, click Next, and then click Finish. You'll see a message that the export was successful. Click OK, then Close, and then OK again to close the Internet Options screen. Later, you'll refer to this .*cer* file from your code to access the PayPal API.

MassPay(), RefundTransaction(), and TransactionSearch(). (BillAgreementUpdate() and BillUser() are not publicly available and are not discussed in this book.)

Change the Web reference name from com.paypal.sandbox.api to PayPalSvc and then click Add Reference. Verify that a new folder named Web References has been created and that it contains a reference named PayPalSvc.

You are now ready to use your PayPalSvc web reference. Using the digital certificate, certificate account name, and password, you can access the PayPal Web Service's methods via this PayPalSvc object.

Getting Started with PayPal's APIClient Tool

PayPal offers immediate gratification for users who can't wait to use the PayPal API. The APIClient application is downloadable from the Help Center tab at Developer Central.

The APIClient was created using Microsoft Visual Studio .NET and is written in C#. The application is a .NET project you'll need to modify and build before you can use it.

Here's how to set up the APIClient application:

1. Download the .NET Code Samples and unzip the *APIClient.zip* file into a folder on your hard drive.

2. Double-click the *APIClient.csproj* file to open the APIClient project in Visual Studio .NET.

3. Expand the Web References folder, right-click on the PayPalSvc reference, and select Properties, as shown in Figure 8-4.

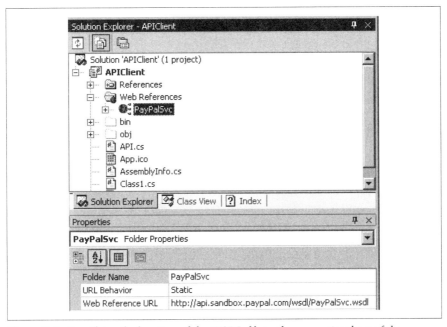

Figure 8-4. Specifying the location of the WSDL file in the properties sheet of the PayPalSvc web reference

4. Point the Web Reference URL to the PayPal Sandbox WSDL file.

5. Right-click the APIClient project name in Visual Studio .NET and select Properties.

6. Select Configuration Properties, and then select Build.

7. In the Properties pane, set the Output Path to *C:* (or whatever drive you are comfortable with; you are going to run this program from the command line, so using something like *C:* is easy on the fingers). Click OK.

8. From the Build menu, select Build APIClient. Visual Studio .NET will build the executable and save it into your Output path; make sure you place it in the same folder as your *certificate.cer* file.

The APIClient is ready to go. All you need now is a transaction to play with.

Setting up a Test Transaction

Before you start using the APIClient, send some money from your Sandbox Personal account to your Sandbox Business account:

1. Log into Developer Central, click the Sandbox tab, click the Launch Sandbox button, and log in with your Personal Sandbox account.

2. Click Send Money and then send some cash (e.g., $10) to your Business account.

3. Next, log out of your Personal account and log back into your Sandbox Business account.

4. The payment you made from your Personal account will appear on the Overview page. Your balance will have increased by the amount you sent (minus the simulated transaction fee).

5. Click the Details link to bring up the Transaction Details. Record the Transaction ID number for use in the next step.

Making Your First Call

That's it for the prep work. Now, it's time to call the Refund Web Service. The APIClient is a .NET console application, so you need to open up a command prompt (*cmd.exe* in Windows XP/2000, or *command.com* in Windows 9x/Me).

Use cd to navigate to the directory where the *APIClient.exe* executable is located (e.g., cd c:\), and execute the client program:

```
APIClient RefundTransaction -t transaction_number -u your_api_username
    -p your_api_password -c certificate_file
```

 For a full description of the arguments for the test tool, please see the APIClient documentation or type APIClient help at the prompt.

If all goes as planned, you will see some output text in your console, as shown in Figure 8-5. Among other things, Ack will be set to Success to confirm that the transaction has been refunded. Also note the number of errors reported by the call (which, in this case, happens to be zero.)

Log into your Sandbox Business account, click History, and look at your transaction log to verify that the payment was refunded successfully.

```
----------RUNNING----------------------------------------------------
Certificate Problem with accessing https://api.sandbox.paypal.com/2.0/
Problem code 0x800B0101-Certificateproblem:CertEXPIRED
Certificate Problem with accessing https://api.sandbox.paypal.com/2.0/
Problem code 0x00000000, Unknown Certificate Problem
----------RESULTS----------------------------------------
+-RefundTransactionResponse:-----------
|   Ack:   <Success>
|   Version:   <1.000000>
|   Build:   <1.0006>
|   CorrelationID:   <>
|   Timestamp:   <4/29/2004 5:49:30 PM>
|   RefundTransaction Errors:   <0>
\----------------------------------
Soap response completed and valid.

C:\>
```

Figure 8-5. Using the APIClient to issue refunds

The APIClient is a nice introduction to the use of the PayPal API, but it demonstrates only a fraction of what the PayPal API can do. In addition, the APIClient was written solely for command-line use and will not scale to other applications. Use the next few hacks to extend the PayPal API into a standalone .NET assembly that any client can use.

—Rob Conery and Dave Nielsen

Create a Wrapper Class for Your API Calls

Create a Windows DLL to call the API and eliminate need for the console application.

Using the API from a console application [Hack #88] is nice for testing, but for real-world applications, you'll want to use an encapsulated module to handle calls to the API. That way, you can reuse the functionality in multiple applications.

> This wrapper class DLL is written in C# and assembled in
> Visual Studio .NET.

The underlying architecture of the PayPal API is the same for each API method, all of which use four basic classes to complete a call:

Type
> This is a generic term for a class that holds information. You fill out the properties in the type and add the type to the request object.

Request
> This object is responsible for creating and sending the SOAP package to the API. It hands the type to the API that contains information specific to the call (the TransactionID for example, in the GetTransactionDetail( ) method).

Response

This object holds the API's response to the call, including whether the call was successful. It also returns a type object, with specifics (transaction details, for example, in the GetTransactionDetail( ) method).

API service

This object executes the call using the request object as an argument and returns a response object.

Handling the Basics

The API wrapper class makes it easier for you to access the PayPal API, and you can reuse it in multiple applications. The wrapper class has four properties (APIPassword, APIPassword, CertLocation, and APIUrl) set by the class constructor method, as well as some additional methods to simplify security setup and formatting.

1. Open Visual Studio .NET and go to File → New → Project.

2. On the New Project screen, select Visual C# Projects and Class Library.

3. Name your project PayPalAPI and click OK.

4. Add a PayPal web reference [Hack #88]. Name it PayPalSvc and click Add Reference.

5. Add a new class file to the project and name it APIWrapper.cs.

6. Copy the following code into APIWrapper.cs, and save the project when you're done:

```
using System;
using System.Net;
using System.Security.Cryptography.X509Certificates;
using System.Text;
using PayPalAPI.PayPalSvc;
using System.Data;
using System.Collections;

namespace PayPalAPI
{
    /// <summary>
    /// Summary description for APIWrapper.
    /// </summary>

    public class APIWrapper
    {
        string _APIUserName="";
        string _APIPassword="";
        string _CertLocation="";
        string _APIUrl="";

        public string APIUserName
```

```
{
    get{return _APIUserName;}
}
public string APIPassword
{
    get{return _APIPassword;}
}
public string CertLocation
{
    get{return _CertLocation;}
}
public string APIUrl
{
    get{return _APIUrl;}
}
PayPalAPIInterfaceService service;
public APIWrapper(String APIUserName, string APIPassword,
    string CertLocation, string APIUrl)
{
    _APIUserName=APIUserName;
    _APIPassword=APIPassword;
    _CertLocation=CertLocation;
    _APIUrl=APIUrl;

    // Add the CertificatePolicy so we can post to an untrusted
        site
    ServicePointManager.CertificatePolicy = new
        MyCertificateValidation( );

    service = new PayPalAPIInterfaceService( );
    service.Url = _APIUrl;

    // Add the X509 Cert to the service for authentication
    X509Certificate certificate =
        X509Certificate.CreateFromCertFile(_CertLocation);
    service.ClientCertificates.Add(certificate);
    SetHeaderCredentials(service);

}
void SetHeaderCredentials(PayPalAPIInterfaceService service)
{
    CustomSecurityHeaderType securityHeader =
        new CustomSecurityHeaderType( );
    UserIdPasswordType userIdPassword = new UserIdPasswordType( );
    userIdPassword.Username = _APIUserName;
    userIdPassword.Password = _APIPassword;
    //userIdPassword.Subject = subject;
    securityHeader.Credentials = userIdPassword;
    securityHeader.MustUnderstand = true;

    service.RequesterCredentials = securityHeader;

}
```

```
string GetAmountValue(BasicAmountType amount)
{
    string sOut="";
    try
    {
        sOut="$"+amount.Value.ToString( );
        amount.currencyID = CurrencyCodeType.USD;
    }
    catch
    {
        sOut="--";
    }
    return sOut;
}

}

}
```

Creating Your Own Certificate Handler

If you have trouble accessing the PayPal API, it might be because your .NET
code does not trust the PayPal digital certificate. But you know that you're
talking to PayPal, so it's not that important. Adding the following code to
your API wrapper overrides .NET's default certificate policy, which is to
challenge certificates issued by untrusted certificate authorities:

```
class MyCertificateValidation : ICertificatePolicy {

// Default policy for certificate validation.
public static bool DefaultValidate = false;

public bool CheckValidationResult(ServicePoint sp, X509Certificate cert,
WebRequest request, int problem) {
    //implement your custom code here
    return true;
    }
}
```

Eventually, you'll need to implement your own code for this class, but for
development purposes, you can simply tell your server to trust every certificate issuer.

—Rob Conery and Dave Nielsen

Use the PayPal API Wrapper Class

#90

Create a simple transaction-lookup form and make an API call with the API wrapper class.

Now that you've created a wrapper class for your API calls [Hack #89], it's time to put it to use. This hack adds one `GetTransactionDetail` function to your wrapper class. It then creates a user interface for the wrapper class from which you can look up the corresponding transaction details.

The first thing to do is log into Developer Central, open up your Personal Sandbox account [Hack #87], and send some money to your Sandbox merchant account.

Sending and receiving money works identically in the Sandbox and on the live PayPal site, except that the money in the Sandbox is not real and you will not receive any email messages from PayPal.

Once you have sent the money, log out of your Personal account and log into your Sandbox merchant account. You should see the money you just sent from your Personal account. Click Details next to the payment and make note of the transaction ID; you will need it later in this hack.

To use the API wrapper class to look up details of a transaction, start by adding the following `GetTransactionDetail` code your wrapper class by appending it to the existing code in the class:

```
public string GetTransactionDetail(string transactionID, string delimiter)
{
  string sReturn="";

  GetTransactionDetailsRequestType detailRequest=
      new GetTransactionDetailsRequestType();
  detailRequest.TransactionID=transactionID;
  GetTransactionDetailsReq request=new GetTransactionDetailsReq();
  request.GetTransactionDetailsRequest=detailRequest;
  GetTransactionDetailsResponseType
      response=service.GetTransactionDetails(request);

  sReturn=response.Ack.ToString()+"\n";

  //build out the response
  StringBuilder sb=new StringBuilder();
  sb.Append("************* Payment Information
******************"+delimiter);
  //payment info
  PaymentInfoType payment=response.PaymentTransactionDetails.PaymentInfo;
  sb.Append("ReceiptID: "+payment.ReceiptID+delimiter);
```

```
        sb.Append("TransactionID: "+payment.TransactionID+delimiter);
        sb.Append("PaymentDate: "+payment.PaymentDate+delimiter);
        sb.Append("GrossAmount: "+GetAmountValue(payment.GrossAmount)+delimiter);
        sb.Append("SettleAmount: "+GetAmountValue(payment.SettleAmount)+delimiter);
        sb.Append("FeeAmount: "+GetAmountValue(payment.FeeAmount)+delimiter);
        sb.Append("TaxAmount: "+GetAmountValue(payment.TaxAmount)+delimiter);
        sb.Append("PaymentStatus: "+payment.PaymentStatus+delimiter);
        sb.Append("PaymentType: "+payment.PaymentType+delimiter);
        sb.Append("TransactionType: "+payment.TransactionType+delimiter);
        sb.Append(delimiter);
        //sReturn+=response.PaymentTransactionDetails.PaymentInfo.ToString();
        sb.Append("************* Buyer Information *****************"+delimiter);

        //receiver info
        ReceiverInfoType receiver=response.PaymentTransactionDetails.ReceiverInfo;
        sb.Append("Business: "+receiver.Business+delimiter);
        sb.Append("Receiver: "+receiver.Receiver+delimiter);
        sb.Append("ReceiverID: "+receiver.ReceiverID+delimiter);

        //item info
        PaymentItemInfoType item=
            response.PaymentTransactionDetails.PaymentItemInfo;
        //PaymentItemType itm=new PaymentItemType();
        sb.Append(delimiter);
        int i=1;
        sb.Append("************* Item Information *****************"+delimiter);
        sb.Append("Custom: "+item.Custom+delimiter);
        sb.Append("InvoiceID: "+item.InvoiceID+delimiter);
        sb.Append("Memo: "+item.Memo+delimiter);
        sb.Append("SalesTax: "+item.SalesTax+delimiter);
        if(item.PaymentItem!=null)
        {
            foreach(PaymentItemType itm in item.PaymentItem)
            {
                //itm=(PaymentItemType)PaymentItem[i];
                sb.Append(delimiter);
                sb.Append("Item "+i.ToString()+":"+delimiter);
                sb.Append("Name: "+itm.Name+delimiter);
                sb.Append("Number: "+itm.Number+delimiter);
                sb.Append("Options: "+itm.Options+delimiter);
                sb.Append("Quantity: "+itm.Quantity+delimiter);
                sb.Append("SalesTax: "+itm.SalesTax+delimiter);
                sb.Append(delimiter);
                i++;
            }
        }

        sReturn=sb.ToString();
        return sReturn;
    }
}
```

Next, create a Windows form in Visual Studio .NET that uses the API wrapper class to call the GetTransactionDetails API function:

1. With the PayPal API solution opened, right-click the solution and select Add → New Project.

2. Select Visual Studio C#/Windows Application.

3. Name your project PayPalTestApp and click OK.

4. Right-click the References entry in the *PayPalTestApp* project and select Add Reference.

5. On the Add Reference screen, select the Project tab and select the PayPalAPI project. Click Select, and then click OK to add a reference to the PayPal API wrapper.

 Check out *Mastering Visual Studio .NET* by Ian Griffiths, Jon Flanders, and Chris Sells (O'Reilly) for help with creating forms in .NET.

When that's finished, create a .NET form (*Form1.cs*) with text boxes and code to look up the details of a PayPal transaction. The form accepts the API username (txtUserName), password (txtPassword), and transaction ID (txtTransactionID) as inputs and submits them to PayPal via the click of a button (cmdDetails). Add a label control (lblResponse) to output the results to. Your form should look something like the one in Figure 8-6.

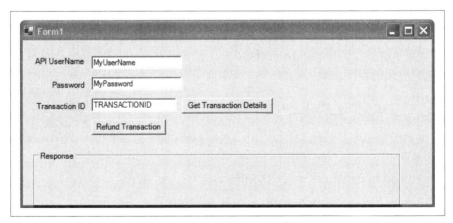

Figure 8-6. Finding transaction details quickly at PayPal

Double-click the cmdDetails button and add the following code to its click event:

```
private void cmdDetails_Click(object sender, System.EventArgs e) {
    string username=txtUserName.Text;
    string password=txtPassword.Text;
```

```
string transactionID=txtTransactionID.Text;
string certPath="C:\\certificate.cer";
string url = "https://api.sandbox.paypal.com/2.0/";

lblResponse.Text="Contacting PayPal....";
PayPalAPI.APIWrapper api=new
                PayPalAPI.APIWrapper(username,password,certPath,url);
lblResponse.Text=api.GetTransactionDetail(transactionID,"\n");
}
```

Set PayPalTestApp, fill out the text boxes with your API username and password, as well as the TransactionID copied from the preceding transaction, and click the Get Details button. The information supplied on the form will be passed to the wrapper class, which will prepare the request and then call GetTransactionDetail. Assuming it's successful, the transaction details will appear in the label control, as shown in Figure 8-7.

Now that you have a reusable class to access the API, you can easily add code to your projects to process refunds [Hack #91], retrieve transaction details [Hack #93], and search your transaction history [Hack #94].

—*Rob Conery and Dave Nielsen*

HACK #91 Refund Payments with the API

Use the API wrapper class to call the RefundTransaction API and refund a payment without logging into the PayPal web site.

Of several things you can do with the API (discussed in the introduction to this chapter), one of the most useful for PayPal's larger businesses is RefundTransaction, especially for customer service reps who have to process refunds routinely. Requiring your customer service reps to log into PayPal to process a refund requires a lot of time and unnecessary access to your account. With PayPal's new Refund API, however, you can create an application that retrieves payment transaction data and processes refunds directly from your own custom application. And just like GetTransactionDetails "Use the PayPal API Wrapper Class" [Hack #90], you can use the API wrapper to handle the basics and just add the refund-specific code.

The refund function call involves the use of three objects:

- RefundTransactionRequestType
- RefundTransactionReq
- RefundTransactionResponseType

The two Type objects are holders for information, while the Request object is used by the API service to send the information to PayPal. Here's an example of the code you need to add to your API wrapper:

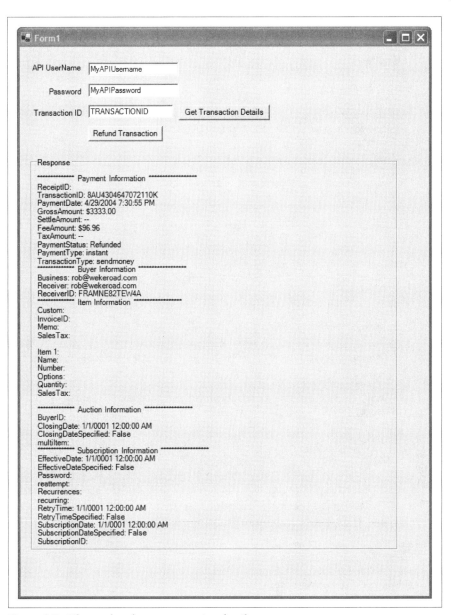

Figure 8-7. The results of your transaction details request

```
public string RefundTransaction(string TransactionID){
   //the variable that will hold the return string
   string sReturn="";

   // Create the Refund Request
```

```
   RefundTransactionRequestType refundRequest = new
RefundTransactionRequestType( );

   //set the memo so you know why you are refunding
   refundRequest.Memo = "test via API";
❶         //refund a full or partial amount

   refundRequest.RefundType = RefundPurposeTypeCodeType.Full;
   refundRequest.TransactionID = TransactionID;
   refundRequest.Version = "1.0";

   RefundTransactionReq request = new RefundTransactionReq( );
   request.RefundTransactionRequest = refundRequest;

try{
   RefundTransactionResponseType response = service.
RefundTransaction(request);

❷    string ErrorCheck=CheckErrors(response);
        //See Hack 92 for Transaction Error Handling
     if (ErrorCheck!="") {
       sReturn=("The transaction was not successful: " + ErrorCheck);
     }
     else {
       sReturn=("Response: " + response.Ack.ToString( )+"\n Correlation ID
         "+response.CorrelationID+"\nTimestamp: "+response.Timestamp.ToString( ));
     }
}catch(Exception x){
     sReturn="SSL Failure, the transaction did not go through. Error: "+
     x.Message;

}return sReturn;
}
```

You have a choice of how much money you would like to refund your customer. The preceding code refunds the full amount, but if you want to issue only a partial refund, specify the amount using PayPal's BasicAmountType by replacing line ❶ with this code:

```
refundRequest.RefundType = RefundPurposeTypeCodeType.Partial;
BasicAmountType amount=new BasicAmountType( );
amount.Value=10.00;
refundRequest.amount=amount;
```

Running the Hack

To use the API wrapper [Hack #89] to process a refund, you must first create a transaction by using your Personal Sandbox account to send money to your Business Sandbox account. First, retrieve the transaction number from your Business Sandbox account [Hack #88].

Next, add the `RefundTransaction` code to your API wrapper class in the same way that `GetTransactionDetail` is added to the API wrapper class in "Use the PayPal API Wrapper Class" [Hack #90]. Then, create a button called `cmdRefund` on your form and add the following code to its `OnClick` event:

```
private void cmdRefund_Click(object sender, System.EventArgs e)
{
  string username = txtUserName.Text;
  string password = txtPassword.Text;
  string transactionID = txtTransactionID.Text;
  string certPath = "C:\\certificate.cer";
  string url = "https://api.sandbox.paypal.com/2.0/";
  lblResponse.Text="Contacting PayPal...";

  PayPalAPI.APIWrapper api = new
      PayPalAPI.APIWrapper(username,password,certPath,url);
  lblResponse.Text = api.RefundTransaction(transactionID);
}
```

The form should look something like the one in "Use the PayPal API Wrapper Class" [Hack #90].

Finally, to run the hack, run your *PayPalTestApp* application, enter the transaction number into the transaction ID field and press the `GetDetails` button. When you've successfully retrieved the details, press the `Refund` button to complete the refund.

Confirm that your transaction has been refunded by logging into your Sandbox Personal account.

The Results

The only response you really need from PayPal once you've executed the refund is one that tells you whether it was successful. The `Ack` property (which indicates *acknowledgement*, not a shriek of pain) contains the status of the refund and is set to `Success` if all went well. If the refund did not go through, you likely violated a PayPal rule, such as issuing a partial refund greater than the purchase price or trying to refund a payment more than 30 days after the payment.

The `CheckErrors( )` function on line ❷ handles this task (see "Handle Transaction Errors within the API Wrapper" [Hack #92] for details). For rules governing PayPal refunds, open your Sandbox Business account and search the online help for *refunds*. See "Get Help from PayPal" [Hack #9] for more information on using PayPal's help system.

—*Rob Conery, Michael Blanton, and Dave Nielsen*

HACK #92 Handle Transaction Errors within the API Wrapper

Write one function to handle all transaction errors and simplify your API code.

If you were to take a close look at the objects created by your web reference in Visual Studio .NET (double-click the PayPal API web reference in your project and navigate to the web reference classes), you'd notice that the ResponseType classes (RefundTransactionResponseType, TransactionSearchResponseType, and GetTransactionDetailsResponseType) extend the same AbstractResponseType class. This unified error-handling approach provides you the same response object, regardless of which transactional class was called. This means you can write one error-checking routine that displays the correct message if an error occurs in any of these API transactions.

> These errors are not application exceptions that you should handle as you normally would. Rather, they are PayPal processing errors that deal with invalid attempts to perform a transaction (such as refunding a payment that's already been refunded).

Just add this code to any of your transaction API calls:

```
string CheckErrors(AbstractResponseType abstractResponse) {
  bool errorsExist = false;
  string errorList="";
  // First, check the Obvious.  Make sure Ack is not Success
  if (!abstractResponse.Ack.Equals(AckCodeType.Success)) {
    errorsExist = true;
  }
  // Check to make sure there is nothing in the Errors Collection
  if (abstractResponse.Errors.Length > 0) {
    errorsExist = true;
    // Do something with the errors
    foreach(ErrorType error in abstractResponse.Errors) {
      errorList+=("ERROR: "
        + error.LongMessage
        + " ("
        + error.ErrorCode
        + ")"
        );
    }
  }
  return errorList;
}
```

This method lets you (or your users) know if anything gets in the way of a successful transaction, even if the code otherwise completes successfully. That way, if something does go wrong, you can pass on information that is needed to enable your user to rectify the problem.

Using the Error Handler

To use the error handler, you must add code in two places. First, add a routine to your *PayPalTestApp* project that checks for errors and handles them appropriately. Second, add the following code to your API wrapper:

```
try{
  RefundTransactionResponseType response = service.
RefundTransaction(request);
  string ErrorCheck=CheckErrors(response);
  if (ErrorCheck!="") {
      sReturn=("PayPal Says: The transaction was not successful:
          " + ErrorCheck);
  }
  else {
      sReturn=("PayPal Says: Response: " + response.Ack.ToString());
  }
}catch(Exception x){
  sReturn="SSL Failure, the transaction did not go through. Error: "+x.
Message;
}
```

For instance, try updating the code from "Refund Payments with the API" [Hack #91] with this error handler and running the code again. Since you've already run a refund against this transaction "Refund Payments with the API" [Hack #91], an error is returned, letting the user know that the type of transaction cannot be refunded, as shown in Figure 8-8.

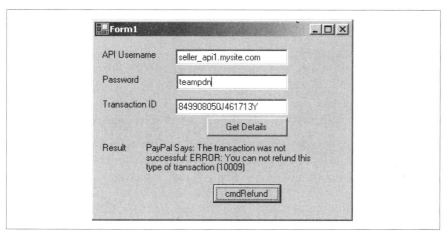

Figure 8-8. An error message generated by the generic error handler

Naturally, you'll want to supplement this error handler with your own messages and additional error traps, but this should help you build more fault-tolerant API applications.

—Rob Conery and Dave Nielsen

Retrieve Transaction Details with the API
#93

Given only a transaction ID, use the GetTransactionDetail API call with the API wrapper DLL to retrieve the details of the transaction.

The GetTransactionDetail API call is a more detailed in terms of the data it returns than the RefundTransaction call "Refund Payments with the API" [Hack #91]. The initiating call is made in the same fashion, but the response object holds many *types* that you need to access to get the transaction details. These types are designed to hold information pertaining to the myriad of PayPal transaction types, so if you use PayPal only to process sales from your Shopping Cart (as opposed to eBay auctions or digital subscriptions), you might not need all the information it returns.

But since retrieving information is so important (not to mention loads of fun), this example puts the call through its paces and retrieves all the available transaction details. The response object has a few Type objects that are of interest, because they hold the details of the entire transaction:

PaymentInfoType
> Information about the payment, including gross payment amount, fee amount, date of payment, and so on.

ReceiverInfoType
> Information about the person or entity who sent the payment.

PaymentItemInfoType
> If you sold items, their details are captured in the PaymentItemInfoType.

AuctionInfoType
> Returns information about the auction (if the payment came from an auction).

SubscriptionInfoType
> Subscription information, including interval, start date, and so on.

The PayPal API uses its BasicAmountType object to store monetary values (e.g., dollar amounts), such as any property of a Type object with the word amount in it. If there is no amount, the property will be null, which can trip up your routines. To return safe values from these fields, the following code makes use of the GetAmountValue( ) function "Create a Wrapper Class for Your API Calls" [Hack #89] to return a string value.

The Code

Here's the GetTransactionDetail() method that retrieves the transaction details for a given PayPal transaction ID:

```
public string GetTransactionDetail(string transactionID, string delimiter){
string sOut="";

//Create the request type, which holds information about the transaction you
//want more information about
GetTransactionDetailsRequestType detailRequest=new
GetTransactionDetailsRequestType( );
detailRequest.TransactionID=transactionID;

//Set the request type of the request object
GetTransactionDetailsReq request=new GetTransactionDetailsReq( );
request.GetTransactionDetailsRequest=detailRequest;

//send the request to PayPal
GetTransactionDetailsResponseType
response=service.GetTransactionDetails(request);

//make sure there is a response
if(response!=null){

//use a StringBuilder as this return uses a lot of resources if you just
//just append a regular string value
StringBuilder sb=new StringBuilder( );

sb.Append("************ Payment Information "+ **************"+delimiter);

//access each response type, gathering the information
//payment info
PaymentInfoType payment=response.PaymentTransactionDetails.PaymentInfo;
sb.Append("ReceiptID: "+payment.ReceiptID+delimiter);
sb.Append("TransactionID: "+payment.TransactionID+delimiter);
sb.Append("PaymentDate: "+payment.PaymentDate+delimiter);
sb.Append("GrossAmount: "+GetAmountValue(payment.GrossAmount)+delimiter);
sb.Append("SettleAmount: " +
    GetAmountValue(payment.SettleAmount)+delimiter);

sb.Append("FeeAmount: "+GetAmountValue(payment.FeeAmount)+delimiter);
sb.Append("TaxAmount: "+GetAmountValue(payment.TaxAmount)+delimiter);
sb.Append("PaymentStatus: "+payment.PaymentStatus+delimiter);
sb.Append("PaymentType: "+payment.PaymentType+delimiter);
sb.Append("TransactionType: "+payment.TransactionType+delimiter);

//item info

PaymentItemInfoType item=response.PaymentTransactionDetails.PaymentItemInfo;
int i=1;
sb.Append("************** Item Information ******************"+delimiter);
```

❶

❷

```
sb.Append("Custom: "+item.Custom+delimiter);
sb.Append("InvoiceID: "+item.InvoiceID+delimiter);
sb.Append("Memo: "+item.Memo+delimiter);
sb.Append("SalesTax: "+item.SalesTax+delimiter);

//The items are returned in an array of PaymentItemType
//loop through the items array, accessing item information
foreach(PaymentItemType itm in item.PaymentItem){
sb.Append(delimiter);
sb.Append("Item "+i.ToString( )+":"+delimiter);
sb.Append("Name: "+itm.Name+delimiter);
sb.Append("Number: "+itm.Number+delimiter);
sb.Append("Options: "+itm.Options+delimiter);
sb.Append("Quantity: "+itm.Quantity+delimiter);
sb.Append("SalesTax: "+itm.SalesTax+delimiter);
sb.Append(delimiter);
i++;
}

//if you are dealing in auctions, the information about
//the auction will be in the AuctionInfoType
sb.Append("*********** Auction Information ************"+delimiter);

AuctionInfoType auction=new AuctionInfoType( );
sb.Append("BuyerID: "+auction.BuyerID+delimiter);
sb.Append("ClosingDate: "+auction.ClosingDate+delimiter);
sb.Append("ClosingDateSpecified: "+auction.ClosingDateSpecified+delimiter);
sb.Append("multiItem: "+auction.multiItem+delimiter);

//Same with Subscriptions
sb.Append("********** Subscription Information ***********"+delimiter);

SubscriptionInfoType sub=new SubscriptionInfoType( );

sb.Append("EffectiveDate: "+sub.EffectiveDate+delimiter);
sb.Append("EffectiveDateSpecified: "+sub.EffectiveDateSpecified+delimiter);
sb.Append("Password: "+sub.Password+delimiter);
sb.Append("reattempt: "+sub.reattempt+delimiter);
sb.Append("Recurrences: "+sub.Recurrences+delimiter);
sb.Append("recurring: "+sub.recurring+delimiter);
sb.Append("RetryTime: "+sub.RetryTime+delimiter);
sb.Append("RetryTimeSpecified: "+sub.RetryTimeSpecified+delimiter);
sb.Append("SubscriptionDate: "+sub.SubscriptionDate+delimiter);
sb.Append("SubscriptionDateSpecified: "+sub.
SubscriptionDateSpecified+delimiter);
sb.Append("SubscriptionID: "+sub.SubscriptionID+delimiter);
sb.Append("Terms: "+sub.Terms+delimiter);
sb.Append("Username: "+sub.Username+delimiter);
sReturn=sb.ToString( );
}
return sReturn;
```

PayPal does not know the type of the transaction for which you are requesting details, so the web service returns every possible bit of information it
can. In this example, all this information is appended to a single string so
that it can be displayed easily. Since the string can be long, you'll need a
StringBuilder object (line ❶). A more practical approach might be to add
tables to a DataSet object (if you are using .NET) or perhaps to create your
own class to handle this information.

If you are developing a typical commerce site, in which items are sold
using PayPal as the payment processor, the section beginning on line ❷
will interest you the most. Each item sold is handed back to you in the
PaymentTransactionDetails.PaymentItemInfo.PaymentItem array. Each item
in the transaction is represented by a PaymentItemType that has pertinent
information, such as item number (a.k.a. SKU), price, quantity, and so on.

Running the Hack

To use the API wrapper class to look up details of a transaction, you need to
add the Auction and Subscription code to the GetTransactionDetail()
method in your API wrapper class and run your *PayPalTestApp* application.
See "Use the PayPal API Wrapper Class" [Hack #90] for further details.

—Rob Conery and Dave Nielsen

H A C K   Search for PayPal Transactions
#94
Use the TransactionSearch API call to find a transaction based on several
different criteria.

The ability to search for transactions is another powerful PayPal API function. You can find transactions by using several different criteria:

Start and end dates
> The bounding time frame of the search, down to the second.

Amount
> The payment amount (e.g., 54.00).

Currency type
> The three-letter currency code (e.g., USD).

Item number
> The item number of a sale item. This item number is the same as the
> product code you might have specified for your product when it was
> sold (a SKU, for example).

Payer email, last name, first name, salutation
> The name and email address of the person or entity who sent the payment.

Receipt ID
> PayPal issues a receipt ID for each transaction, much like the transaction ID. If a customer has a question or an issue about her order, she might offer this number to you.

Payment status
> This can be pending, completed, failed, denied, refunded, or canceled_reversal. For instance, specify completed here to show only completed transactions.

Payment type
> This can be payment, bill, refund, and so on (see the *PayPal API Developer's Guide*, available at PayPal Developer Central, for the full list). Using the payment type as a search parameter, you can show only those payments that were refunds, or perhaps those received by billing.

The search is an *inclusive* search: the more parameters you specify, the more limited your result set will be. At the time of this writing, partial values, Boolean, wild card, and regular expression terms are not supported, although PayPal might add support for these types of searches in the future. Figure 8-9 shows an example of the output.

The Code

The following code sets up a separate class for holding search parameters to be passed. The results of the search are put into an array object, through which you can loop to view the return information:

```
❶   public class TransactionSearchParam
    {
    public DateTime EndDate=DateTime.Now;
    public string TransactionID="";
    public string Amount="";
    public string Currency="";
    public string ItemNumber="";
    public string PayerEmail="";
    public string LastName="";
    public string FirstName="";
    public string Receiver="";
    public string ReceiptID="";
    public string PaymentStatus="";
    public string PaymentType="";
    }

    //the search wrapper method; the StartDate is required so pass
```

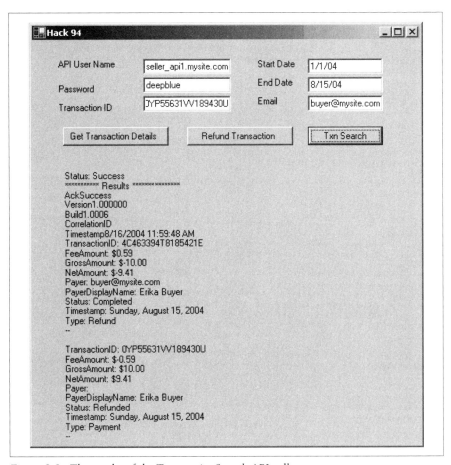

Figure 8-9. The results of the TransactionSearch API call

```
//it in as an argument
public DataTable RunTransactionSearch(DateTime StartDate,
      TransactionSearchParam param, string delimiter){

//setup the return string object
string sReturn="";

//create the Type object, which will hold the search parameters
TransactionSearchRequestType transSearch=new TransactionSearchRequestType( );

// Set up the TransactionSearch
TransactionSearchReq request=new TransactionSearchReq( );
transSearch.StartDate=StartDate;

//set the params
transSearch.StartDate=StartDate;
transSearch.EndDate = param.EndDate;
```

```
//count the number of arguments to be passed in
//you may want to have some mininum logic involved
int args=0;
if(param.TransactionID!=""){
transSearch.TransactionID = param.TransactionID;
args++;
}
```

❷
```
if(param.Amount!=""){
transSearch.Amount = new BasicAmountType( );
transSearch.Amount.Value = param.Amount;
args++;
}
if(param.PayerEmail!=""){
transSearch.Payer = param.PayerEmail;
args++;
}

if(param.Currency!=""){
transSearch.CurrencyCodeSpecified = true;
args++;
}

if(param.ItemNumber!=""){
transSearch.AuctionItemNumber = param.ItemNumber;
args++;
}

if(param.LastName!=""){
transSearch.PayerName = new PersonNameType( );
transSearch.PayerName.LastName = param.LastName;
args++;
}

if(param.FirstName!=""){
transSearch.PayerName = new PersonNameType( );
transSearch.PayerName.FirstName = param.FirstName;
args++;
}

if(param.PaymentStatus!=""){
transSearch.StatusSpecified = true;
args++;
}
if(param.PaymentType!=""){
transSearch.TransactionClassSpecified = true;
args++;
```
❸
```
}
//set the request type object with the one
//filled out with params
request.TransactionSearchRequest=transSearch;
```

```
//run the transactioon
TransactionSearchResponseType response = service.TransactionSearch(request);

//make sure the response was created
if(response!=null){
StringBuilder sb=new StringBuilder();
sb.Append("Status: "+response.Ack.ToString()+delimiter);

sb.Append("*********** Results **************"+delimiter);

❹   sb.Append( "Ack"+response.Ack +delimiter);

❺   if(response.PaymentTransactions!=null){
    // Loop through and return the values
      foreach(PaymentTransactionSearchResultType trans in
          response.PaymentTransactions){
        sb.Append("TransactionID: "+ trans.TransactionID+delimiter);
        sb.Append("FeeAmount: "+ GetAmountValue(trans. FeeAmount)+ delimiter);
        sb.Append("GrossAmount: "+ GetAmountValue(trans.GrossAmount)
          + delimiter);
        sb.Append("NetAmount: "+ GetAmountValue(trans.NetAmount)+ delimiter);
        sb.Append("Payer: "+ trans.Payer+delimiter);
        sb.Append("PayerDisplayName: "+ trans.PayerDisplayName+delimiter);
        sb.Append("Status: "+ trans.Status+delimiter);
        sb.Append("Timestamp: "+ trans.Timestamp.ToLongDateString()+ delimiter);
        sb.Append("Type: "+ trans.Type.ToString()+delimiter);
        sb.Append("--"+delimiter+delimiter);
      }
}
sReturn=sb.ToString();
}else{
  sOut=sb.ToString()+delimiter+"No Results!";
}
```

Passing search parameters with a dedicated class, TransactionSearchParam
(on line ❶) eliminates the extra coding involved when passing parameters as
arguments. If the parameters ever change, there is little work to do to bring
your code up to date. But the best part is that your method signature doesn't
change and break all your code. The section of if statements from line ❷ to
line ❷ fills out the TransactionSearchRequestType object that the PayPal API
needs to run the search. If your search returns any values, Ack is set to
Success on line ❹. Then, provided that the result set is not empty (line ❺),
the code starts looping through the collections to retrieve the information.
This example is pretty straightforward, and it holds all the transaction information for each returned transaction.

Running the Hack

Add the RunTransactionSearch code to your API wrapper class [Hack #93].

Next, add three text boxes (txtStartDate, txtEndDate, and txtEmail) and a button (cmdSearch) to From1. Then, add the following code to the button's Click event:

```
private void cmdSearch_Click(object sender, System.EventArgs e)
{
  string username=txtUserName.Text;
  string password=txtPassword.Text;
  string transactionID=txtTransactionID.Text;
  string certPath="C:\\certificate.cer";
  string url = "https://api.sandbox.paypal.com/2.0/";

  PayPalAPI.APIWrapper api=new
  DateTime StartDate = DateTime.Parse (txtStartDate.Text);
  DateTime EndDate = DateTime.Parse(txtEndDate.Text);
  string Email = txtEmail.Text
  lblResponse.Text = "Contacting Paypal...";
  PayPalAPI.APIWrapper api = new PayPalAPI.APIWrapper(username, password,
      certPath, url);
  PayPalAPI.API.APIWrapper.TransactionSearchParam param =
      new PayPalAPI.APIWrapper.TransactionSearchParam();
  param.EndDate = EndDate;
  param.PayerEmail=Email;
  lblResponse.Text = api.RunTransactionSearch(StartDate, param, "\n");
}
```

Run the form, fill out the text boxes with your date range and email address, and click the Search button. The information supplied on the form will be passed to the wrapper class, which will prepare the request and then call the RunTransactionSearch API. When successful, the list of transactions will appear in the label control.

—*Rob Conery and Dave Nielsen*

HACK #95 Hack the API Wrapper

Create a master-detail report with information collected directly from PayPal.

Looking up order information for your buyers can be hard work, especially if you process many orders a day. Here's an order-searching form in Visual Studio .NET that allows you to search the PayPal history by date range (which you can expand later to include other parameters). The results are displayed in a *master-detail report*, which consists of a list of transactions in a DataGrid and a transaction detail form for any given transaction, all with information obtained directly from PayPal!

Add two new forms to your test application, and change the code a little bit for the RunTransactionSearch( ) method to return a DataTable instead of a string:

1. Add a new form to your test application, call it frmSearch, and make it your startup form.

2. Add two DateTimePicker controls, and name them dtStart and dtEnd, respectively, and give each descriptive labels (e.g., Search, Start).

3. Add a DataGrid control and name it dg.

4. Add a button to the frmSearch and name it btnSearch.

5. Add a label and name it lblStatus. This label tells the user what's going on while he waits for the request to be returned from PayPal.

Figure 8-10 shows an example of the complete form.

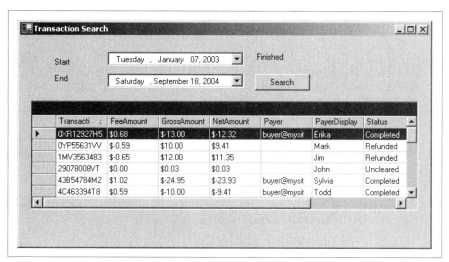

Figure 8-10. The new transaction search form

The Code

Update the RunTransactionSearch() method to return a DataTable instead of a string:

```
public DataTable RunTransactionSearch(DateTime
StartDate,TransactionSearchParam param){
  DataTable table=new DataTable("results");
  TransactionSearchRequestType transSearch=new TransactionSearchRequestType();

  // Set up the TransactionSearch
  TransactionSearchReq request=new TransactionSearchReq();
  transSearch.StartDate=StartDate;

  request.TransactionSearchRequest = new TransactionSearchRequestType();
  transSearch.Version = "1.0";
  transSearch.CurrencyCodeSpecified = false;
  transSearch.EndDateSpecified = false;
```

```
        transSearch.StatusSpecified = false;

        //set the params
        transSearch.StartDate=StartDate;
        transSearch.EndDate = param.EndDate;

        #region args list
        int args=1;
        if(param.TransactionID!=""){
          transSearch.TransactionID = param.TransactionID;
          args++;
        }

        if(param.Amount!=""){
          transSearch.Amount = new BasicAmountType();
          transSearch.Amount.Value = param.Amount;
          args++;
        }
        if(param.PayerEmail!=""){
          transSearch.Payer = param.PayerEmail;
          args++;
        }

        if(param.Currency!=""){
          transSearch.CurrencyCodeSpecified = true;
          args++;
        }

        if(param.ItemNumber!=""){
          transSearch.AuctionItemNumber = param.ItemNumber;
          args++;
        }

        if(param.LastName!=""){
          transSearch.PayerName = new PersonNameType();
          transSearch.PayerName.LastName = param.LastName;
          args++;
        }

        if(param.FirstName!=""){
          transSearch.PayerName = new PersonNameType();
          transSearch.PayerName.FirstName = param.FirstName;
          args++;
        }

        if(param.PaymentStatus!=""){
          transSearch.StatusSpecified = true;
          args++;
        }

        if(param.PaymentType!=""){
          transSearch.TransactionClassSpecified = true;
          args++;
        }
```

```
    #endregion

    request.TransactionSearchRequest=transSearch;

    //if there are more than 0 args set, run the transaction
    if(args>0){
      //run the transactioon
      TransactionSearchResponseType response =
            service.TransactionSearch(request);

❶    if(response!=null){
        if(response.PaymentTransactions!=null){
          //build the columns out
          DataColumn cTransactionID=new DataColumn("TransactionID");
          DataColumn cFeeAmount=new DataColumn("FeeAmount");
          DataColumn cGrossAmount=new DataColumn("GrossAmount");
          DataColumn cNetAmount=new DataColumn("NetAmount");
          DataColumn cPayer=new DataColumn("Payer");
          DataColumn cPayerDisplayName=new DataColumn("PayerDisplayName");
          DataColumn cStatus=new DataColumn("Status");
          DataColumn cTimestamp=new DataColumn("Timestamp");
          DataColumn cType=new DataColumn("Type");

          table.Columns.Add(cTransactionID);
          table.Columns.Add(cFeeAmount);
          table.Columns.Add(cGrossAmount);
          table.Columns.Add(cNetAmount);
          table.Columns.Add(cPayer);
          table.Columns.Add(cPayerDisplayName);
          table.Columns.Add(cStatus);
          table.Columns.Add(cTimestamp);
          table.Columns.Add(cType);

          DataRow dr;
          foreach(PaymentTransactionSearchResultType trans in
                response.PaymentTransactions){
            dr=table.NewRow();
            dr["TransactionID"]=trans.TransactionID;
            dr["FeeAmount"]=GetAmountValue(trans.FeeAmount);
            dr["GrossAmount"]=GetAmountValue(trans.GrossAmount);
            dr["NetAmount"]=GetAmountValue(trans.NetAmount);
            dr["Payer"]=trans.Payer;
            dr["PayerDisplayName"]=trans.PayerDisplayName;
            dr["Status"]=trans.Status;
            dr["Timestamp"]=trans.Timestamp.ToLongDateString();
            dr["Type"]=trans.Type.ToString();

            table.Rows.Add(dr);
          }
        }

      }

    }else{
```

```
        throw new Exception("You must specify at least one search parameter");

    }

    return table;
}
```

Line ❶ begins the main change to the code and is responsible for building out the DataTable. Its execution is pretty straightforward and follows the same principal as appending the return values to a string: just loop through the results, adding a row for each array element.

Running the Hack

Add this code to the btnSearch Click event to call the API wrapper and set the DataGrid.DataSource property:

```
private void btnSearch_Click(object sender, System.EventArgs e) {
    string username = "MyAPIUserName";
    string password = "MyAPIPAssword";
    string certPath = "MyCertPath";
    string url = "https://api.sandbox.paypal.com/2.0/";

    DateTime dStart = dtStart.Value;
    DateTime dEnd = dtEnd.Value;

    //let the user know what's going on
    lblStatus.Text = "Contacting Paypal";
    PayPalAPI.APIWrapper api =
            new PayPalAPI.APIWrapper(username,password,certPath,url);
    PayPalAPI.APIWrapper.TransactionSearchParam param =
            new PayPalAPI.TransactionSearchParam();

    param.EndDate = dEnd;
    System.Data.DataTable table = api.RunTransactionSearch(dStart,param);
    dg.DataSource = table;
    lblStatus.Text = "Finished";
}
```

This code, activated when the Search button is clicked, performs the search and displays the results in the DataGrid, as shown in Figure 8-11.

Finally, create a detail form that calls the GetTransactionDetails() method of the API wrapper, and output the results to a label control:

1. Add a form named frmDetail.

2. Add a label named lblTransactionID.

3. Add a label named lblResponse.

4. Add three public string fields named UserName, Password, and TransactionID.

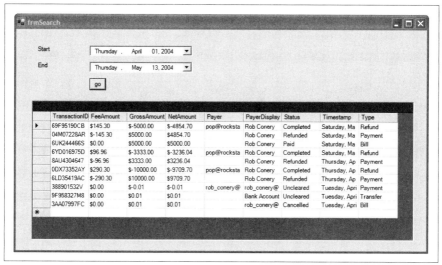

Figure 8-11. Nicely formatted search results

5. Add an event handler for the form's load event and call it `Form_Load`.

Add an event handler for the double-click event of the DataGrid, and insert code to grab the selected transaction ID:

```
private void dg_DoubleClick(object sender, EventArgs e) {

    DataGridCell cell=dg.CurrentCell;

    //the transaction ID is in the first column
    string transactionID = dg[cell.RowNumber,0].ToString( );

    frmDetail detail=new frmDetail( );

    //set the form values
    detail.TransactionID=transactionID;
    detail.Show( );
}
```

Finally, add code to the Load event of the detail form, which calls the API wrapper `GetTransactionDetail( )` method:

```
private void frmDetail_Load(object sender, System.EventArgs e) {
string username = "MyAPIUserName";
string password = "MyAPIPassword";
string certPath = "c:\\mycertificate.cer";
string url = "https://api.sandbox.paypal.com/2.0/";

    //let the user know what's going on
    lblResponse.Text="Contacting Paypal....";
    PayPalAPI.APIWrapper api=new PayPalAPI.
APIWrapper(UserName,Password,certPath,url);
    lblResponse.Text=api.GetTransactionDetail(TransactionID,"\n");
```

```
        lblTransactionID.Text=TransactionID;

    }
```

When you perform a search, the results will look something like Figure 8-12.

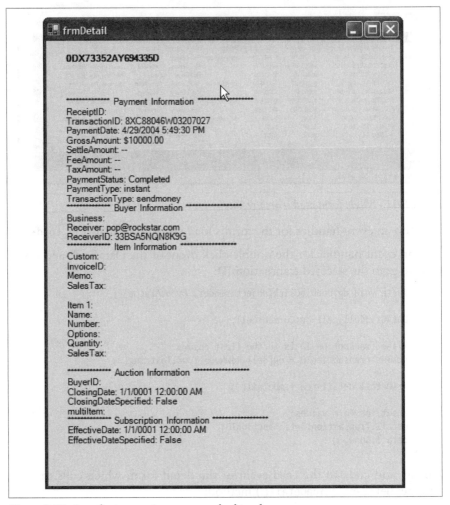

Figure 8-12. Just the transaction you were looking for

With the master-detail report generated by this project, you'll be effectively duplicating the History tab from the PayPal web site, albeit in your own application, fully customized and supplemented with your own feature set. See the next section for an example of how this approach can be especially useful.

Importing into Quicken and QuickBooks

If you're a Quicken or QuickBooks user, you've probably discovered that PayPal's "Download My History" feature (found in the History tab) provides nothing more than rudimentary support for converting transaction data into a form that Quicken or QuickBooks can understand. Fortunately, the PayPal API provides the perfect opportunity to build your own customized—and, most importantly, automated—means of importing your PayPal transactions into your accounting software.

Regardless of the type of accounting software you're using, you need to start by assembling a table of transaction data from your PayPal history using the `RunTransactionSearch` method described earlier in this hack. The tricky part is to make sure you don't import the same transaction twice, and there are a few ways to accomplish this. The easiest way is probably to confine the table to a fixed date range using the `StartDate` and `EndDate` parameters. So, if you run your importer project once a week, restrict your search results to those transactions between 12:00:01 a.m. Monday morning and 12:00:00 midnight the following Sunday.

The next step is to get your data into Quicken or QuickBooks. The easiest approach is probably to have your application create an Open Financial Exchange (OFX) file and then manually import the file into Quicken or QuickBooks. For details on the OFX format, go to *http://www.ofx.net*.

 Previously, you would have had to create a Quicken Interchange Format (QIF) file for Quicken or an Import Interchange Format (IIF) for QuickBooks. However, both of these formats appear to be deprecated in favor of the more universal OFX schema.

If you really want to make the connection between PayPal and QuickBooks as slick as possible, you'll want to dispense with the task of manually importing your data. Instead, you can connect your application to QuickBooks via Intuit's QBXML Request Processor API and send your transaction data to QuickBooks seamlessly (and automatically). For documentation and an SDK, visit *http://developer.intuit.com/*.

—*Rob Conery, Dave Nielsen, and David A. Karp*

Issue Payments en Masse with the Mass Pay API

#96

Send out a large number of payments all at once with the Mass Pay feature through the API.

As described in "Use Mass Pay to Create an Affiliate System" [Hack #77], PayPal allows you to send many payments at once through the PayPal web site. Using the Mass Pay API and some slight modifications to the code in "Make Your First API Call" [Hack #88], you can also do this from your own applications.

> You can pay up to 250 payees at once using Mass Pay. To make more than 250 payments, you'll need to call Mass Pay repeatedly.

Setting up the Request

The first thing to do is set up a simple tab-delimited text file that contains all the information about your payees, as shown in Figure 8-13.

Figure 8-13. Using a simple tab-delimited text file to store the information about the recipients of your payments

List the recipients' email addresses in the first column and the corresponding payment amounts in the second column. Include an optional third column to list a unique identifier for each recipient for tracking and reconciliation purposes. The optional fourth column lets you include a customized note to be sent to each of your recipients.

The Code

This code uses the MassPayReq, MassPayRequestType, MassPayRequestItemType, and MassPayResponseType objects generated by the web reference in order to process the Mass Pay request.

> This code requires the SSL certificate generated in "Make Your First API Call" [Hack #88].

```
// Load the Certificate
X509Certificate certificate = X509Certificate.CreateFromCertFile(certPath);
// Create the API Service
PayPalAPIInterfaceService service = new PayPalAPIInterfaceService();
service.Url = url;

// Add the X509 Cert to the service for authentication
service.ClientCertificates.Add(certificate);
// Create the MassPay Request Item
```
❶
```
MassPayRequestItemType masspayRequestItem = new MassPayRequestItemType();

// create the Amount
BasicAmountType amount = new BasicAmountType();
amount.currencyID = CurrencyCodeType.USD;
amount.Value = "0.67";
masspayRequestItem.Amount = amount;

// create the recipient email
masspayRequestItem.ReceiverEmail = "your-recipient@domain.com";

// create the optional unique id (for your own benefit)
masspayRequestItem.UniqueID = "some unique id";

// create the optional Note
masspayRequestItem.Note = "some note";
// Create the MassPay Request
```
❷
```
MassPayRequestType masspayRequest = new MassPayRequestType();

// you can set an email subject if you want to.
// This will be the subject of the email that your payees are going
//    to receive
masspayRequest.EmailSubject = "some email subject";

masspayRequest.MassPayRequestItemDetails = new MassPayRequestItemType[ 1 ];

// add the previously created MassPayRequestItemType object to this array
masspayRequest.MassPayRequestItemDetails[0] = masspayRequestItem;

MassPayReq request = new MassPayReq();
request.MassPayRequest = masspayRequest;
// Build the Security Header
CustomSecurityHeaderType securityHeader = new CustomSecurityHeaderType();
UserIdPasswordType userIdPassword = new UserIdPasswordType();
userIdPassword.Username = ""; // Insert your API username here
userIdPassword.Password = ""; // Insert your API password here
userIdPassword.Subject = "";
securityHeader.Credentials = userIdPassword;
securityHeader.MustUnderstand = true;
service.RequesterCredentials = securityHeader;
MassPayResponseType response = service.MassPay(request);

Console.WriteLine("Ack: " + response.Ack.ToString());
Console.WriteLine("Correlation ID: " + response.CorrelationID);
Console.WriteLine("Timestamp: " + response.Timestamp.ToString());
```

Running the Hack

When you successfully execute the code [Hack #90], the Ack code returned will
be Success:

```
Ack: Success
CorrelationID:
Timestamp: 4/27/2004 10:25:30 AM
```

Each payee is represented in the code as a `MassPayRequestItemType` object.
Create the initial `MassPayRequestItemType` instance (line ❶) and a
`BasicAmountType` instance that contains the amount, and add it to the item
request. Also create the recipient's email, unique ID, and note, and add
them to the item request.

Note that this code creates only one `MassPayRequestItemType` object (line ❷).
You can repeat the steps to fill in as many objects as you want and thus
overcome the limit of 250 payees. Typically, the way to do this is to read the
individual item details from the tab-delimited file and create the objects on
the fly. That way, you should be able to create a list of
`MassPayRequestItemType` objects.

When you send a payment with Mass Pay, you pay the seller
fees [Hack #14] that would otherwise be assessed to your recipients.

—Souvik Das, Rob Conery, and Dave Nielsen

H A C K #97 Pay Affiliates and Suppliers on a Schedule

Automate Mass Pay API calls to schedule mass payments at regular intervals.

When you have a lot of people to pay, setting up and executing online payments one at a time can quickly get tedious. Likewise, repeatedly setting up
Mass Pay requests can get tedious if you have to do it every month or every
week. Here is a great real-world example that shows you how to give away
your money faster than you thought possible.

The Code

Start with the code from "Issue Payments en Masse with the Mass Pay API"
[Hack #96] and extend it with two new classes: `MassPayee` and `MassPayeeTable`
(which supplements the `ArrayList` object):

```
//a class which holds the payee info
public class MassPayee{
  public string Note="";
  public string Email="";
```

```
    public string EmailSubject="";
    public string ReferenceID="";
    public double Amount=0;
}

//a class which holds the MassPayees
public class MassPayTable:ArrayList{

  public void AddPayee(MassPayee payee){
      //the API will only allow 250 payees
      if(Payess.Count=250){
          throw new Execption("A maximum of 250 payees are allowed");
      }else{
          Payees.Add(payee);
      }
  }
  public void ClearPayees( ){
      Payees.Clear( );
  }
  public int Count{
      get{return Payees.Count;}
  }
}
```

Here's the code for the RunMassPay routine:

```
public string RunMassPay(MassPayTable PayeeTable){

  // Build the Security Header
  this.SetHeaderCredentials(service);

  // Create the MassPay Request
  MassPayRequestType masspayRequest = new MassPayRequestType( );
  //allocate the array for the ItemTypes
  masspayRequest.MassPayRequestItemDetails = new
                      MassPayRequestItemType[PayeeTable.Count];

  // create the Amount
  BasicAmountType amount;

  // Create the MassPay Request Item
  MassPayRequestItemType masspayRequestItem;;

  //our indexer
  int counter=0;

      //loop through the MassPayee List and add the
      //information to the PayPal API objects.
  for(int i=0;i<PayeeTable.Count;i++){
      masspayRequestItem= new MassPayRequestItemType( );
      amount= new BasicAmountType( );
      amount.currencyID = CurrencyCodeType.USD;
      MassPayee payee=(MassPayee)PayeeTable[i];
```

```
        amount.Value = payee.Amount.ToString( );
        masspayRequestItem.Amount = amount;
        masspayRequestItem.ReceiverEmail = payee.Email;
        masspayRequestItem.UniqueID = payee.ReferenceID;
        masspayRequestItem.Note = payee.Note;
        masspayRequest.EmailSubject = payee.EmailSubject;

        // add the previously created MassPayRequestItemType object
            to this array
        masspayRequest.MassPayRequestItemDetails[counter] =
            masspayRequestItem;

        counter++;
    }

    MassPayReq request = new MassPayReq( );
    request.MassPayRequest = masspayRequest;

    MassPayResponseType response = service.MassPay(request);
    string sReturn=CheckErrors(response);
    if(sReturn==""){
        sReturn=response.Ack;
    }
    return sReturn;
}
```

To use this routine, gather the payee information from your site database
and execute the call:

```
public string SendMassPay( ){

    //get the payees from the database
    string sql="MyPayeeSQL";
    SqlConnection conn=new SqlConnection("MyConnectionString");
    SqlCommand cmd=new SqlCommand(sql,conn);
    SqlDataReader rdr=cmd.ExecuteReader(CommandBehavior.CloseConnection);
    APIWrapper api=new

APIWrapper("MyUserName","MyPassword","MyCertLocation","APIUrl");

    APIWrapper.MassPayeeTable Payees=new APIWrapper.MassPayeeTable( );
    APIWrapper.MassPayee payee;
    while(rdr.Read( )){
        payee=new APIWrapper.MassPayee( );
        payee.Note=rdr["Note"].ToString( );
        payee.Email=rdr["Email"].ToString( );
        payee.EmailSubject=rdr["EmailSubject"].ToString( );
        payee.ReferenceID=rdr["ReferenceID"].ToString( );
        payee.Amount=(double)rdr["Amount"];
        Payees.Add(payee);
    }
    string result=api.RunMassPay(Payees);
```

```
    rdr.Close( );
    conn.Close( );
    return result;
}
```

Running The Hack

To pay affiliates and suppliers on a schedule, implement the code by following these steps:

1. Create a new project: select Visual C# Projects and then Console Application.

2. Add the MassPayee and MassPayTable classes to the *Class1.cs* file.

3. Add the RunMassPay routine to the *Class1.cs* file.

4. Add the SendMassPay routine to the *Class1.cs* file.

5. Replace the MyPayeeSQL value with the name of a procedure stored in your database that you've created. The stored procedure should return the following fields: Email, EmailSubject, Amount, Note, and ReferenceID. Make sure one of the email addresses is your Sandbox Personal account so that you can confirm you sent the money.

6. Replace the MyConnectionString with your own database connection.

7. Compile and run the console application.

The response from PayPal will either be Success or a list of errors. See "Handle Transaction Errors within the API Wrapper" [Hack #92] for more information on errors and return codes.

Confirm that your payments have been sent and received by logging into your Sandbox Personal account.

—Souvik Das, Rob Conery, and Dave Nielsen

HACK #98 Search eBay for Listings that Accept PayPal

Use the eBay API to search for PayPal-enabled listings.

eBay and PayPal are a natural fit. eBay buyers love to pay with PayPal because it's quick and easy, so the vast majority of items listed for sale on eBay accept PayPal. This hack uses the eBay API to search for listings at *http://www.ebay.com* that accept PayPal.

Like PayPal API applications, eBay API applications can be written using any programming language and operating system. This hack uses the eBay Software Development Kit (SDK) for Windows and the C# programming language. eBay SDKs abstract away some of the implementation details of programming the API to make it easier to create an application. In addition to the SDK for .NET, eBay also provides an SDK for Java, as well as XML over HTTPS POST and SOAP interfaces. See *eBay Hacks* by David A. Karp (O'Reilly) for further coverage of the eBay API.

To create a search application with the eBay SDK, you must first perform a few preliminary setup steps:

1. Sign up for the eBay Developers Program at *http://developer.ebay.com*. When you complete the registration process (which is free), you'll receive a set of developer keys you need to begin developing eBay applications against the eBay test environment, known as the Sandbox (different than the PayPal Sandbox [Hack #87]).

2. Download the eBay SDK for Windows and install it on your computer. Remember, even if you're not using Windows and .NET, you can still write applications using the eBay API. For instance, much of the API code in *eBay Hacks* is written in Perl, which can, of course, be used on virtually any platform and without needing to be supported by an SDK.

3. Create a test user account on the eBay Sandbox. Go to *http://sandbox. ebay.com*, click Register at the top of the page, and fill out the form. Although the form looks just like the sign-up form used by eBay, an eBay Sandbox account is similar to a PayPal Sandbox account, in that it is merely a pseudo-account used just for testing your software application.

4. Create a security token using the token generator located at *http:// developer.ebay.com/tokentool*. This page takes the developer keys from step 1, as well as your sandbox user ID and password, and converts them into a security token that you can use for testing purposes. You pass the token to the eBay API server each time your application makes an API call.

The Code

Now that you've done the preparatory work, it's time to write your application. Create a Windows forms application with a small text box called txtSearch, a button called btnSearch, and a listbox, lstItem, in which to store the search output.

To call the functions in the SDK, begin by making a reference to the assembly *eBay.SDK.dll* from your project in Visual Studio .NET. Then, insert the appropriate include files at the top of your form's code window:

```
using eBay.SDK;
using eBay.SDK.API;
using eBay.SDK.Model;
using eBay.SDK.Model.Item;
```

Finally, create a Click event handler for the button that performs the search and displays the results:

```
private void btnSearch_Click(object sender, System.EventArgs e)
{
    IItemFoundCollection items;
    GetSearchResultsCall search = new GetSearchResultsCall(CreateSession());
    search.Query = txtSearch.Text;
    search.PayPalItemsOnly = true;
    search.MaxResults = 20;    // can be up to 200; more if you use paging
    items = search.GetSearchResults();

    foreach(IItem it in items)
    {
        lstItem.Items.Add(it.Title);
    }
}
```

Because the majority of the communication and data-handling code is wrapped by the classes provided by the SDK, the code you have to write is fairly straightforward. To do the search, this procedure simply creates an instance of the GetSearchResultsCall object, assigns values to its properties, and then calls the object's GetSearchResults method.

> Setting the PayPalItemsOnly method to true filters out non-PayPal items.

The return value of GetSearchResults is a typed IItemFoundCollection that is populated with IItem objects, each of which represents an item listed for sale on eBay. After the function returns the collection of eBay items, the foreach loop uses it to populate the listbox with their titles.

There's one part of this code that can be a little tricky: creating a session object. The eBay ApiSession object is required to be passed to the server along with every eBay API call. Our event handler gets an ApiSession object by calling a function called CreateSession, which looks like this:

```
private ApiSession CreateSession()
{
    ApiSession sess = new eBay.SDK.API.ApiSession();
    sess.Developer = ConfigurationSettings.AppSettings["DeveloperID"];
```

```
    sess.Certificate = ConfigurationSettings.AppSettings["Certificate"];
    sess.Application = ConfigurationSettings.AppSettings["ApplicationID"];
    IApiToken t = new ApiToken( );
    t.Token = ConfigurationSettings.AppSettings["Token"];
    sess.Token = t;
    sess.Url = ConfigurationSettings.AppSettings["ServerUrl"];
    return sess;
}
```

Running the Hack

This code expects to find the configuration information it needs in a .NET
XML configuration file, called *Web.config* if you're writing a web application or *ExeName.config* (where *ExeName* is the name of the executable) if
you're creating a compiled binary application. A typical configuration file of
an eBay application written in any .NET language looks like this:

```
    <?xml version="1.0" encoding="utf-8" ?>
    <configuration>
      <appSettings>
        <add key="DeveloperID" value="mydevid" />
        <add key="ApplicationID" value="myappid" />
        <add key="Certificate" value="mycert" />
        <add key="ServerUrl" value="https://api.sandbox.ebay.com/ws/api.dll" />
        <add key="Token" value="AgAAAA**AQAAAA**aAAAAA**n8yAQA" />
      </appSettings>
    </configuration>
```

For this to work, you need to replace the italicized values in the appSettings
section (*mydevid*, *myappid*, and *mycert*) with your developer keys (sent to you
from eBay after registering in step 1, earlier in this hack) and your security
token (generated in step 4). Finally, the ServerUrl value provided here is the
correct URL for the eBay development Sandbox. (You'll use a different URL
to take the application live.)

Compile your application, and give it a whirl!

Hacking the Hack

There are many more things you can do with the eBay API besides search.
One of the most common operations involves automatically listing items for
sale, typically to save time in the selling process or provide integration
between your inventory database and eBay. You can also use the eBay API to
obtain details about listings in progress, download high-bidder information
for completed items, and even create notifications when a bidder with negative feedback bids on one of your auctions! There are more than 70 calls in
the eBay API, and the SDK provides quite a few code examples in a number
of different programming languages.

—*Jeffrey McManus*

Test IPN and PDT in the Sandbox

Test Instant Payment Notification (IPN) and Payment Data Transfer (PDT) in the PayPal Sandbox.

Once you've deposited money into the Personal account in your Sandbox "Set up the Sandbox" [Hack #87], you'll need to configure your Sandbox Business account to use either PDT or IPN (both of which are discussed at length in Chapter 7). This hack shows how to configure PDT.

As with the live PayPal site, to use PDT with the PayPal Sandbox, you must first configure some options in your Sandbox Business account Profile.

 PDT works only when Auto Return is turned on. You must set this before using PDT in your web site.

To enable Auto Return and the PDT feature, follow these steps:

1. Open the Sandbox, launch the Sandbox Business account, and log in.
2. Click the My Account tab, and then click Profile.
3. Click Website Payment Preferences and turn on the Auto Return option.
4. Finally, turn on the Payment Data Transfer option.
5. Click Save when you're done.

 When you save your PDT preferences, an ITidentity token is generated and appears in a message at the top of the Website Payment Preferences page. In future visits, your ITidentity token will appear in the Payment Data Transfer section, below the On and Off options.

See "Process Payments like a Credit Card with PDT" [Hack #85] for additional PDT setup instructions and tips.

Now, when sending order information to PayPal, you can do it through a URL (GET) or via an HTML form (POST). Either way, you need to tell PayPal that the payment is going to a Sandbox account. Just add the parameter test_pdt=1 (or test_ipn=1 if you are using the IPN) to the URL (or include it as a variable in your HTML form).

When the transaction is complete, the pseudobuyer will be redirected to the URL you supplied in the ReturnURL parameter, along with several transaction parameters appended to the URL, including:

Transaction number (tx)

You'll use the transaction number to get the full set of transaction information [Hack #93].

Status (st)

The status of the transaction is normally Completed. See "Receive Instant Payment Notifications" [Hack #65] for explanations of the other status flags you might see here.

Amount of sale (amt)

The dollar (or whatever currency used) amount of the sale.

Currency (cc)

The currency used for the sale.

Once the Sandbox has sent you this information, you can set up your IPN or PDT logic as you need without worrying about real orders and real money being transacted. The return information from PayPal won't specify that it's a Sandbox transaction, though, so if it's important to you to know this, you can append a flag to your return URL, like this:

```
http://www.myreturnurl.com?test=1
```

PayPal appends its transaction information to this URL for both PDT and IPN, preserving your test parameter and thus helping you to distinguish test transactions from real ones.

—*Rob Conery and Dave Nielsen*

H A C K
100
Go Live

Take the training wheels off your Sandbox application and start working with real money.

Once you've finished developing your application and have completed your testing in the Sandbox [Hack #87], you'll ultimately want to take your application live. You'll need to do the following:

1. If you haven't done so already, set up a real, verified Business or Premier account on the live site *outside* the Sandbox, as described in the introduction to Chapter 3.

2. Obtain a new digital certificate with a new certificate ID and password.

3. Log into your PayPal Business account and click the Profile tab.

4. Click the API Access link and then click the API Certificate Request link.

5. All accounts need to be verified [Hack #2] before requesting a certificate (otherwise, you won't see a Request link). When you have finished this

process, you will receive a link to a new certificate with a new user ID and password.

Unlike the Sandbox, when you have finished the request process, you will not automatically be given the option to download a certificate. Some businesses will even be denied because they do not have an account in good standing. Others might be denied because they are too new. The exact reasons for being denied a certificate are not clear, but it if it happens to you, contact PayPal Customer Service and try to get it resolved.

6. Change the URL of the PayPal API in your application. If you've built a modular application, it should reference the URL for the API in one or two locations. Find those locations and change the URL from:

```
https://api.sandbox.paypal.com/2.0/
```

to:

```
https://api.paypal.com/2.0/
```

If you're using the API wrapper [Hack #89], you'll find the URL inside the wrapper class.

Performance and Efficiency

Since access to the PayPal API is currently free, you don't have to worry about tracking and limiting the number of calls your application makes over a given time period. However, since web services calls hamper the performance of your application, you should be thinking about efficiency as you develop. For instance, you might want to cache repeatedly accessed information so that your users don't have to wait while your application retrieves data unnecessarily.

Finishing Up

Once you've made these changes to your application, it's prudent to test your application with real money on the live site before distributing it or installing into a production environment. When you feel your application is ready, go ahead and launch, sit back, and enjoy.

—*Rob Conery and Dave Nielsen*

Index

We'd like to hear your suggestions for improving our indexes. Send email to *index@oreilly.com*.

cmdDetails button, 291
cn variable, 94
code tampering, preventing, 109–113,
    230–233
    with encryption, 113–118
colors not allowed in custom pages, 164
Component Inspector feature
    (Macromedia), 133–135
Conery, Rob, ix
confirming
    purchases to customers by
        email, 218
    Sandbox email addresses, 276
Continue buttons on Payment Sent
    pages, 165
Continue Shopping button,
    displaying, 151
contributors to political campaigns,
    getting required information
    about, 128–131
conversion rate, measuring, 259
cookies
    magic, used for checking valid
        subscribers, 193–195
    personal information and, 45
    setting for tiers, 198
    tracking buyers with, 166–168
CountDonated variable, 248
count_inventory variable, 243
coupons, discount, 181–185
CreateSession(), 321
credit cards
    accepting payments of, 3
    adding to PayPal accounts, 6–9
    chargebacks, protecting yourself
        from, 80
    discouraging customer use of, 56
    forgotten passwords and, 9–11
    funding payments with, 32
    Personal accounts and, 52
    setting identifying strings on
        statements, 57
    stolen, repercussions of using, 11–13
cross-border payment fees, 55
crypt(), 206
cryptographic keys, encrypting buttons
    with, 114–118
cs variable, 94
    incompatible with Custom Payment
        Pages, 163

currency
    avoiding currency conversions, 68
    bogus, accepting payments in, 146
    foreign, accepting payments in, 55
    searching for transactions by, 301
    support for subscriptions funded by
        multiple currencies, 206
    (see also money)
currency (cc) transaction
    parameter, 263, 324
currency_code variable, 94
custom checkout page styles
    header banners, getting the most
        from, 162
    using multiple, 161
Custom Payment Pages, 160–164
custom variable, 94, 105–107
    Aggregate Cart feature, 156
    tracking sales using, 109
Customer Service, contacting, 26
customers
    capturing information with
        IPN, 252–254
    getting to know, 82
    identifying yourself to, 57
    offering discount coupons, 181–185
    paying seller fees when
        buying, 40–42, 78
    protection when shipping goods
        to, 82
    returning to web pages, after making
        purchases, 227–230
    sending purchase confirmation
        email, 218
    tracking
        before/after PayPal
            transactions, 266
        site visitors, 165–168
    upselling, 236–237
CVV (Card Verification Value),
    unavailable with virtual debit
    card, 37

D

Das, Souvik, ix
databases
    adding product information to, 173
    adding tier fields to, 196
    building dynamic
        storefronts, 168–171

Colophon

Our look is the result of reader comments, our own experimentation, and feedback from distribution channels. Distinctive covers complement our distinctive approach to technical topics, breathing personality and life into potentially dry subjects.

The tool on the cover of *PayPal Hacks* is a money changer. The money changer is a container clipped to one's belt that stores, organizes, and dispenses coins to facilitate making change on the go. It is typically divided into four barrels, so that pennies, nickels, dimes, and quarters can be held separately. The money changer is extremely useful for people who need to make frequent cash transactions while in transit, and is often used by train conductors and traveling vendors.

Jamie Peppard was the production editor and proofreader for *PayPal Hacks*. Brian Sawyer was the copyeditor. Darren Kelly and Claire Cloutier provided quality control. Judy Hoer wrote the index.

Hanna Dyer designed the cover of this book, based on a series design by Edie Freedman. The cover image is a photograph from the Stockbyte Work Tools CD. Clay Fernald produced the cover layout with QuarkXPress 4.1 using Adobe's Helvetica Neue and ITC Garamond fonts.

David Futato designed the interior layout. This book was converted by Julie Hawks to FrameMaker 5.5.6 with a format conversion tool created by Erik Ray, Jason McIntosh, Neil Walls, and Mike Sierra that uses Perl and XML technologies. The text font is Linotype Birka; the heading font is Adobe Helvetica Neue Condensed; and the code font is LucasFont's TheSans Mono Condensed. The illustrations that appear in the book were produced by Robert Romano and Jessamyn Read using Macromedia FreeHand 9 and Adobe Photoshop 6. This colophon was written by Sanders Kleinfeld.